T0147192

THE SAVING HERITAGE FOR AWARENESS

Book II

REV. ALFRED A. ADAMS

authorHOUSE®

AuthorHouse™
1663 Liberty Drive
Bloomington, IN 47403
www.authorhouse.com
Phone: 1 (800) 839-8640

Published by AuthorHouse 05/08/2019

ISBN: 978-1-7283-0936-1 (sc)
ISBN: 978-1-7283-0935-4 (e)

Library of Congress Control Number: 2019905033

Print information available on the last page.

Contents

CHAPTER FOUR

Acknowledgement

My deepest gratitude to The Almighty God, and Jesus Christ our Savior and our advocate, comforter and Helper The Holy Spirit, who through His grace had made this project possible. I also give my heart fell thanks to the following persons : my daughter Jill Adams and her husband David Seide for their wonderful love towards this project. I extend my appreciation to my sons Melvin Adams and Reuben Adams for their strong support in this work. Also my daughter Elizabeth Adams for her love. Not left behind, Diana Nyakoh, one of the sponsors, and my friend, William Aduam.

THE GLOBAL SPIRITUAL SOLUTION

This book, is a book that takes the reader deep into Christianity, and make one understand and find fate in God which helps for the acquisition of the capacity to understand the spiritual things of life for incorruptible of the heart, because when the soul is corrupt, wisdom departs and knowledge hides in the understanding to depart, but wisdom is the treasure of the heart, which attracts knowledge to understand. A sizeable number of our modern world population are tormented with mental disabilities, which is Satan's greatest weapon for destruction and keep expanding in physical and psychological attacks against the global inhabitants. It is a confusion, being cause by current technological civilization and must be taken care of, not by human intelligence but by spiritual globalization solution, that has the capacity to bring it to an end for a global peace. Spiritual laws are more severe than physical laws and their consequences are more severe, knowing that all things originated from the spirit and by the spirit there is solution for every situation. When situation become condition then there will be no solution, but when it is seen as a spirit, then it can be rebuked and a change will occur forever. In the spirit realm, words are object. The purpose of this book is to send spiritual awareness to the inhabitants of the world to see what is going on in the spiritual realm and to equip them to victory.

CHAPTER ONE

THEOLOGY MADE EASY

The Bible:- The divine doctrine which has been put together by inspiration of the proof of the existence of God.

Theology :- The study of the concept of the understanding of religion in relation to the nature of God. The theological study takes one deep into the bible to unveil the things of God to discover what He has already revealed about Himself hidden to man. It is the explanation of religious faith, practice and experience. This step enable us to know Him as creator, the source of life, the master and Father of all creation. The study of theology is profitable because it helps one to know God for who He is, so He shall be glorified. Theology is the intense study about God which make one knows God and love Him to obey onto eternity. It brings about the concept of life and death, and life after death, and helps one to love everything which has life and obey to worship. The word theology was derived from Greek, "Theos" meaning "God" and "Logos" meaning "word or utterance." So "Theos-logos is God's Word." Therefore Theology is the science of the proof of the existence of God and His miracles which are the deeper acts of God in science. It comprises of the terminology which makes it possible about all the necessary technical applications that describes this subject into a study theory in this word-science-profession of God. Theology opens ones understanding in the scriptures which is the ministerial science, revealing and declaring the hidden part of God and godliness. It is the primary function place in order of science, of the works of God.

Luke 24:45 "And He opened their understanding that they might comprehend the scripture."

The scripture is full of parables because it contains the language of heaven and that was the language Jesus was speaking. And whoever wants to know the scripture needs his understanding to be opened to comprehend the scripture. And only the God Head Bodily, that is THE FATHER, THE HOLY SPIRIT and THE WORD HIMSELF which is Jesus Christ, only these three could open ones understanding to comprehend the scripture by submission. It is a great advantage and a great asset when one had already received a theological education, having knowledge of all the under mentioned theories, and with the help of the Holy Spirit, *the scripture* becomes an asset and life. The following are some theological tittles :-

PASTORAL THEOLOGY:- Pastoral theology looks into the issues and the challenges with religious truth in relation to spiritual care to the church. Being a pastor, must edify the relationship between a pastor and the people under his spiritual care. Pastoral theology is church ministry. It involves homiletics (the preparation and delivery of sermons), pastoral care, faith, baptism, communion, liturgy, salvation, ordination, ethics, ceremonies etc. It entails the office of the pastor, overseer or bishop. Pastoral theology is practical science and concludes all religious theologies dealing with epistical functions in Christianity and even in some other religions.

PRACTICAL THEOLOGY:- It is the study of the practical science of everyday life intending to make it more meaningful and applicable, and it involves homiletics and Christian education which embodies the handling of effective ministry in families, youth and children. The application of practical theology is the introduction of the ministries in the church and raises effective communicators of visionary scriptural leaders for the spiritual growth of the believers. It emphasis on how the impact of the scripture will really affect the lives of the believers in this technological era to effectively contribute to the affairs of the world for the proper functioning of the world to justify God's intention of the creation of the earth and the heavens. It also involves counseling in marriages and life in general, and also practical clinical programs.

FAITH :- Faith is the divine formula that exterminates every problem which is delivered into the hands of human beings and makes the word of God a formula and GPS(global positioning system) of life. It is a spiritual force that causes change, growth, development and prosperity. Faith releases the power in you, otherwise that power will be dormant in your heart which has been in you since you were in your mother's womb. Anything that has a name exists which is a spirit, and faith has a name, so it exists and is a spirit. Spirit works miracles that's why faith works miracles. So faith is the evidence of things we do not see with our eyes but hope to receive and received, no matter what the situation, that's faith. When situation becomes spirit and not condition, miracles happen and that's by faith.

It is that which recognizes the power and authority over diseases, sicknesses (demons) and witches and wizards, and capable to edify broken lives, in the name of our Lord Jesus Christ, the Son of the Living God. With faith as the divine formula, there is no negativity in actions.

The tremendous power of faith is the conclusive word of Jesus Christ on the subject of divine healing. It is the foundation of all things, leading as far as creation unto salvation. Medical science is good and purposed to glorify God but the science of the miracles of Jesus Christ is the greatest. Nothing is made or created without faith, therefore faith is older than the person having the faith because through faith he was created. Faith is not something one can acquire but have it from the womb. There is no power like the power of faith. It is the master key to everything, the master key to unlock the prison doors, the master key that breaks the chains of the captive, the master key that brings the axe from the bottom to the surface of the water, the master key that raises the dead. Mark 10:27 "And Jesus looking upon them saith, With men it is impossible, but not with God: For with God all things are possible."

This means, whosoever has faith can find favour with God because that person is connected to God. And whosoever is connected to God, angels will always do him service.

DOXOLOGY:- The part of theology which deals with the study of the doctrine of adoration of Jehovah. "Doxo" is Greek word which means "glory or to adore" and Logia which also means "word" in Greek, meaning a form of praise that is made into song. Hence Doxology means ADORATION(word of glory). Doxology is the Christian worship dedicated to the ALMIGHTY GOD as being the OMNIPOTENT (all powerful), the OMNISCIENT (the all knowing and seeing) and the

3

OMNIPRESENT (all present, everywhere). This is what theology is all about and renders exaltation to the Almighty God, the Creator. Theology itself is the concept of religion which declares the nature of God. In this case, praising, praying and studying the bible are all in the adoration. The book of Psalms is in adoration to the Almighty, likewise the book of Genesis which exhibits the power of the creator, the God Almighty, the Father of our Lord Jesus Christ. Rom. 11:33-36, Rom 1:20, Isaiah 40:28-29, 1Tim. 6:16.

CHRISTOLOGY:- This word was derived from Greek as any other theological term, Christos means "the Anointed One or Christ." It is the study of the doctrine of Jesus Christ: His prophecy, His birth, His Ministry, His death, His resurrection, His ascension and His deity. This study gives clear view of Jesus Christ, making it clear that Jesus is God according to Heb. 1:8-9. Psalm 93:2, 45:6-7, Isaiah 9:6, John 1:1-2, 14, 34; John 20:31. His birth was made known by the Angels which carried the message to Mary and confirmed His status in Luke 1:35, 26-32. Jesus was born as a baby and lived among us, Luke 2:7,27-32, Jesus was baptized, Luke 3:21-22. The Ministry of Jesus began Luke 3:23. Luke 4:18 was the confirmation of the beginning of His ministry. He carried on with His deliverance Ministry Mark 9:1-43, Luke 7:11-17. Jesus was arrested, condemned and crucified, John 18:2-14, John 19:14-19,39-42. Jesus resurrected, John 20:1-9,26-30; Acts 1:3, 2:24. The ascension of Jesus, Acts 1:9-10, Luke 24:51-53. The Deity of Jesus, Acts 2:34, Eph. 1:20-23, Heb. 1:5-6,8-9; Psalm 45:6-7.

THEOLOGY OF JESUS AS GOD :- Exo. 33:20 "And He said, thou canst not see My face: for there shall no man see My face and live."

Even Moses was not qualifies to see the face of God, why because he had blood on his hands, and violated the law of God by marrying an Ethiopian. So no man shall see God and live. Exo. 33:12-17 my presence shall go with you. Exo. 33:11 He spoke unto Moses face to face. Exo. 34:5 He stood with Moses. Deut. 7:3 No intermarriages.

Ezek. 39:29 "Neither will I hide My face any more from them for I have poured out My Spirit upon the house of Israel, said the Lord God."

God wanted to come closer to us this time because of the Love He loved us. Because of the love He loved us, He wanted to live in our midst, so He said, I will no longer hide My face from man, I will come among you for you to see Me and be in your midst, but I cannot live in your midst with the name Emmanuel - "God with us" which means God physically wanted to live permanently among mankind but because we often turn to worship idols and some are continually addicted to idols and all kinds of sin. God could not permanently stay with us but came into our midst as Jesus Christ - The Anointed One has visited us - The Savior and went back to where He was, after the visit. And now He is seated on His THRONE. The name JESUS means God has visited us, and CHRIST means The Anointed One, So JESUS CHRIST means The Anointed One Has Visited us. The name Jesus was given to Mary and Christ was given to the shepherds, the three wise men. Matt. 5:8 Blessed are the pure in heart, for they shall see God.

Then Christ came, the Anointed One, Jesus, God has visited us - Savior, and those who believed in Him saw Him, walked with Him and did things in common with Him - The pure in heart, those who have been drawn by the Father, whom the Father has poured out His spirit upon them, those of the house of Israel, meaning the followers of Christ, shall see Him and do see Him.

When we say Jesus is God people do not believe, But of truth I say to you, He is God. If anyone does not believe that He is, the day you will close your eyes and you are dead, you will see that He is God, that time there is nothing you can do, it will be too late. There will be no way you can correct this mistakes. Can you believe how many people have died and regretted after seeing Jesus who He is. Brethren if a witch or wizard (Satan) can leave his or her body down, come out of the body, as a spirit and go and do the evil he or she desire to do to people who are weak in spirit and after that successful evil mission comes back and take the body, and be normal human being in the day time, walking by you in the street, Is it hard for God, the creator to make His body to exit from the spirit, and come down to accomplish whatever mission and go back and allow the spirit to come down to be with us, as He gave to Adam in the garden of Eden which was stolen by Satan being used by witches and wizards? God left His spirit in Heaven and came down to be born in the person of Jesus Christ, lived among mankind and save the world that once we confess the name JESUS CHRIST, we are saved, a name that carries so much anointing and power, a name once mentioned, the blind receives his sight, the lame walks, the deaf hears, the dead is risen, the sea paths into two, a name when mentioned enable one to walk on the sea. Because he is God, He can live without His spirit and his Spirit also can live without the body. So Jesus said in John 16 :7 "It is expedient for you that I go away; for if I do not go away, the comforter (the Holy Spirit) will not come unto you; but if I depart I will send him unto you." So His spirit is with us on earth without His body, and He is still God. That one, we say, we do not accept it, but that of the witch who go out with the spirit to do evil, we do accept and believe that to exist and is real because those witches and wizards go out to torment, oppress and afflict mankind, but that of GOD INCARNATE in the Person of JESUS CHRIST which has established us, the grace of redemption, justification and salvation, we say is not acceptable. Lord have mercy on our unbelief. In Jesus name. Believe in God for after this life, where will you go? We cannot or do not recycle human life, no one can bring those who are dead back to life with exception of what the Creator has said. You can be a magician or a miracle worker or one who has been raising the dead, you will also die one day and you cannot save yourself, neither those raised. In John 6:44 Jesus said, No man can come to Me, Except the Father which hath sent Me, draw him: and I will raise him up at the last day.

In Heb. 1:8 the bible says, But unto the SON, He said, "THY THRONE, O GOD" is forever and ever, a sceptre of righteousness is the sceptre of thy kingdom. Jesus Christ loves us and His love is without condition.

JESUS WAS A CITIZEN OF BETHLEHEM, the city of David:

The Jews were expecting the Messiah to be a citizen of Bethlehem. They rejected to accept Jesus as the Messiah because they thought, since the mother Mary and Joseseph came from Nazareth, so Christ also came from Nazareth, that is the reason why they called him "Jesus of Nazareth." But Jesus was born in Bethlehem. When Philip told Nahtanael in John 1: 45 -47 "Philip findeth Nathanael, and said unto him, we have found Him, of whom Moses in the law, and the prophets, did write, Jesus of Nazareth, the son of Joseph. And Nathanael said unto him, Can there any good thing come out of Nazareth?" Again they held strongly their believe that, Christ will never come from Galilee, because no prophet had ever risen from Galilee and it was true that Christ was not born in Galilee but in Bethlehem. The scripture says in, John 7:40-42,52 "Many of the people therefore, when they heard these saying, said, of a truth this is the prophet. Others said, This is the Christ. But some said, shall Christ come out of Galilee? Hath not the scripture said, that Christ cometh of the seed of David, and out of the town of Bethlehem, where David was? They answered and said unto him, Art thou also of Galilee? Search and look; for out of Galilee arise no prophet." Jesus was a citizen of Bethlehem because He was born in Bethlehem and was raised in Nazareth and Joseph was seed of David, confirmed in Luke 2:4-7 "And Joseph also went up from Galilee out of the city of Nazareth, into Judaea, unto the city of David, which is called Bethlehem; because he was of the house and the lineage of David. To be taxed with Mary his espoused wife, being great with child. And so it was, that, while they were there, the days were accomplished that she should be delivered. And she brought forth her first born son, and wrapped Him in swaddling clothes, and laid Him in a manger; because there was no room for them in the inn." Luke 2:11 "For unto you is born this day in the city of David a Savior, which is Christ the Lord." The bible said nothing about the den in which the manger was, but we believe that the owner of the den might probably be a descendent of David. If that is so then Christ was born directly in the house of David and in the city of David, while Joseph was a descendant of David, Matt. 1:16. Know that God is always right and will never make mistake. So Christ will never be born in Bethlehem without the house of David.

LOVE OF GOD : *what* is Love of God? "It is the physical and spiritual feeling of attraction in connection, which creates a strong and constant unity unconditionally. "This is the kind of love displayed by Our Lord and Savior Jesus Christ. John 15:13 "Greater love hath no man than this, that a man lay down his life for his friends." Everything Satan does is an imitation of what God does. When man was living soul he could exit from the soul and go anywhere with the body while the soul was lying down and afterwards came back into the soul and be normal, a LIVING SOUL, and Satan saw this wonders of God in the life of man. When man sinned against God, he became a LIVING BEING, and this changed the plan of God for creation, the man could no longer leave down the soul neither the body, now that he is a living being. So Satan stole this miracle. Only the creator whom we will all go before Him to give account of our existence on earth and in the world has the final decision. Because there is judgment, there is heaven and there is hell, which every human being dead or alive have the audacity to enter into one of the two. Which one of the two, heaven or hell are you prepared and preparing to enter?

Nebuchadnezzar prepared a furnace with seven times higher temperature to get rid of Shadrach, Meshach and Abednego, but inside the furnace (the hell) THE SON OF GOD, was in the furnace with them and turned the burning internal fire space of the furnace into an air conditioned compartment (heaven) and they were found singing and dancing in the furnace. Likewise Jesus (THE SON OF GOD) will turn your hell into heaven, if you will accept and confess Him tonight. John 6:33 Jesus said, For the bread of God is He that comes down from heaven and give life to the world. John 14:8-9 "Philip saith unto Jesus, Lord, show us the Father, and it sufficeth us. Jesus saith unto him, Have I been so long time with you, and yet hast thou not known Me, Philip? he that hath seen Me hath seen the Father; and how sayeth thou then, show us the Father.

EPISTEMOLOGY:- The study of the doctrine of the theoretical nature of the knowledge of the word of God as the correspondence to the congregation. These are the books which Apostle Paul wrote eg. Romans, Corinthians, Galatians, Ephesians, Philippians, Colossians, 1st and 2nd Thessalonians, 1st and 2nd Timothy, Titus, and Hebrews. Then was the 1st and 2nd Peter by Apostle Peter; and the 1st, 2nd and 3rd John, by Apostle John; which are more or less laws in the new testament. The Christian Epistemology is based on reason and evidence for acquiring knowledge in God. It is the exhibit of the proof of receiving the knowledge in God. Gen. 1:21-27, 2:19. Adam received the proof of the knowledge of the Lord God and witnessed the creation of birds and animals with his eyes.

Gen. 6:13-17, 7:5-6, 11-12, 17-22, Noah received the proof of the knowledge by which God spoke to him about a flood which did happened.

Gen. 18:2 Abraham received living proof of the knowledge of God and physically welcome the three angels and dine with them, which predicted divinity unto Sarah to have a son at the age of ninety and hundred respectively. It goes on and on. Exo. 3:2 Moses also saw the proof of the knowledge of God by his encounter on Mount Sinai. We also saw the wonderful living proof of the Knowledge of God by the hand of Jesus Christ which He confirmed with miracles: healing, raising the dead, feeding the thousands, walking on the sea, commanding the weather to obey Him and His resurrection after His burier. Luke 24:6.

The confirmation of the arrival of the Holy Spirit upon the apostles and the miracles they performed was a living proof of the knowledge of God. Acts 2:43, 6:8, 8:6-13, 15:12, 19:11; Heb. 2:4. Finally Apostle Paul on epistemology gives us the knowledge of God by which there is no excuse to believe that God is real according to the miracles and prophecies. Rom. 1:20.

ESCHATOLOGY:- The study of the doctrine of the tribulation, rapture, predictions and the prophecies of the end times. Rev. 13:5-10,Thess. 2:1-12, 1Pet.1:5, 4:13, 5:1, Matt. 24:4-28,Mark 13:19, 1Cor. 4:3-5, 1Cor. 3:13-15. The major section of theology which deals with the end of the age and life, the end of the world and the nature of the Kingdom of God and also deals with life after death. Eschatology is the events to come, especially those of the revelation (apocalypse), the Rapture as Jesus says in Matt.24, impersonation of Christ, wars and rumors of wars, nation against nation, hatred and killing, false prophets misleading even the elects, the gospel will be preached in every nation, both the sun and the moon will be darkened, and we shall hear the shaking of the heavens. We know what things, these books say about the end time and all of the prophecies and the tribulations involve which will come and the believers who will be raptured. The anti-Christ, 666, the beast will be revealed before the rapture, etc. We all think the anti-Christ to be a human being, that's what the world thinks, who knows, if it turns out to be substance eg., government, network, a country or a company. You never know.

EXEGESIS:- It is the study of the critical interpretation or explanation of the biblical text. It deals with explanation, discovering and exploring or critical analysis and involves research or the thorough investigation of the text. A systematic process by which a person arrives at a reasonable basic or fundamental knowledge of the meaning of the subject or the text of the scripture in order to make it available to the understanding of the ordinary man. The word exegesis is a Greek word meaning "to define or dig out to the least." It involves the explanation and interpretation of the particular text of the scripture. There is science in every area of life and those who have the knowledge take advantage. Study to show thyself approved unto God, a workman that needed not to be ashamed but rightly dividing the word of truth. 2Tim. 2:15. The word of God must be handled properly through careful studies, under the principles below:

1. BASIC PRINCIPLE OF EXEGESIS - Grammatical principle - the structure of the language.
2. LITERAL PRINCIPLE OF EXEGESIS - Meaning of the passage.
3. HISTORICAL PRINCIPLE OF EXEGESIS - Culture, Tradition and Paraphrasing according to how the scripture is viewed.
4. SYNTHESIS PRINCIPLE OF EXEGESIS - in relation with surrounding passages, the context, link to other quotations.
5. PRATICAL PRINCIPLE OF EXEGESIS - paraphrasing and relations to present the word of God, rightly applying the text to our lives and to be responsible as a life changing application.

SAMPLE OF EXEGESIS:- 1Pet. 2:9-10 "But you are (1)a chosen generation, (2)a royal priesthood, (3)a holy nation, (4)His own special people that you may (5)proclaim the praises of Him who (6)called you out of darkness (7)into his marvelous light, who (8)once were not people, (9) but now the people of God, (10)who had not obtained mercy (11)but now have obtained mercy."(Exo. 3:8)

1. A chosen generation	Carefully called out of all His creation.
2. A royal priesthood	People empowered to command and to control the world.
3. A holy nation	Who are of a nation without fault.
4. His own special people	People so valuable in His sight.
5.Proclaim the praises of Him	The only people whose praise is acceptable by Him.
6. Called out of darkness	Delivered from Satan.
7. Into His marvelous Light	Into His precious Jesus.

8. Once were not people	when we did not know Christ, we were not considered as people, speaking anyhow without the divine reason and lost.
9. But now people of God	But now we are His children and people given power and friends, known and approved.
10. Who had not obtained mercy	We were destroyed often without God's intervention.
11. But now have obtained mercy	But God is now with us and have His intervention.

When you are able to break the word to the best of your understanding, then it becomes spirit and fills your body. So it shall always speak to you and reminds you of the present and the future. It becomes the Light and makes you Light.

ECCLESIOLOGY:- The study of the doctrine of churches, especially church building and decorations, the theology as applied to the nature and structure of Christian churches. It means assembly and word, a Greek word. The purpose and activities of the church. The study of the doctrine of the church, constitution, government of the church, and discipline or rules or laws of the church as the body of Christ. Ecclesia which is church and **Logia** which is word hence it is the study of the doctrine of the church structure, offices and governance of the church. 2Chro. 20:5, 1Kings 8:13, 1Kings 7:51. It is simply to teach us our roll as individuals and the roll of the church as followers of Christ which is the body of Christ. Ecclesiology involves things like, (1)place of fellowship, (2)partaking in the Lord's supper, (3)ushering of baptism, (4) engaging in serious prayers, (5)taking care of the poor, (6)the sick, (7)the widows and (8)the elderly.

HOMILETICS:- The study of the doctrine of the composition and delivery of sermon or the study of the composition, analysis, preparation, classification, and delivery of sermon. In theology, more focus is given to homiletics. The purpose of the preaching of Jesus Christ was to disseminate or spread the word leading to salvation and ordination of the apostle for soul winning and establishments of churches; Matt. 28:19, Mark 16:15, Mark 3:14, Luke 9:2. Apostle Paul appointed Timothy and Titus to preach the word with distinctiveness. The practice of the early church was for someone to read from the scriptures of the apostles or the scriptures of the prophets, that is reading from what is currently known as the Holy Bible and another to explain but the New Testament era has changed the whole concept of modeling. The person who reads can equally be the same person who explain. In some case both are in use, one at an instance.

HERMENEUTIC :- The study of the doctrine of the science or the knowledge of the verse interpretation, especially of the biblical text, the wisdom, the literature and ideal verse. It's the science that delves into the investigation of the exact methodological principle of the interpretation of the scripture. The term hermeneutics is sometimes used in collective argument. It includes written, verbal and none verbal communications which focuses on the verse of the sermon. It refers to the analysis of the verse to achieve basic interpretation. The books of the bible are all prophecies and every single verse carries prophetic power which are revealed through the reasoning of the hermeneutics dissemination and discerning prophetic contents of the word. The early Christian churches were more concerned of the reality of the prophetic utterances and the identification of the prophet. They were also more careful and more concern of the defense of Christianity against other religious sects, since prophetic utterances and miracles were the foundation of Christianity and charismatic establishments. 1Con. 14:32-33 "And the spirits of the prophets are subject to the prophets. For God is not the author of confusion but of peace, as in all churches of the saints."

HEMATOLOGY:- The study of the physiology of the blood, the diagnosis, the treatment and prevention of disease of the blood and the bone marrows and as well as clotting of blood. In theology this has nothing to do with treatment of the blood. It basically concerns man and sin, and the blood of Jesus Christ being shed to cleanse us. In Hebr. 9:22 And according to the law, almost all things are purified with blood and without shedding of blood there is no remission. Matt. 26:28 "For this is the blood of the new covenant, which is shed for many for the remission of sin." Exo. 24:8 "And Moses took the blood and sprinkled it on the people and said, this is the blood of the covenant which the Lord has made with you according to all the words." In the medical field hematology has only to deal with blood, infusion of the blood when necessary and cleaning the blood system but in theology, it is the best offer made by God to cleanse us with the blood of Jesus Christ to purify us to be fit for His presence.

SYNCRETISM:- The study of the doctrine of the practice of the combination of multiple faith which is not acceptable by the Christian concept and mostly relevant in philosophy and religious confusion (all religion believe in some form of God). Such conflicting situation occurs by the introduction of alien beliefs or imposition of alien beliefs in a society of indigenous beliefs. Religious syncretism does disagrees with Christianity and may be termed heresy which is the opinion contrary to either side. The bible shows us the true religion and the following scriptures give the picture of true religion. Deut. 6:4-5 "Hear, O Israel: the Lord our God, the Lord is One! You shall love the Lord Your God with all your heart, with all your soul, and with all your strength." Acts 17:23-24,29 "For as I was passing through and considering the objects of your worship, I even found an altar with this inscription: "TO THE UNKNOWN GOD." Therefore the one whom you worship without knowing, Him I proclaim to you: God, who made the world and everything in it, since He is Lord of heaven and earth, does not dwell in temples made with hands. Therefore since we are the offspring of God, we ought not to think that the Divine Nature is like gold or silver or stone, something shaped by art and man's devising." Acts 4:12 "Nor is there salvation in any other, for there is no other name under heaven given among men by which we must be saved." John 6:46 "Not that anyone has seen the Father, except He who is from God: He has seen the Father." John 20:30-31 "And truly Jesus did many signs in the presence of His disciples, which are not written in this book; but these are written that you may believe that Jesus is the Christ, the Son of God, and that believing you may have life in His name."

SOTORIOLOGY:- It is the study of the doctrine of Salvation. The Greek word "Soteria means Salvation" and "Soter also means Savior." It is the study of how God reconciled the separation between man and God because of Sin, by first Repentance, followed by Confession and then Acceptance of Jesus Christ, as the Son of God and being the Lord and Savior. Soteriology, basically concerns with how an individual is saved through the mercy, compassion, grace and faith in Jesus Christ which reunites us to God. Once we are saved we must be willing to the separation from sin and learn to walk with God. Gen. 17:1 "When Abram was ninety nine years old, the Lord appeared to Abram and said to him, "I AM ALMIGHTY GOD; WALK BEFORE ME AND BE PERFECT."

John 3:3 "Jesus answered and said to him, Most assuredly, I say to you unless one is born again, he cannot see the kingdom of God."

Phil. 2:12 "Therefore, my beloved, as you have always obeyed, not as in my presence only, but now much more in my absence, work out your own salvation with fear and trembling."

APOLOGETICS:- Apologetics is the study of the doctrine of the justification of the Christian faith and the divine wisdom. It is the theoretical and practical defense of the Christian faith. This may bring to mind the word apologize which only deals with when one is wrong and come to the state of being remorse but in this case it has nothing to do with being remorse but a systematic argumentative discourse in "DEFENSE" because it was derived from the Greek word "apologia". So apologetics is the defense of the claim against principles and objections. Apologetics is the doctrine which pertain directly to the development of the defense and the use of defense of the truth of the Christian faith. 1Pet. 3:15 But sanctify the Lord in your hearts, and always be ready to give defense to everyone who asks you for a reason for the hope that is in you, with meekness and fear. 2Cor. 10:5 Casting down arguments and every high thing that exalts itself against the knowledge of God, bringing every thought into captivity to the obedience of Christ. Apologetics serves three purposes:

1. To strengthen the faith of Christian believers.
2. To aid in the task of evangelism.
3. To clear people's wrong view of the deity of Jesus Christ, the miracles of Christ, the Trinity, and of sin and the argument of the existence of God.

Apologetics is a way of putting up a defense for the Christian faith using methodological apologetics and principle of apologetics of Christianity as the true religion. John 14:11, 20 "Believe Me that I am in the Father and the Father in Me, or Believe Me for the sake of the work themselves; At that day you will know that I am in the Father and you in Me and I in you." John 20:17 "Jesus said to her, do not cling to Me for I have not yet ascended to My Father, but go to My brethren and say to them, I am ascending to My Father and your Father, and My God and your God." 1John 5:7

"For there are three that bear record in heaven, the Father, the Word, and the Holy Ghost: and these three are One." These are the confirmation of the TRINITY and the Deity of Jesus Christ and the Holy Spirit according to the scriptures. When world leader or governments usher a new establishment which is against God's laws or what the bible is against, the Christian has every right to argue by apologetics methodological approach and correct the minds of the people because we are part of the world and that is the reason why we are Christians. We shall be responsible for the effect of human abominable decisions or human errors, being strongly backed by demons, without the Christian intervention to correct them.

ANGELOLOGY:- The study of the doctrine of theological knowledge concerning Angels. Angels are celestial bodies which act as intermediaries between Heaven and Earth, and man and God. They are also guardian spirits. They protect and guide humanity and carry out the instruction of God. When were angels created? Job 38:7 "When the morning stars (archangels) sang together, And all the sons of God (angels) shouted for joy." For the Angels to shout at the foundation of creation, they need to be created before the foundation, so they existed before the foundation. Angels were not mentioned in the physical creation because Angels do not belong to the physical creation. They were before the creation and for that reason they shouted joyfully when the foundation of the earth were laid. Job 38:6-7. Angels have the quality of God, Exo. 23:21. They have God's name in them. Angels have the ability to enter and exit at will into the physical realm, also they can be visible and invisible. Jacob wrestled with the Angel, Gen 32:24. Angel spoke with Joshua, 5:13-14 and as well Daniel saw angel, Dan. 10:12-13. Abram saw angels as humans and spoke and dine with them, Gen.18:2. Angel were created by God, Eze. 28:15.

PNEUMATOLOGY:- The study of the doctrine of the operation of the Holy Spirit. It's simply the study of the Holy Spirit. The term pneumatology comes from two Greek words namely "pneuma" meaning wind, breath, or spirit and "logia" meaning word or matter. It is the study of the biblical doctrine of the Holy Spirit. There are many evidences in the New Testament which confirms the personality of the Holy Spirit, in John 14:16 Jesus promised us the arrival of the Holy Spirit and He arrived in Acts 2:1-4. So it makes sense to say, He is a person, who according to Jesus enables, encourages and comforts which requires that the Spirit is a person and His functions are personal. The deity of the Holy Spirit like Jesus is also related to the Father on an equal bases, hence He is entitled to receive worship as to the Father and the Son. 2Cor. 13: "For if I pray in a tongue, my spirit prays, but my understanding is unfruitful." He is a miracle worker as we all know from the scriptures, an inspiring scriptures. 2Pet.1:20-21 "Knowing this first that no prophecy of the scripture is of any private interpretation. For prophecy never came by the will of man, but holy men of God spoke as they were moved by the Holy Spirit." It is by the function of the Holy Spirit that make Church planting and existence possible because he is the helper. John 14:26 "But the helper, the Holy Spirit, whom the Father will send in My name, He will teach you all things and bring to your remembrance all things that I said to you." The Holy Spirit is given metaphor of "HE" meaning the Holy Spirit is a person and could take any form like as Dove, Water, Fire, Wind, Clothing. Acts 2:2-4, Acts 19:11-12.

POLEMICS:- The look and the attitude of the congregation and congregational dispute. The word polemics was derived from Greek word "polemikos" meaning warfare "polemos," a strong verb or written attack against someone or something. It is the contention and the dispute that is intended to establish the truth of a specific understanding and to avoid the false edification of a contrary situation. Polemics are mostly seen in arguments about controversial topics over religious matters. The most important thing to consider by the Christian in polemics is to be aware at all times the goal of Christ to be achieved. This perception must continue for the basic purpose for discussion about polemics topics. This branch of theology does not make the aim of winning arguments or how powerful we are as Christians, but how faithful we must be to Christ and winning of souls. Christ is always the center of polemics in Christianity, exposing unbeliever to the truth of Christ and the light of God.

SATANOLOGY:- The doctrine of the study of the worship, practices, teachings and works of Satan. He is a fallen archangel with his demons and are classified under angelology because they were once angels and all the doctrine pertaining to his hideous kingdom (Rev. 12:7-12). Satanology teaches the none existence of God and the liberalism and naturalism leading human to believe nature and not God. We as Christians, we cannot believe in God without considering that Satan exists. Consideration of this brings spiritual warfare and leads to Pentecostal and charismatic believes which deals with deliverance and warfare against demons. There are several quotations in the scripture showing the activities and the person of Satan. Isaiah 14:12 which speaks of the son of the morning who has fallen from heaven and Eze. 28:2 (13-17 "Son of man say to the prince of Tyre, Thus says the Lord God: Because your heart is lifted up, And you say, I am god, I sit in the seat of gods, in the midst of the sea, Yet you are a man, and not a god, behold, you are wiser than Daniel!" These scriptures confirm the description and pride of Satan. Angels do not marry, Matt. 22:30 so if a spirit marries a human being, its demonic and it should be dealt with. Angels do take human form. Hebr. 13:2 'Do not forget to entertain strangers, for by so doing, some have unwittingly entertained Angels." Gen. 18:2 "So he lifted his eyes and looked, and behold, three men were standing by him: and when he saw them, he ran from the tent door to meet them, and bow himself to the ground. And said, My Lord if I have now found favor in thy sight, do not pass on by your servant." Angels were created by God, and Satan was created by God. Eze. 28:15 "You were perfect in you ways from the day you were created, till iniquity was found in you." The devil made the first human to loose their estate and cause them to be rebellious which caused them their dominion which was the light from Christ Jesus. 2Cor. 11:3 "But I fear, lest somehow as the serpent deceived Eve by his craftiness, so your minds may be corrupted from the simplicity that is in Christ." Satan also prevents human of the light of the scripture to shine unto them 2Cor. 4:4, and made Christians join occult sects, even pastor who become captive under demonic possession. The study of the doctrine of Satan teaches us about his character, purpose and his temptations to make the Christian alert 1Pet. 5:8-9. Satan's name is seen from Genesis to Revelation, and because people are ignorant of him they serve God and serve Satan at the same time. If you know him you will avoid him.

Reason for possession:- Family practices and power are sometimes handed down by inheritance or transfer, involving both past and present acquired charms, mediums, occultism etc Deut. 18:9-13. These can include tarot cards, voodoos, jujus, chancellors, spirit guides, idle words which gives Satan opportunity for possession 2Cor. 4:2. These are hidden things of shame and must be renounce or else your salvation could be taken captive, if we allow Satan's influence again in our lives, Luke 22:3.

Deliverance:- Through persistent prayer and commanding faith, demons are cast out if they are in existence. To battle with Satan involve prayer. Eph. 6:18, Mark 6:7, Luke 10:17. Even someone who was not with the disciples and never came to Jesus was casting out demons in the name of Jesus Christ, because he had a strong believe that by the mention of the name Jesus Christ demons are cast out. Mark 9:38-40. This shows that it is a principle of authority in such situation of Godly qualities.

Fallen Angel :- Satan is a fallen angel with supernatural powers. Satan is a person who is a spirit being who appears lovely, polite in the eyes of humanity, who pretend to be good but dangerous with weapons of fiery darts, a foolish wise military leader who refuses defeat and proud to repent and aggressive in his wiles.

NAMINOLOGY :- It is the study of the doctrine of naming and it is the most important ceremony of humanity. Anything that does not exist has no name but only that which has name exists. A name of a child is the acceptance of a child into a community and into the world. A name can affect one's success in life. The name you give your child plays an important role in the life of the child. The child will hear this name every day and if there is a curse behind this name, this child will receive this curse every day all his or her life. You can imagine the harm and the damage you might have caused to the child by giving him or her a name you do not even know what it is or with a curse behind it. Likewise if there is blessing behind the name, this child will receive this blessing every day all his or her life. So as Christians we do not just give any name to our children, but ask from God. When God gives a name, that name cannot be broke, that name cannot be cursed, that name cannot be poor, that name cannot be sick.

Gen. 17:19 "Then God said, No, Sarah your wife shall bear you a son, and you shall call his name Isaac.

Luke 1:13 Your wife Elizabeth will bear you a son and you shall call his name John.

Luke 1 :31 You will conceive in your womb and bring forth a Son and shall call His name Jesus.

Sometimes we look at the problems, the troubles and challenges we go through and name it after our children. If the name is not God ordained, it will be wrong and torment and jeopardize the child's destiny. This is a human mistake and a tremendous chaos.

When God wanted to be friend of Abraham, He changed his name meaning God ordained Abraham's name by adding His name "H" of the "YAHWEH."

Jacob which is Ya'aqov "Y' of the "YHWH" to Isra-el which has the Godhead name "EL" of the "ELOHIM."

Likewise Sarai the wife of Abraham was changed to Sarah having the "H" of the "YHWH."

Even to Ishmael having double portion of God's name the "H" of the "YHWH" and the "EL" of the "ELOHIM."

Jesus which is Yeshua meaning Jehovah that is "YHWH" or "Yahweh" the beginning "Y" and the end "H."

In 1Chronicles 4:9-10 Now Jabez was more honorable than his brothers and his mother called his name Jabez, saying, Because I bore him in pain. The mother named him after her situation, the pain she went through. When Jabez saw the torment of his name, he called on the name of God of Israel saying:

1. That You bless me indeed :- Prosper me indeed, Even though I am called sorrow or pain let my name reflect not the curse but prosperity - "Tzellakh."
2. Enlarge my territory:- Elevate me, let me be great, let the world hear of me, Elevation - "Hatzlakh."
3. That Your hand be with me:- That I will succeed in all that I do, be successful - "Umatzlakh"
4. That You will keep me from Evil :- Give me sound wisdom, that I will always be careful and obedient - Sound Wisdom - "Tuwshiyyah"
5. That I may not cause pain :- That I may build wealth and be wealthy, when I am wealthy I will not cheat that I may be cursed. I shall not be corrupt but edification of wealth will be my portion - "Umatzlekhim."

Jabez was honorable but was being tormented, being afflicted and being oppressed and saw his only solution was God of Israel and cried onto Him and the bible says God granted his prayer. God is always ready to grant our prayer. If there is a man to pray, there is a God to grant that prayer. Jabez was specific, he touched the root of his problem, his name.

1. Today with the power and anointing of Tuwshiyyah (sound wisdom) any curse behind my name, be removed and replaced with the spirit of Tuwshiyyah. In Jesus name.

2. I command the spirit of umatzlekhim (building of wealth to fill me). In Jesus name.

3. Umatzlakh (the spirit of success) cover me and fill me and be my portion. In Jesus name.

4. I soak myself with Tzellakh (spirit of prosperity). Tzellakh soak me. In Jesus name.

5. Hatzlakh (spirit of greatness) you are my portion. I will prosper and be prosperous and prosper in prosperity. In Jesus name.

6. Every negative attachment to my name be removed and replaced with prosperity(Tzallakh), success(Umatzlakh), sound wisdom(Tuwshiyyah), greatness (Hatzlakh) and building of wealth(Umatzlekhim) in life. In Jesus name. Every pride, every power consciousness be removed. Where is God of Elijah, fill me with Your spirit. In Jesus mighty name.

ETHICOLOGY:-The study of the doctrine of Christian ethics being the nature and approach of good and evil, the behavioral analysis or the moral principle that qualifies a believer to be the follower of Jesus Christ and a good citizen, when we depend our life basically on the word of God. Christian Ethics is based on the concept of Obedience, Courage, Prudence, Temperance, Charity, Justice, Hope, Love and Faith in Christ. Whoever rejects Jesus as the Christ and refuses to accept Him as the Son of God is Anti-Christ and does not have the Father but whoever accepts and receives Jesus as the Christ and Son of God is a believer and follower of Christ, 1John 2:22-25. Christian Ethics teaches that all is passing away that is in the world and will not abide forever but he who does the will of God will abide forever, 1John 2:16-17. We have been made to understand that there are three in heaven, the Father, the Word and the Holy Spirit and are one which constitute God. 1John 5:7. And until we believe in this Trinity we may not know God, who He is. We are born again by the confession of the sacrifice of Christ 1John 4:15. Lastly we are to love one another because that was the ultimate commandment from Jesus Christ. John 15:12-13 and without this love, we cannot claim to be Christians. Ethics means having these qualities; courage, temperance, hope, faith, love or charity, justice and prudence.

1. Courage is the ability to ignore and avoid fear. It does not care how long it will take. It gives strength and endurance. It removes limitation and cause one to act with the principle of using reasoning. Courage is hereditary and could be copied from others. There are two types of courage, 1. spiritual and 2. physical. Luke 18:1-8 the unjust judge and the widow. She had the courage, the prudence, the temperance, hope, faith and justice. Likewise in Act 2:4 the apostles were filled with the Holy Ghost and boldly came out to preach the gospel.

2. Prudence is basically the use of wisdom which enable one to know and have the insight of situations and the knowledge, which could be acquired. The combination of all these give the capacity to judge with courage. A cardinal virtue which is the ability to take a risk and receive the power to do business. The word 'prudence' is derived from the Latin word "prudencia" which in its principle of application, unveil the gift of descending spirit which is the ability to rule and govern, using reason of discipline by the Holy Spirit.

3. Temperance is the ability to refrain from the things which leads onto sin. It is the reformation of behavior ethics and enable one to calm down, even at the worse situation which demands retaliation. It is the modest of self control.

4. Hope is the expectation unseen. This is normally common with Christians. It is the believe in miracles. Miracles are things not seen but believed to be in existence and are received or could be received. They believe Jesus Christ is capable to do miracles by the mention and the believe in His name over a particular expectation and it is the result of the covenant that those who believe in Jesus Christ have future with the Father.

5. Faith is the central focus of life. Faith is the trust to live tomorrow, the trust to wake up tomorrow from sleep. Many people do not pray to wake up from sleep but they do, many do not pray to live tomorrow but they do, because we are already empowered with

that faith. Every human being have some kind of faith, whether we believe in God or not, it's a form of faith. Christianity is based on faith and without faith Christianity is depleted. Faith is strong believe and trust in something or someone.

6. Charity is an unconditional love. The word charity was derived from the Latin word CARITAS, which means favor and favor is not fair and does not measures who receives the favor. It is an unconditional love, known as agape love. It is the theological virtue that demonstrate the love of God upon mankind unconditionally. Likewise God expects us to love one another unconditionally. It is the healing faculty in the estate of world inhabitants.

7. Justice is fairness, Jesus said in Matt. 23:23 Justice, mercy and faith, these you ought to have done without leaving the others undone. Luke 18:1-8 the unjust judge and the widow. Ethics is more than we anticipate, it can go on and on.

TONGUESONOLOGY:- It is the doctrine of speaking in tongues. One thing we have to know is speaking in tongues is a spiritual activity.

Tonguesonology is a two way word combination, tongue and sonology

1. Tongue - the muscular organ in the mouth used for articulating speech.

2. Sonology - is a neologism (new expression or word) used to describe the study of sound in a variety of disciplines. In medicine, the term is used in the field of imaging to describe the practice of medicine. eg ultrasonography or ultrasounds. So tonguesonology is the doctrine of the sound by the tongue through the mouth being a new expression or new word or new term or new phrase which communicates with the heavenlies who understand it. 1Cor. 14:39 Therefore, brethren, desire earnestly to prophesy and do not forbid to speak in tongues. So speaking in tongues is a sign of the Holy Ghost anointing. Those who desire to speak in tongue can use Matt 7:11 as a scriptural base to desire to speak in tongues, which says, "If ye then being evil know how to give good gifts unto your children; how much more shall your heavenly Father give the Holy Spirit to them that ask Him." Using this verse as a faith base, will successfully lead to speaking in tongues not excluding

fasting, for fasting will bring one to God quicker than any other thing. Anointing comes by spending time with God, through the word of God, prayer and fasting, preparing the heart for the Holy Ghost assignment. We have the Charismatic way of speaking in tongues and the Pentecostal way of speaking in tongues. The interpretation of the tongues is the words that flows through your mind or another person at the same time the tongues flows from the Holy Ghost.

In these modern days we see people who learn and practice to speak in tongues. But tongues is a language given by God to communicate with Him. It is inspirational and not motivational, therefore it cannot be imitated or learned. What is the contrast between those who speak in tongues and those who do not speak in tongues? Speaking in tongues is the greatest secret of communication in the spirit, God has given to Christians. Even some witch doctors speak unknown language to command the demons under their control. A believer in the comfort of human is not complete till that believer moves out from the human comfort to the spiritual comfort and that makes a Christian a child of man to live as child of God because the day you receive Jesus Christ you are no more son of man because you have been born by God for the scripture says, as many as received Him to them He gave power to become children of God, to those who believed in His name. The first question a person or a Christian will ask is how do we speak in tongues. It's simple, it is a command from Jesus himself that believers shall perform the under mentioned in Mark 16:16-18. There is secret in speaking in tongues and there is a level a person must attain to penetrate into the spiritual realm. Tongues is a sign to Christians, which says these signs shall follow those who believe the gospel and are baptized:

1. In My name, they will cast out demons.
2. In My name, they will speak with new tongue.
3. In My name, they will take up serpents.
4. In My name, they will drink deadly substance and will not hurt them.
5. In My name, they will lay hands on the sick, and they shall recover.

Our tongues must start "in the name of Jesus." The mistake most of us do is we end our prayer in the name of Jesus and do not start in His name.

Know that He is the beginning and the end. So in the mighty name of Jesus Christ, then you begin to pray in tongues, the same way you lay hands on the sick in Jesus name and they get healed. Because you mention the name of Jesus Christ and the heart is connected to Him, you must begin to speak in tongues and tongues will begin to discharge from your bowel and flow out of your mouth in that same name of Jesus. In 1Cor. 14:2 "He who speak in tongues does not speak to men but to God for no one understands him; however in the spirit he speaks mysteries." The devil knows every language of the nations of the world, because he is the ruler and the prince of the world, John 12:31 and John 14:30, and none of the languages of the nations of the world can cast him out, except the heavenly language which was used to cast him unto the earth. That's the reason why when believers command him to come out, he obeys because we speak heavenly language and have heavenly relationship. We have the Holy Spirit and <u>He is our helper who assign to us angels.</u> The devil can hold your miracle in every language but not in tongues. What do Christians speak at the presence of God and His angels these days? Is it a language or a sound. Many make noise but tongues is a language and not sound. There is difference between language and sound. "Language is a combination of word spoken or written, of a particular origin in communication which carry a message." Know that tongues is a language and not a rattling sound of an object. With tongues, you are talking by fire, every blessing of yours, declaring and decreeing blessing into your life which only heaven understands it. There is fire in tongues. Apostle Paul said if I speak in tongues my understanding is fruitful because the devil does not understand what I am talking and that makes my prayer fruitful and bear fruit because the devil does not know what I am speaking and gets confused for I am speaking a new language, a language created after Satan was thrown out of heaven. God is an intelligent God, for He knows if tongues is given before the devil was cast out of heaven, believers will have no power, so first of all, the devil must be cast out of heaven, then send Jesus Christ to come and deal with the Satan and after Him send the Holy Spirit with pouring of the speaking in tongues to give Christians the ability to frustrate the devil and overcome him. There are quite a number of tongues but the most common are:-

1. **Foreign tongues :-** (Acts 2:6-8), it could also be called tongues of languages. This is a language given by God to a believer

through prayer who has not the ability to speak a particular language whom He desire him to communicate His message to another person of the same language (eg. prophesy) and after that communication that language exterminates. Because God wants to communicate at a particular time so He gives that language for his own communication. It is a language which comes by the power of the Holy Ghost to fill the believer and energized him with boldness to deliver that message and after the work is done that language ends

2. **Worship tongues:-** The bible says those who worship the Lord must worship Him in Spirit and in Truth. John 4:24. When we worship in spirit we are edifying, in otherwise we are building and 1Thess 5:11 says, Comfort each other and edify one another. So speaking in tongues is building your spiritual life, building your finances, building your marriage, building your business, building your education, building your future and so on. Speaking in tongues puts the devil in trouble and the more we speak in tongues the more explosions we create and experience

3. **Gift of Tongues:-** Apostle Paul quoted in 1Cor. 12:4,10d "There are diversities of gifts, but the same spirit. To another different kinds of tongues." Speaking in tongues is a gift and the gift of speaking in tongues is for believers. It is an inheritance for believers according to Mark 16:17. There are people who receive the speaking in tongues as gift but for those who shall believe according to our Lord Jesus Christ, it is a right which is a promise. The gift of speaking in tongues is given to specific people who have specific assignment because they have to pray for something to change, who communicate in the office of intercession and prophecy. It is not for everyone to receive the gift of speaking in tongues but the promise of speaking in tongues is for every Christian.

4. **Prophetic tongues:-** The scripture calls it a none tongues which always carry message and needs interpretation. 1Cor. 14:5 I wish you all speak with tongues, even more than you prophesied; for he who prophesies is greater than he who speak with tongues, unless indeed he interprets, that the church may receive edification. And in many occasions we experience it, when we gather for

worship. Speaking in prophetic tongues means prophesying over the church, about your business, your family, your career etc., every work that comes out in this section of speaking in tongues is prophecy.

5. **Angelic Tongues:-** Angelic tongues are meant to give instruction to angels. Angelic tongues are tongues which angels speak in heaven. If you speak angelic tongues, angels hear you. These tongues are given to Christians because every Christian have been given angels, assigned by God. Matt. 18:10 "For I say to you that in heaven their angels always see the face of My Father who is in heaven." So if the believer does not give the angels instruction, it's not the fault of God, it's the believer's fault. The business of devil is to disturb your business, your future, your education, your finances, even your prayer life etc. So the Christian also enter into his closet with tongues in Jesus name and fire is released. There will be always chaos in the kingdom of Satan. Speaking in tongues means speaking tons of fire by angels and quickly they will be there. As many as received Him, them He gave the right to become the children of God, so from the day you were born by God, your language was changed, you see things differently, you are given a new nature. The problem is you are still seeing and doing things the same way as before, you are talking the same way as before. The bible says, if any man be in Christ, he is a new creature, old things have passed away, new things are regenerated.

There is tongues of angels, and if we speak these tongues, we give instruction to angels, what they must do. Tongues is a language given to believers who do not have the ability to speak a particular language but as they pray, God give them a language for His purpose of communication. The witch doctor command incantation upon an evil altar or shrine to give instruction to charms and they go and perform whatever the witch doctor commanded them. The Christians are more powerful than the witch doctor. Believers have hosts of angels and personal angels who have mighty power which can put out every power and make the witch doctor prostrate and nothing. Witch doctors operate from powers, principalities, dominion and authorities. The Christian operates from the THRONE OF GOD - the greatest power, from which the whole universal power is released.

THEOLOGICAL SCIENCE OF GOD THE TRUE LIGHT

As humans beings, we have to understand that there is no life without Light, and we cannot live without it. Light is the foundation of Science and without it there is no "LIFE." The bible says, God is light and in Him there is no darkness, meaning we cannot live without God because God is full of science. "SCIENCE" is the study of the proof of the wonders of God, which confirms the reality of the existence of God. Hence, without God there is no "LIGHT" and without light there is no science, which is the knowledge of the absolute truth and the law of life. The Scientist believes in science, yes, he is right, and the Christian believes in God, yes, he is also right, both science and God exist, and that, there is God who is the originator of science. The Christian generally believes in science because everything around him is all science and the Scientist also believes in God because there are circumstances beyond human science. Whatever God created was by the art of science because the revolutions, the rotations, the orbiting, distances between orbits, planet, stars etc. were all perfectly calculated which was the art of the Scientific God. This title is to set a coalition between God and Science and to bring to the attention of both Scientists and Christians, the conflicting mindset to break the gap between God and Science and to know that God is full of science and believing in God is believing in science and accepting Science to be part of God is equally believing in God. So what is being emphasized here is that, creation was through science, and it's the purpose and glory of scientific creations. John 1:9 says, That was the "TRUE LIGHT" which gives "light" to every man coming into the world." Both the old and new testaments and most especially this verse is saying that Jesus is LIGHT and it's Him who approves of every man which comes to this world and equips us with "HIS LIGHT" to see the past, present and the future. Without "CHRIST" no man shall enter into this world. But when we come into this world, because of the generational and ancestral sins, the wicked, "Satan" takes advantage and snatches and withhold that light till we are drawn by the hand of the Holy Spirit to salvation and the Light is once again restored.

Gen. 1:3 says, Then God said, Let there be "LIGHT" and there was "LIGHT." The bible says, the Light shined in the darkness, and the darkness comprehended it not. This Light talks about Jesus who showed up at the command of the Father to stop Satan who is darkness, from opposing the "HOLY GHOST" for further creations, exactly as it happened in Daniel 10:13-14. and 1John 1:5 says "This then is the message which we have heard of Him, and declare unto you, that God is "LIGHT," and in Him is no darkness at all." Only God is light who gives light to the world and He expect us to be His likeness, to maintain the light in us.

LIGHT which is the base of this title, is electromagnetic radiation having the properties of waves possibly divisible by many wave lengths through the electromagnetic spectrum. It is the scientific side of the "TRUE GOD." Light involves two spectrums:

1. The Visible Spectrum. 2. The Invisible Spectrum.

1. VISIBLE SPECTRUM or Light :- This is the Son of the True Living God with the following properties: Radiant from which originates all colors; violet, Blue, Green, Yellow, Orange, Red etc. emanates the expression of love, happiness and confidence; Cosmic rays; X-rays; Radio-waves; Ultraviolet Rays; Gamma-rays; Infrared rays. Infrared ray is measured in nanometers, a billion of a meter 0.000,000,0001, used in nanotech which are small devices. That is why God creates out of nothing and the least. Visible spectrum is responsible for the sense of sight and define as having wave lengths impossible to measure but in human aspect it ranges from 400 - 700nm and between the infrared and the ultraviolet has frequency range of eg. 400-750 terahertz (thz) by scientists, that's human standard. These are in the Son whom the father has delivered all power of the universe into His hands. Matt. 27:18 says, "And Jesus came and spoke unto them, saying All power is given unto Me in Heaven and in Earth." Again in John 14:8-9 "Philip saith unto Him, Lord, show us the Father and it sufficeth us. Jesus saith unto him, I have been so long time with you, and yet hast thou not known Me, Philip? he that hath seen Me hath seen the Father; and how sayest thou then, Show us the Father?" All these confirm that Jesus Christ is the God incarnate and without Him nothing consists. His name Emmanuel meaning God with us, and Jesus which is Savior meaning God has visited us and that was the name the Angel Gabriel gave to Mary his mother, so He went back after the visit to His Father by fulfilling the prophesy.

So Jesus is that God, because there is no way a man can see God the Father

2. INVISIBLE SPECTRUM or Light :- (God - the Father) the Light, is with the following properties. Cosmic-rays, X-rays, Radio-waves, Gamma-rays, Ultra Violet-Rays, Infrared-rays, Radiant, Micro-Waves.

John 1:18 "No one has seen God at anytime. The Only begotten Son who is in the Bosom of the Father, He has declared Him." These are His properties that is why humanity must fear and be obedient to Him. Cosmic Rays, Gamma Rays, Ultra Violet Rays, X-Rays, Infrared waves, Micro Waves, Radio waves, Radiant. Acts 17:24 "God who made the world and everything in it, since He is Lord of heaven and earth, does not dwell in temples made with hands." So it is wrong to imagine God to be some old man with white long bear touching the ground and long silver hair. He is God who is everywhere and fills everything, that is why He is LIGHT and has ordained nature to be the agent of God under the assignment of the Son, Jesus Christ, who punishes those who sin against Him and blesses those who do His will. We cannot belittle God to be doing little things. God is so extreme that nobody can withstand His physical or direct punishment or receive equally same in blessing. We have to understand and know that as we of the human race have government with branches copied from Him, even so is God whose government is vast. It is necessary to elaborate on these properties in God that makes human what we are:-

(a) Cosmic Rays = Highly energetic atomic nucleus travelling through space at a speed of light. In our universe they originate outside the solar system and from distance galaxies to the earth atmosphere. "Cosmic rays make celestial travel the most fastest in less than seconds and make it possible through every substance". Dan. 9:21 "While I was speaking in prayer, the man Gabriel whom I had see in the vision at the beginning, being caused to FLY SWIFTLY, reached me about the time of the evening offering. "Luke 24 : 31" And their eyes were opened, and they knew Him; and He vanished out of their sight."

(b) Gamma Rays = penetrating electromagnetic radiation arising from radioactive decay of the atomic nuclei or nuclear explosions or lightening. Gamma rays are so powerful that they cannot be captured by mirrors and if mirrors did, they become damaged. It has greater energy and penetrating power than X-Rays but limited to the earth atmosphere. "These carry the curses from God which no one can remove, unless God Himself." 1Sam. 16:14 But the spirit of the Lord departed from Saul, and a distressing spirit from the Lord troubled him. In Gen. 3:14-19 Both the serpent, Adam and Eve were cursed, and this is how far the curse has brought mankind.

(c) Ultraviolet = Beyond the visible spectrum (unapproachable), the electromagnetic spectrum whose wavelengths are shorter than visible light (100nm) and longer than x-rays (400nm) and powerful. The ultraviolet radiation is an invisible rays released by the sunshine which was created with it, and completely reduced by the oxygen in the Earth atmosphere for the safety of humanity, according to science. When applied on human, it produces dark skin and could be dangerous to living tissue. This property in God make demons, witches and wizards burn and deform at deliverance services." Heb. 12:29 "For our God is a consuming fire."

(d) X-Rays = Electromagnetic wave of high energy capable to pass through the most opaque and robust material and mostly used in detecting and unveiling internal fractures for examination and treatment in medical purposes, especially radiograms and radiographs. "This exposes every hidden secret by the Holy Ghost, during deliverance service as these rays pass through the people, demons begin to confess every hidden secret." Heb. 4:13 "And there is no creature hidden from His sight, but all things are naked and opened to the eyes of Him to whom we must give account."

(e) Infrared waves = Remote power, which, the source is known but can't be seen. eg. TV remote. It is also use in scientific, military, medical appliances, industrial and law enforcement devices. Infrared allows information to be stored in cloud and make it possible to be retrieved whenever desired. It is used in security cameras and imaging equipments and cameras, even high powered detectors. It is very important and profitable in our modern technology, it serves an important role and is the part of science that has made astral technology possible. "Infrared makes invisible images visible to human eyes and reveal every hidden secret. We see miracle and we know is from God but we cannot see Him, it is the prophetic tool of the prophet, from which the prophetic word is revealed, so without infrared there will be no prophecy." 2Cor. 3:17 "Now God is spirit; and where the Spirit of God is, there is liberty."

(f) Micro waves = Highly Electromagnetic energy with billions of cycles and wavelength ranging from 0.001 - 0.3m with frequencies 300MHz (100cm) and 300GHz (0.1cm) according to science, with large infrared waves and short radio waves that is used in radio communications and heating. Micro wave generally is not an object but a media filled with wave lengths capable to create heat. And this is a media in God that makes Him impossible to touch or unapproachable. So this produce heat without physical source. This is His presence at deliverance gathering; where people receive their deliverance and demons are caged in these cycles and make them scream. Matt. 4:41 "And demons also came out of many, crying out and saying, You are the Christ, the Son of God! And He rebuking them, and did not allow them to speak, for they knew that He was the Christ." In the Lord Jesus this is hid in Him so that humanity can come closer to Him, but not to the dark world.

(g) Radio Waves = An electromagnetic wavelengths having transmitting power to communicate universally but not visible, eg. radio communications. It also allows transmitting power to communicate between planets, permitting recipients to hear and speak to one another. We hear the voice of God but we do not see Him, even from heaven His voice reaches us on Earth. Acts 9:7 "And the men who journeyed with him stood speechless, hearing a voice but seeing no one." And also

Rev. 12:10 "Then I heard a loud voice saying in heaven, Now is come salvation and strength, and kingdom of our God and the power of His Christ have come, for the accuser of our brethren, who accused them before our God day and night has been cast down."

(h) Radiant = All colors; sending out light, brilliant and glowing steadily brightly, and it's transferrable by electromagnetic radiation producing light, x-rays, gamma-rays or heat radiation, cause by energy known as continuous electromagnetic waves (photon). The radiant enable us to express happiness, create beauty and maintain hope. With radiant in contact and in us, we send out smiles to each other as humans. The radiant make humans to come closer and connect to each other. "This enable us to connect to God and use us to glorify Himself." 2Cor. 4: 18 "While we do not look at the things which are seen, but at the things which are not seen. For the things which are seen are temporal, but the things which are not seen are eternal." Radiant is not seen but its reaction could be felt and seen. For one to shine, it is the effect of the radiant.

The presence of these properties or any of them means God is present. The combination of these will make God physically present, but it's impossible, so God cannot be seen but be heard, by voice, that is why the deity of Jesus is a reality. This is the presence of God which represents HOLINESS. Holy Ghost constitutes all the properties which are invisible to the ordinary eyes but visible only at works. When wave lengths of visible light are present, the eyes will see it as bright light or visible light. And if JESUS is "LIGHT" which is the image of the invisible God, commanded by the unapproachable LIGHT, then Jesus is the VISIBLE LIGHT and that "UNAPPROACHABLE LIGHT" is the "INVISIBLE LIGHT" which is "GOD the FATHER" and that is the INVISIBLE SPECTRUM - The True God. Without the TRUE GOD there will be no light, and without this True God, there will be no energy. Without Him no light bulb will give light because the light we see all over the earth, invented and natural is the refraction from the True God. That is why our True God is full of science. So you can imagine how deadly it could be to see the face of God. Seeing the Face of God means burning completely without ashes. Rev. 16:18 "And there were noises and thunderings and lightenings, and there was a great earthquake, such a mighty and great earthquake as had not occurred since men were on the earth." Also Rev. 11:19 "Then the temple of God was opened in heaven, and the ark of His covenant was seen in His temple. And there were lightenings, noises, thunderings, an earthquake and great hail." Only the opening of the temple without seeing His face resulted in such lightenings, thunderings, earthquakes, noises and hails, how deadly it will be to see His face. God used the Ark to represent Him but the Ark could not demonstrate His physical expressions, so He has to show up as God incarnate in the form of Jesus Christ which is the True name of the TRUE GOD. And if the ark produced such Lightenings, Thunderings, noises, earthquakes and hails, what do you think will happen if He is seen physically? If no wave lengths and rays are present in our eyes, it is assumed as Dark and this is an empty space without light which means there is no electromagnetic radiation or power in that space and make that space, where all kinds of wickedness and evil originates and practiced, which is the kingdom of Satan. All the above waves and rays being the properties in God, that is the reason why no one shall see the face of God and live. John 5:26/3:16b - For as the Father has life in Himself {to give life}, so He has granted the Son to have life in Himself {to give life}, that whosoever believes in the Son, should not perish but have eternal life {in himself also to give life}. Light is life, where there is light there is life, as such one must have light to have life and with the light such one can give life. This is the reason why Jesus raised the dead and whoever believes in Him and has this light can also raise the dead in the name of Jesus Christ. The bible says He gives this light to those who believe in Him.

The Radiant (violet, blue, green, red, orange, yellow) and infrared, are the joy properties in EMMANUEL, and because of these visible colors, that is why we see Him and live and we are part of Him because we are created of these colors which is by His approval and empowerment.

The Ultraviolet, Radiant and the infrared signifies His holiness, and that makes Him superior and different from all. This is the more reason why people go to where the Spirit of God is present and they begin to feel the heat of the Holy Ghost. The ultraviolet and the Radiant makes man

33

the likeness of God but not God. Witches and Demons are trapped and perpetually caged in this "TRUE LIGHT." Where the Spirit of God is present, where all the rays and waves are present, whoever fumbles with the Spirit of God at that time in that vicinity will be trapped in the burning heat. This is the more reason why Moses saw the burning bush and was surprised and afraid. For this reason the bible says in :

John 6:46 Not that anyone has seen the Father, Except He who is from God, He has seen the Father.

John 1:18 No one has seen God at anytime. The only begotten Son who is in the bosom of the Father, He has declared Him. Once you accept Christ, your soul becomes the likeness of God. You become the light unto the world. God is light and there is no darkness in Him. So is the power and the wisdom of God, which is Christ Jesus. 1John 1:5.

Exo. 33:20 But He said, You cannot see My face; for no man shall see My face and live.

FATHERHOOD OF GOD :- Because only Jesus Christ was able to live unto the will of the Father, among the inhabitants on the earth to date, so Jesus is ordained by God, His Father, to be God of the universe. Acts 17:31 "Because He had appointed a day, in the which He will judge the world in righteousness by that MAN whom He had ORDAINED; whereof He had given assurance unto all men, in that He had raised Him from dead." Again in Acts 10:42 "And He commanded us to preach to the people, and to testify that it is He which was ORDAINED of God to be the judge of the quick and the dead. "The claim of Jesus of God as his Father is based on the creation, Let there be Light, and there was Light, Gen. 1:3. He was inside God as word and was called forth into existence as Light by God the Father, that's the reason why Jesus said, a little while is the light with you, walk while ye have the Light, lest darkness come upon you, for he that walk in darkness does not where he goes, while ye have the Light, believe in the Light that ye may be the children of Light. John 12:35-36. So Jesus was born by God at the creation, that was the meaning of His claim as THE SON OF GOD, which is not metaphor but a reality. The Father sent Him physically to dwell among us on this our earth without human father. This is the reason Jesus never called Joseph, the husband of Mary, His mother, "father" and said human being is not our father but brought to existence through them and they do not own us.

Matt 23:9 "And call no man your father upon the earth, for one is your Father, which is in heaven." He continued to explained: John 16:27-28 "For the Father Himself loves you, because you have loved Me, and have believed that I came out from God. I came forth from the Father and Am come into the world; again, I leave the world and go to the Father." Meaning the Father love the disciples, because they had believed that He came out from inside the Father to join Him, and He sits with the Father. He continued to say He came from the Father who sent Him and He is come into the world for a purpose and the purpose is almost accomplished, so He was going to leave the world once again to join the Father. This gives the exact picture of His claim. And whoever does not accept the claim of Jesus Christ to be the Son of God the Father can also not be a child of God. Only Christ was obedient to the Father and has been ordained "the Son" and only Him Christ has whole heartedly accepted the offer of the Father as His Son, stated in, Heb. 1:5, 8 "For unto which of the angels said He at anytime, thou art My Son, this day have I begotten thee? And again I will be to Him a Father, and He shall be to me a Son? But unto the Son He said, Thy Throne, O God, is forever and ever: a sceptre of righteousness is the sceptre of thy kingdom." Christ is ordained our God and the God of the universe and all power is given unto Him in heaven and the earth. Heaven and earth means the whole universe. In our time, in every family, the husband who is called the father by the children and even some wives call their husbands Father, that's OK because he represents God in the family and that is great for God to reveal Himself in every family, so God is in every family as Father. If we can give this Fatherhood to God by every husband or family, God will reign in Families and families will be at peace. But because husbands claim the glory of Fatherhood so we have so many troubles in families.

THE REAL ASPECT OF JESUS CHRIST.

Creation is the beginning of the UNIVERSE and all things in the universe. It is the value access of all things. Gen. 1:1. "In the beginning God created the HEAVEN and the EARTH". By His word all these great works were made. Gen. 1:26 "Then God said, let us make man in Our image, according to Our likeness; let them have dominion over the fish of the sea, over the birds of the air, and over the cattle, over all the earth and over every creeping thing that creeps on the earth." God created Adam and Adam was alone in the Garden of Eden from the beginning. Even so God was alone in the firmament, moving in the firmament, a light unto the darkness. God being a creator, decided to create the Heavens and the Earth for His glory. The Heavens were the planets called THE SOLAR SYSTEM with a living planet called the Earth and beyond. Many do not believe there is God.

The creation of man is not the decision of a creation. Man has two eyes, two ears, two legs, two hands, two nose and one mouth. This means Somebody perfectly designed man. That master designer and the master architect is God. That's the reason why man has only one mouth because God has only one mouth, so He can not lie, that is why lying is a sin. Lying is double tongue but man has only one tongue, so once we lie, we are trying to have two mouth which God did not create us to be so. If man is of the wisdom of mankind, one day mankind will create a man with four mouths, like the exhaust pipe of some cars. A car originally had one exhaust outlet but some now have two, even four, that is the wisdom of man. This shows that God specially designed man to be His image and His own likeness as the bible says. So there is God and we must believe that He is. God is Someone no one can see with His eyes. Once we see God with our eyes, God has become like one of us, then He is no more a creator, and no more Almighty but a human Being. But God is not a human being, He is a combination of all rays and all waves and fills the universe. God is The True Light which no darkness can comprehend since that Light is the combination of all Rays and All Waves. Therefore for one to see Him, that person must be perfectly holy with a specific anointing on him. Anything with any form of sin in himself that sees God will burn without ashes. 1Timothy 6:16 "Who alone has immortality, dwelling in unapproachable LIGHT, who no man has seen or can see, to whom be honour and everlasting power." This is the more reason why JESUS CHRIST has to come physically and dwelled among us by God so that when you see Christ you see God, because God Himself said in Exo. 33:20 "And God said, Thou canst not see My face: for there shall no man see Me, and live." God saw Moses as an angel because Moses was doing what angels do, yet God told him, you cannot see My face. Jesus is the most

PERFECT HOLY Person on earth. Jesus Christ is the only person who can see God, who can go close to God, Who can sit with Him. Anyone who wants to see God can only see Jesus Christ and whatever He says is final. Jesus Himself said it in John 6:46 "Not that any man has seen the Father (God), save He which is of God, He hath seen the Father." He Jesus Christ has proved His deity by performing many miracles. Giving sight to the blind-man born with blindness from his mother's womb, healing the lame and sick, raising the dead, walking on the sea, casting out demons from people's lives to set them free, taking money from the mouth of a fish to pay the taxes of the apostles and finally rose from the dead when He was crucified. God does not die. If God dies then He has become the likeness of man. So Jesus Christ rose from the dead after three days as He prophesied to the disciple and the believers. If there is anyone who does not believe that Jesus Christ is God, at least he will believe that He was the greatest prophet who did miracles no prophet or no religious leader ever did, and until now there is no one, even His name raise the dead and heal the sick and give sight to the blind. So Jesus Christ is God who came in the flesh and is the Father and God of the universe.

John the Baptist also said in John 1:18 "No man hath seen God at any time, the only begotten Son, which is in the bosom of the Father, He hath declared Him." John is saying only Jesus Christ has seen God, and He has described Him. John the Baptist knew what he was talking about. He knew who Jesus was. He knew Jesus came out of the Father as light and was sent by the Father into the world to prove His deity and to take back what was taken by force pretence. In the kingdom of God, Jesus rules, being the Son of God, so when you see Jesus you have seen God. Likewise, in the kingdom of Satan, when you see the devil you've seen Satan, that is why Satan is also called devil. All things of Satan are imitation of Heaven, be vigilant and avoid him as much as possible. As Jesus Christ is the Son of Living God, even so the devil is the son of Satan. The bible has made us to know that, God created the heavens and the earth, but the earth was without form, and void: and darkness was on the face of the deep. And the spirit of God was hovering over the face of the waters. And God said, Let there be LIGHT and there was LIGHT. And God divided the LIGHT from the DARKNESS." So He created the heavens and the earth. He already had laid down the BLUE PRINT of the earth. For His intention was to create man and put him on the earth to display and demonstrate His glory. So BLUE PRINT was first created by God. His concentration was very much on the earth and Lucifer was aware because He saw the BLUE PRINT and began to oppose the Spirit of God against further creation in the form of Darkness. Gen.1:2 says "The earth was without form and darkness was on the face of the deep. And the Spirit of God was hovering over the face of the waters." The darkness that came with the earth and covered the face of the earth was a SPIRIT, preventing further creation, and this was LUCIFER, an OPPOSING SPIRIT now known as SATAN, that is the reason why he did not have the GODHEAD name, The ELOHIM which is EL. God could not continue with the creation without someone call LIGHT, which was in Him because Darkness, LUCIFER who is now Satan had covered the earth. 2Thess. 2:4 "Who opposes and exalt himself above all that is called God, so that he sits as God in the temple of God, showing himself that he is God."

Satan covered the earth while the creator God covers the universe. 1John 3:8 "He who sins is of the Devil (Satan was the first to sin) for the devil has sinned from the beginning. For this purpose the Son of God was manifested, that He might destroy the works of the devil." The earth was not solid soil at that time and not water but was a mixture of soil and water and for man to live on this earth was impossible. These two elements, the water and the soil must separate and the soil must hardened and the water gathered around and at specific areas of the solid soil and such occurred. Satan in the form of darkness wanted to take dominion over the earth and God being the Almighty will not strive with Satan because He had created him. So the Almighty God whose face there is always lightening and thundering, had to call the LIGHT {HIS SON} to come and drive away the spirit of Darkness {SATAN}. The LIGHT which is Jesus Christ who was known as EMMANUEL, who was Word in the Father, came out of the FATHER by His command; Let there be Light and there was Light and the Darkness (SATAN) could not stand before Him. John 1:4-5, says "In Him was life and the life was the LIGHT of men. And the LIGHT shines in the DARKNESS, and the DARKNESS did not comprehend it." He is LIGHT which pierced through every substance and every element, the first time Light appeared. He was a WORD in the Father and was spoken out to be LIGHT and He is THE LIGHT of the world. 1John 5:7 says "There are three that bear witness in heaven: the FATHER, the WORD and the HOLY SPIRIT; and these three are ONE". The Darkness which is the spirit of opposition was driven aside by the LIGHT OF GOD, who is the image of the invisible God. John 3:19 "And this is the condemnation, that the LIGHT has come into the world, and men love DARKNESS rather than LIGHT, because their deeds were evil." If there is no Satan, man will not search for God because life will be so easy and man will not even think of a creator. God's plan of the BLUE PRINT was to create man to care for the earth for His glory and Satan knew this. Satan knew that one day, he will be driven out of the kingdom of God, that is heaven and the next destination for him was the earth, that is the only planet with life and for this reason he did not want the creation of the earth, so that there will be no place for him to be casted to and remain with the Godhead to continue with his opposition to accomplish his aim. Now the earth has come into existence with the herb whose strength waited on the rain and because there was no rain, the herbs was in the earth, in wait of the rain to sprout. Because of this, man was not created till the rain came as in Gen. 2:4-5 "This is the history of the heavens and the earth, when they were created in the Day that the Lord God made the earth and the heavens. Before any plant of the field was in the earth and before any herb of the field had grown. For the Lord God had not cause it to rain on the earth and there was no man to till the ground. But a mist went up from the earth and watered the whole face of the ground." God could not create man because He needed clay to create man, whose life will depend on the moisturized soil. Man will need food and the food must come from the ground. So God made the relationship between man and the earth inseparable.

Because God created Satan, He did not reject or abandon him. Satan was crowned the Chief of the Archangels and all angels. Satan still disagrees and refuses that he was created by God, because he thinks God did not command the darkness into existence but rather came with the earth which God commanded into existence. Satan feels no one created him and claim to be equal with God, not thinking that without the earth he would not be in existence. And that was the problem of Satan. He was the mediator between the angels and God, and for this he took advantage and claim to be God. Isaiah 14:13-14. "For you have said in your heart: I will ascend into heaven, I will exalt my throne above the stars (angels) of God: I will also sit on the mount of the congregation, on the farthest side of the North. [14] I will ascend above the heights of the clouds, I will be like the MOST HIGH." Satan is described in Ezekiel 28:13-17 it portrays the picture of Satan and who he is. These were the pride of Satan and was cast down to the earth with his supporters from heaven. So Michael, the light of God with Gabriel, Raphael, Uriel and the angelic host of heaven which worship God, casted Satan and his angels out of heaven and he landed on earth with a third of the angels of heaven which supported him. (Rev. 12:4 - 12); for he knew the plan of God about the earth and man, because he read the BLUE PRINT of the creation and knew this. The earth was so precious to God and in His sight, and it was very dear to His heart when it was created, so God did not just created it, but created it with an angel to protect it, an angel who is so mighty and ordained with all power, beauty and anointed, and that angel was Lucifer, very handsome angel. Lucifer as head of the angels took advantage of the angels and tried to take advantage to control the earth by preventing farther creation in the form of darkness, but God knew all his intention which showed his desire to be on earth and take over the earth from the beginning, so when he made the war in heaven, the angels made him faced the war and was casted out of heaven and thrown unto the earth. So in this way, Satan chose to land on the earth to oppose man. If his opposition against God, about the creation did not work, his opposition against man, to destroy him against the plan of God for His glory will work. One of his main purpose is to harass and to threaten the whole population of the earth. The earth is at war with him.

Satan knew God's desire was to have human family to share his life and love, that He could entrust the rest of the physical creation into the hands of man and that from time to time, He would visit them as He did to Adam and his wife from the beginning. Gen. 3:8 "And they heard the sound of the Lord God walking in the garden in the cool of the day, and Adam and his wife hid themselves from the presence of the Lord God among the trees of the garden." The Lord God himself was coming down from His throne and was visiting them, every cool of the day, that is four o'clock in the morning in the winter time and three O'clock in the morning in the summer time, God came to pray for them every cool of the day, but now, things had changed because of rebellion, man has to pray to God, for His mercy, compassion and His favor which in the beginning it was not so. This He did because of the great love He had for them, an unconditional love, a love from the spirit and not from the flesh. Man was at that time a physical entity in a spiritual body but now a spiritual entity in a physical body.

Gen. 2:7 "And the Lord God formed man of the dust of the ground and breathed into his nostrils the breath of LIFE and man became a LIVING SOUL."

When God created man, he was made a living soul, meaning he was a physical entity covered with a spirit entity. You can see him but you cannot feel or touch him. The flesh was inside the soul, you can see a human being, a person you can name but if you reach out your hand to touch him, your hand will go through space, you will touch nothing and feel nothing, that was the reason why the Lord God was visiting man because he was HIS likeness physically and spiritually, for it was the soul that was visible and since the flesh was inside the soul, it was invisible, and was minding spiritual things and not earthly things, not the things of the flesh, meaning the man also loved God from the spirit. When man begins to mind spiritual things relating to the Lord God, he becomes God's partner who will always look for us and works with us. The bible says, the IMAGE AND the LIKENESS : Gen. 1:26 "And God said, let us create a man in our image, after our likeness." God created man in His image, someone we can see with our eyes, images are visible, so He made man to be visible, which means God is visible in spirit but we need a spiritual eyes to see Him, like Hagar, Gen. 21:19 and the servant of Elisha, 2Kings 6:17 and Balaam, Numb. 22:31. After our likeness, the image that we see cannot be touched, it is not material, you can't feel that image that we see at that time, if one tries to hold it, his fingers will go through space. There will be nothing to hold, nothing to feel, empty image. John 20:17 "Jesus said to her, Do not cling to Me, for I have not yet ascended to My Father, but go to My brethren and say to them, I am ascending to My Father and your Father and to My God and to your God." Meaning I am now in the likeness of My father, you are seeing My image, you will be shocked if you touch Me and find your fingers go through empty space. Jesus left heaven as SON OF GOD, was conceived as SON OF GOD, born as SON OF MAN, lived as SON OF MAN, crucified as SON OF MAN, buried as SON OF MAN, and raised as SON OF GOD. When man allowed himself to be deceived to rebel against the Lord God, the creator and refused to accept his fault, then the soul was sucked into the flesh and man became a LIVING

BEING, from a living soul to a living being. When Satan landed on earth, he was so happy because he thought he also has his own kingdom. But when he saw man unexpectedly, and saw the wonders man was doing, he marveled and was angry. Man could make the physical body come out of the soul by the spirit, in short, exit from the soul, while the soul would be lying down till the body return and enter into the soul again and stands up and begins to walk and angel with him wherever he goes, Satan marvel about the greatness of man. Meaning God made man to be god above all creation. When Satan saw man doing such wonders and most especially being guarded by angels wherever he goes, he marveled, and was jealous and hated man and conceived evil to do whatever it take to destroy him. Man therefore was a living soul who was greater than Angels because he Satan has no flesh, and no soul. Angels, like Satan have only one category with man, that is "SPIRIT." Satan was nowhere match to man at that time. After he had made man to fall, he stole that wonders and the marvel he saw with man, and because he was not the rightful owner of those wonders, he only copied it and made it's counterfeit and now witches and wizards could make their spirit come out of the body instead of the body coming out of the soul, and also for the fact that man is now a living being. The wish of Satan was for man to completely die. He knew about the living soul but had no idea about the Living Being, if he knew about the living being he would have attacked the living being also. This procedure of the Living Being is a second chance for man to live again to recover to restore the Living Soul through which the godly relationship could be restored. So this present life in this world is a SECOND CHANCE. Man lost the glory of God upon him and become a living being and has to take care of his flesh, so he needs to toil to feed the flesh. Gen. 3:19 "In the sweat of thy face shalt thou eat bread, till thou return into the ground; for out of it was thou taken: for dust thou art, and unto dust shalt thou return." Because man was a living soul at that time, they did not see themselves naked. Man became naked when the physical being was realized and exposed. So man died in spirit as the bible said, he died a spiritual death and from that time there was a separation between the LIVING BEING and GOD. Now man could not see the Lord God any more, he could not see the Angels of the Lord God any more but could only see earthly things, animals, birds, trees etc. while he was before seeing both Celestial and Terrestrial entities and was not seeing himself to be naked but now he saw himself to be naked. He could no more see celestial beings but only terrestrial things. Gen. 3:5 "For God knows that in the day you eat of it your eyes will be opened, and you will be like God, knowing good and evil." So from this very time man died completely in the spirit. Gen. 2:17 "But the tree of the knowledge of good and evil, thou shall not eat of it: for in the day that thou eatest thereof thou shall surely die." Man lost his spiritual values, the light and the dominion on the earth, after which they were crying for restoration but there was nothing they could do except the intervention of God Himself. Satan now saw a woman, Eve with Adam the man and purposed in himself to use her to cause the fall of man. He said to the woman, *look*, now you only see and know good and positive things around you but if you eat the fruit of the tree of the knowledge of good and evil which is in the garden because of Satan, you will also see and know the bad and negative things around you, fighting against you. It was Eve who made the devil to realize that the tree of the knowledge of good and evil was purposely in the garden to eliminate him, Satan. So Satan tried all that was in his power to make the tree eliminate Adam and his wife but God knew this before their creation and provided an intermediary which transformed them to living beings instead of eliminating them, and Satan also knew that the soul will be sucked into the flesh for them to become living beings but did not know they could continue to live. When Adam and Eve were living souls, they were caring and satisfying the soul, but now that they became living beings, they only cared for the body and labored for the mouth to nourish the body (the flesh).

God does not entrust responsibilities without related power. Once He calls you, you do not need to ask him for the related power. He had already deposited in you that power needed, therefore if you ask Him to give you that power, He will not mind you because He knows you do not know what you are talking about. All that you need is the help of the Holy Spirit to be able to perform and the love relationship with God. You may be your own enemy for not knowing and not being able to use such power. There is a great power in man. So Satan was able to destroy man against the will of God and snatched that Light which Jesus Christ gives every man coming into this world to see the past, present and the future. God our Father also gives us glory which is the spirit of prosperity to prosper for His glory, and Satan is not worried about the glory because he knows demons are capable to snatch it. The Holy Ghost helps us to succeed when we are able to maintain the glory. Now Satan was able to achieve his purpose against man, by snatching the LIGHT from man and making them to blame God to loose the GLORY also, which is to make man prosper. Satan is not interested in the glory, for the glory could be taken by his witches, demons, even human beings, it could be a family member, a midwife, a doctor, whoever avails himself, Satan will take advantage. "This was the REASON FOR JESUS CHRIST TO COME DOWN ON EARTH TO TAKE BACK THOSE SPIRITUAL VALUES (the Light and the dominion) so that, once we turn back to Him and believe in His name, He restores that Light and the dominion." In John 1:9 says "That was the TRUE LIGHT (JESUS) which gives LIGHT to every man coming into the WORLD." this shows that every person coming into the world is approved and equipped with Light by Jesus Christ, who Himself is LIGHT, before dispatching you to the world to be born, and John 5:26 says, For as the Father hath LIFE in HIMSELF(to give life), so He has granted the Son (Jesus) to have life in HIMSELF (to give life): {Psalm36:9, 1Pet.2:9} and in John 3:16b says, "that whosoever believes in Him should not perish but have everlasting life," (in himself to give life.) How can one give light if he has no light? How can one give life if he has no Life? One must have Light in yourself to give light, likewise one must have Life in yourself to give life. The bible says by Him all things were made and for him all things were made. With this life in us we are equipped to reverse pre-mature death, disaster, sickness, afflictions and oppressions which are demons.

Whenever the Lord Jesus approved man to come into the world, He also made the spare part of every organ of the body of man, stand-by in the preservation room in heaven, that whenever any part of the body goes wrong, either internal or external, you can request by ordering from heaven, so angels will be dispatch from heaven with those parts to come and replace it. But there are certain principles to obey now for this to come into reality. The answer is Malachi 3:8-9. If you pay your tithe and offering correctly that individual is qualified to request for those replacement. Those parts are paid for with your tithe and the surgical procedure is paid for with your offering. If you don't have enough tithe in your heavenly account to pay for the organ you are disqualified. If you don't have enough offering in your heavenly account for the procedure, you are disqualified. Every human being has two accounts in heaven, the tithe account (for blessing) and the offering account (for protection). There are certain health situation, only God can deal with it and depends on the person's faithfulness and obedience to God that is your tithe and offering and the word of God. You have to know exactly, what is wrong to request for the right parts or organs for replacement. This is needed to call on heaven for diagnosis by angels or physical diagnosis sometimes. Jesus said in John 3:11-12 "Most assuredly I say to you, we speak that we know and testify that we have seen, and you do not receive our witness. If I have told you earthly things and you do not believe, how will you believe if I tell you heavenly things? No one has ascended to heaven but He who came down from heaven, that is the Son of Man who is in heaven." Only the Son of God through His Holy Spirit which Only Him can give, reveals to those who avail themselves to receive. Due to ignorance, many who are dead did not request for their spare organs and now they are dead and prompted the preservation establishment to discard their preserved organs which was kept for replacement of the faulty organs. When there is the need for an organ to replace a bad organ of a patient, which needs immediate care, someone must die or be killed to have his organs for that patient, when the devil kills someone for your sake to give you his organs, Satan is always happy to do so, if heaven does not provide, because you and your descendant will be his captives, he will have the right to lay hands on your descendants. If you are a Christian and you are not well established in Christ, you and your descendants will be captives to Satan. This is the whole purpose of physical surgery of the organ replacement at the, but if you are a Christian, a real follower of Christ, you will do the surgery and walk away and Satan will have no power over you because of the blood of the Lamb which washes our sins.

And God said to Christ (the Prince) the ruler of the kingdom of Heaven, as the bible testifies in Jn. 1:1 and Jn. 1:14 : "In the beginning was the word and the word was with God and the word was God. And the word was made flesh and dwelt among us, and we beheld his glory, the glory as of the only begotten son of the Father, full of grace and truth." So said God the Father to Christ, "Satan has corrupted the earth and made man to infect the creations on earth with his corruption. Satan now rules the planet that I love, the planet of my heart. Satan has also infected the earth with suffering, problems, sicknesses, killings, molestations, bulling and more, which is the result of corruption. Satan has filled the earth with evil. Man could not stand against Satan, and is now a slave to him." Rom. 6:16 "Do you not know that to whom you present yourselves slaves to obey, you are that one's slave whom you obey, whether of sin leading to death, or of obedience leading to righteousness." So God was seeking who will go and take back the Light, the Dominion and the Earth. Angels could not do it because they were under him so he had no regard for them and overcame them (Gen. 6:2-3). So in said Eze. 22:30 So I sought for a man among them who would make a wall, and stand in the gap before Me on behalf of the land, that I should not destroy it; but I found no one." God then said to Emmanuel (Christ) in Isaiah 6:8 Now, "Whom shall I send, And who will go for Us, and Emmanuel (God with us) replied, Here AM I, FATHER! Send ME." The Father said, then, I am delegating you (Jesus Christ meaning the anointed One the true God has visited us) to visit the earth and teach the whole world how they could overcome Satan and save the whole earth with your blood, because your blood will be a terror on Satan. In (Mk. 2:28 and Mt. 9:38) Christ the Lord of the Sabbath and the Lord of the harvest, accepted the challenge. What happened, in the kingdom of heaven? As soon as Christ accepted the challenge from the father, to come to the earth to save man from his sins, and out of the bondage of Satan and restore the light, the dominion and the earth, back to man, the whole atmosphere of the kingdom of heaven turned to the color of gold. Michael and his battalion matched through the streets and the whole population of angels jubilated singing and dancing in the kingdom saying, "Glory be to God in the highest." Why? Because the son of God has accepted to sacrifice to the Father's will to rescue the captive, the lost and the kingdom on earth. The Father then said to Christ, You now bear my name as a Son, I God your father in You and You CHRIST in me. You have my holy spirit and my holy spirit is in You and always with You forever. Jn. 14:10-11. God then said to Christ, after You have come back, Your decision in this kingdom is final and nothing else. Only You and You alone, even I your Father has nothing to say, for this Jesus said in, "Whatsoever ye shall ask in my name, that I will do, that the Father may be glorified in the Son.

If ye shall ask anything in My name, I will do it. If ye love Me keep My commandments. And I will pray the Father and He will give you another comforter that He may abide with you forever." Matt. 28:18 "All authority has been given to Me in Heaven and on earth." and Matt. 11:27 All things have been delivered to Me by My Father. So whosoever believes in Him, John 14:13-16 God said to Christ, no single person will be left on earth if I should appear on the earth Myself. Christ then said to God His father, if I Christ, I am to appear on earth in spirit, the people that I am going to save cannot bear my appearance, because things that will happen to purify the earth, before my appearance will be too hectic for the inhabitants of the earth to handle, beginning with storm, earthquake, volcanoes, hurricanes, tornados, thunderstorms and lightening etc. to clean up the earth of every sin for six days, and the seventh day my appearance, (Rev.16:18 "And there were noises and thundering and lightening; and there was a great earthquake, such a mighty and great earthquake as had not occurred since men were on the earth." So I Christ, will like to appear on the earth in the human form, conceived nine months and through the human process, live among them, do things in common with them, perform miracles to prove my deity, then I can teach them to overcome Satan. God the Father also accepted and granted His request. John 3 : 16 - 17. "For God so love the world that He gave His only begotten Son, that whosoever believeth in Him should not perish, but have everlasting life. For God sent not His Son into the world to condemned the world, but that the world through Him might be saved."

Jesus is really the SON of God, if you believe it or not. He is God because the son of a king is also a king (he is the next king), so the Son of God is also God. Christ, God of creation, called the Angel Gabriel and made Himself "WORD", and entered into "ANGEL GABRIEL" then asked Gabriel to take Him to Mary, the daughter of JOACHIM and ANNE. A family that devoted itself to helping the poor and the work of God. Every year this family will divide whatever earnings they accrued into four. The first part for the priest, the second part for the work in the synagogue, the third part for the poor, and the forth part for their family. They had incredible love for God, who also offered their daughter who is their first born to God who was brought up by the synagogue, a virgin who was betrothed by Joseph. So this way Christ came to the earth. Luke

1 : 26-30 says : "And in the sixth month the Angel Gabriel was sent from God unto a city of Galilee named Nazareth. To a virgin espoused to a man whose name was Joseph of the house of David. And the virgin's name was Mary. And the angel came in unto her and said, HAIL, thou that art highly favored, the Lord is with thee, Blessed art thou among women. And when she saw him she was troubled at his saying, and then taught in her mind what manner of salutation this should be and the angel said unto her, fear not Mary, for thou has found favor with God. Thou shall conceive and bring forth a son and shall be called JESUS." Mary accepted the challenge and was conceived by Angel Gabriel (Holy Spirit), through the WORD and by the WORD. So the uncontainable Immortal, contained Himself in the womb of the mortal. As soon as JESUS CHRIST was born unto the earth, the seven curtains dividing the earth and Heaven was unveiled to allow communication between Christ and God, His Father alone. All other communications between God and all prophets were closed. And Heaven and Earth became visible to each other. The whole Angels of the kingdom of Heaven were seen singing songs of praises, saying "glory be to God in the highest," because "THE LORD" the son of God is born and has landed unto the earth. The bible confirms this: Luke 2 : 11-14." For unto you is born this day in the city of David a savior, which is Christ the Lord. And this shall be a sign unto you, ye shall find the baby wrapped in swaddling clothes lying in a manger. And suddenly there was a multitude of the heavenly host praising God and saying Glory to God in the highest and on earth peace and good will towards men." That day Satan and his son devil and his demons, all over the universe song songs of praises because God has come down with power and authority, thinking the mistake of Adam still exists since He is also a living being. But watch, the evil spirits and Satan their boss were deprived, no power or authority allotted them and the name of Jesus Christ became a terror upon Satan and his host, that is why Jesus Christ said when you bind the devil, bind him in my name and he will be bound in heaven. Jesus did not come for war with man so the angelic host with him always obeyed his instruction and never for the sake of Christ, Angels attacked man till he returned to his seat. For this Jesus Christ advice us not to fight against blood neither against flesh but to love one another. If we must be angry, it should be against Satan and his demons. Ephesians 6 : 12. "For we wrestle not against

flesh and blood but against principalities, against powers, against the ruler of darkness of this world, spiritual wickedness in the high places." Jesus Christ is the God whom the Father has given all the authority and power both in Heaven and on the Earth. Matth. 28:18 and Matth. 11:27.Without him we shall not see the Father and when we see Jesus Christ, we've seen the Father. Salvation was the mission of God and for this Christ came to the earth. Jesus gave himself to be arrested and be crucified as the bible states: that which is written in the scripture might be fulfilled. John 18:4-9. and Isaiah 53:7,10. As soon as Jesus Christ was arrested, the angels in Heaven joyfully began to sing songs of praises saying, "OUR GOD IS ABOUT TO CONQUER THE WORLD, He is the greatest warrior, till He was crucified." There was heavy rainfall which was not for fancy, it has significance which stands for purification of the earth. Immediately Jesus Christ breathed his last as he cried out and gave up his soul, Angels were seen descending to welcome Him saying,

THIS IS OUR GOD, THE KING OF THE UNIVERSE, PRAISE THE LORD AND PRAISE HIS NAME. CHRIST JESUS IS THE GOD WHOM THE FATHER HAS GIVEN ALL THE AUTHORITY AND POWER BOTH ON EARTH AND IN HEAVEN. WITHOUT HIM WE SHALL NOT SEE THE FATHER,WHEN WE SEE HIM, WE SEE THE FATHER. AMEN.

This went on until Jesus rose from the death. The angels waited in songs of praises until Jesus had completely finished his job on earth, both in the grave and on the surface of the earth. The father honored him with great honor. He was accompanied in mezzo of the angels with songs of praises to his throne. When a spear was pierced in the side of Jesus, he oozed blood unto the earth. The blood that dropped unto the earth spread and covered the whole earth. In this wise Jesus bought the sins of the whole world with his own blood, and died for every human being and for the world's salvation, and the third day, He rose to life. In John. 10 : 17-18 Jesus said, "Therefore doth my Father love me, because I lay down my life, that I might take it again. No man takes it from me, but I lay it down of myself. I have power to lay it down and I have power to take it again. This command have I received from my father." Jesus Christ promised and did it. Matt.17:9, 22-23. "And as they came down from the mountain, Jesus charged them saying : Tell the vision to no man, until the Son of Man be risen again from the dead." You don't need to expose your vision or mission until it is accomplished, that's what Jesus is saying, because when the mission is accomplished, it will be exposed and it could not be hid. "And while they abode in Galilee, Jesus said unto them, the son of man shall be betrayed into the hands of men, and they shall kill him and the third day he shall be raised again, and they were exceedingly sorry." So God gave up His Perfect SON to win the imperfect children. Amen.

After his resurrection He then went to meet his disciples on many occasion and performed miracles John 20:30-31 and John 21:25. After that Jesus appeared unto many of the believers and anointed his disciples whom he gave authority to continue with the work of God to baptize, and to teach. As we have learnt, the blood of Jesus is a terror on Satan and his son the devil. When we bind him, with the blood of Jesus, Satan becomes congested and begins to struggle, when we continue to bind him, he is conquered. Jesus set foot on the land, the river, the sea, these has purpose. Why? Because his blood has to save the world as the Father had commanded, therefore if one should live on the sea, since Jesus had set foot on the sea, his blood will spread to wherever he had set foot to save all. Jesus loves all and he is the savior of all. No one has ever seen God, even the angels, with exception of Christ Jesus. Jesus Christ, the love of God is the only one, who does sits with God the Father, and knows the Father. John 6 : 46. The angels do hear the voice of God, but do not see his face. John 1:18." No one has seen God at any time. The only begotten Son, who is in the bosom of the Father, He has declared Him." Angels take instruction from God, converse with him but no one of them can tell how God looks like. Therefore whatever you need, is better you ask from Jesus Christ and better still ask from God in the name of Jesus Christ. Request directly to God do not come as we wish. Request to God through Jesus Christ yields immediate result or a little while after. Let's put our faith in Jesus Christ and we shall see the power of God. The help we are looking for is close to our feet but because is on our feet we do not regard it. I hope you have taken Jesus Christ as your savior so you will have what you want in the name of Jesus. This is the Christ, God the son, the living God who is the most popular since the creation of the universe. He did not write a single book but has more books than ever and over all mankind, he did not sing a song but has more songs in his name than all in the universe. This is the real aspect of the Son of the Living God, Jesus Christ.

CREATION THROUGH SCIENCE AND PURPOSE:

God's desire was to have a human family in his likeness and image, to share his life and love that he could make fellowship with his physical family who will continue with the rest of his creation, that HE God, would appear physically and move in his glory in the responsibilities of man.

Gen. 2:4. "These are generations of the heavens and of the earth when they were created, in the day that the Lord God made the earth and heavens."

This verse is purely scientific which is describing how great and endless the universe is. It also describes the creative intelligence of the Creator who is full of science and the master of science, because looking at our solar system and distance between the planets, how they rotate and revolve, the speed of each planet, their seizes and shape, cannot be coincidence and it's not the matter of big bang. It was carefully calculated, meaning someone carefully created the universe, the solar systems and the planets, as we carefully calculate the parts of automobile and carefully assemble them, even so the universe was carefully created and all that is in it. Does it make sense if someone says the automobile is the result of chemical explosion from the earth? So the big bang does not make sense in terms of creation of the universe and the earth. Man invented the automobile for transportation and his glory, even so God created the universe and man for His glory. So God creates and man invents.

Now heaven means a complete solar system, and one generation of heaven is equivalent to so many tens of solar systems. So generations of heavens is millions of solar systems and billions of planets. One solar system comprise of quite a number of planets with their moons, the asteroids, meteoroids, comets, kuiper belt etc. So this verse is speaking purely science because God is full of science and master of science and never created anything without science. When God wanted physical glory, He decided to create man whom He will use to glorify Himself beside the angelic glory. So it came to the point to find where the man will live. It must be an environment that can enhance life and give life. God then decided to created an earth to put the man. But the earth alone cannot be hanging in that universe atmosphere without stability. It needs to be balanced to be stable. So there was the need for other solar systems to balance our solar system for man to be able to live on this Earth, and those solar systems also needed to be balance with other solar systems and went on and on till finally the earth became balanced and stabilized. That is the reason the bible said generations of heavens. The bible never mentioned Earths because apart from our solar system which has the Earth, made so unique and cannot be duplicated. The millions of solar systems out there have no Earth. You can imagine, only on this our earth you can walk more comfortably. The planets in our solar system are much more stable than those outside. This shows how much God loves the inhabitants of the earth. So if one heaven represents one solar system then the generations of heavens are millions of solar systems and billions of planets in the universe. All the creations of God was first laid down in a BLUE PRINT which become a format before creation, found in Genesis chapter one; and in chapter two we found the physical creation. Since the creation of Adam the first man, we have not been able to finish the discovery of our solar system. We have only been able to discover only nine planets and even the ninth, some scientists do not consider it as a planet. Some say it is a star, others say it is a planet. When shall we finish the discovery of our solar system and move to the next? <u>Spiritual laws are more complicated and can travel and see far than physical laws which are limited.</u> We are human and we are limited. Every planet has it's own moon which shines only on that planet. Gen. 2:1. <u>Thus the heavens and the earth were finished and all the host of them</u>. The host means the billions of the solar systems and their kuiper belt, the meteoroids and the asteroids and other elements which are not yet discovered. There are more in the heavens which are not yet discovered. Since the creation of man, thousands of years we have not gone nowhere with the discovery in our solar system. This should tell everybody, so far as you live on this earth, that, there is God, and there is heaven and there is hell, whether we believe it or not, when the time comes people will regret. No one is in heaven and no one is in hell. What we know and hear is PARADISE for the righteous and SHEOL for the unrighteous. So it is your choice to choose paradise or sheol. Know that paradise is a place of protocol for the righteous, where angels of God welcome them to receive the crown. 1Pet. 5:4 "And when the chief shepherd shall appear, ye shall receive a crown of glory that fadeth not away." And Sheol is as well a place of protocol for the unrighteous, where the unrighteous are hurled into fiery lake of burning fire. Rev. 21:8. "But the fearful, and unbelieving, and the abominable, and murderers, and whoremongers, and sorcerers, and all liars, shall have their part in the lake which burneth with fire and brimstone: which is the second death." Matt. 13:42 "They will throw them into the blazing furnace, where there will be weeping and gnashing of teeth." If you do not believe what this book is telling you, ask yourself where did I come from and where am I going after this life. The day you close your eyes and dead, you will see what is in this book "life and colored." It is that time you will regret and wish to come back to correct your mistakes, and that will be too late and all will be over. Many have died and regretted but there is nothing they can do. You are fortunate to be alive for a moment like this, it is your second chance, so don't miss it.

But man has deny himself and come under bondage, not knowing that he was created to inherit everything God has made and fell short of the glory of God.

After God had created the earth and all was set, there was the need of someone to care for the earth, so the bible says in:-Gen. 2:5 "And there was not a man to till the ground." This means there was not someone to work on the surface of the earth. God would have put an angel to take care of the earth. God decided to put a physical being at the care of his physical creation because:-

1. God needed a physical being and not a spirit being to take care of the physical creation, because physical things must be taken care of by physical being.
2. Due to the behavior of Lucifer, a chief angel who is now called Satan, God loved man more than the angels (because he was an opposing spirit and God knew his future) and gave power to man, power which is more potent than that of the angel. The bible confirms this because there had not been any occasion in the bible where God blessed the angels and gave dominion to them to subdue the earth but God gave power to man.

The bible confirms this in:- Gen.1:28 "And God blessed them and said unto them:

1. Be fruitful
2. And multiply
3. Replenish the earth

4. Subdue the earth
5. And have dominion over the fish of the sea, and over the fowl of the air, and over every living thing that moves upon the earth."

This shows that there is abundant power, an unlimited power stored in man by the almighty God, because of the great responsibility which is put before man by the creator of the universe. God is power and power belongs to God alone. And He who has power gives power. So God gives power to whom he had ordained to assume his responsibilities meant for.

When God created us, He knew us before creation. Jeremiah 1:5. "Before I formed thee in the belly I knew thee, and before thou comest forth out of the womb I sanctify thee, and I ordained thee a prophet unto the nation."

So God knew the responsibilities He had for man. God then commune with his board of directors, that's the prince of the Universe, both Heaven and Earth, Christ Jesus and his CEO of heaven and earth, the Holy Ghost, the comforter, the advocate and the Fire Works.

So it is writing in Gen.1:26-27. "And God said let us make man in our image, after our likeness and let them have dominion over the earth and all in it. So God created man in his own image, in the image of God created he him, male and female."

Man is created to take the form of the Lord God- the Father, and to take the form of Jesus Christ- God the Son, and to take the form of God the Holy Ghost. Before man was created, God looked at all the kingdoms of the earth and selected a suitable kingdom for each individual, which is so rich and so loving. But people out of their own mistakes accuse God for nothing, eg. Why God has made me poor? Why am I black or white? Why me in the third world? Why God made me male or female? I have male or female qualities. People refuse to believe in God and worship Him because of these complains. God is the creator, all things both physical and spiritual were created by him, and that makes Him God. Our faith in God change nothing about God. God is the same yesterday, today and forever.

Hebr. 13:8. Romans 9:20-21." Nay but, O man, who art thou that replies against God? Shall the things formed say to him that formed it, Why hast thou made me thus? Has not the potter power over the clay, of the same lump to make "one vessel unto honor, and another unto dishonor?

What if God, willing to show His wrath, and to make his power known, endured with much longsuffering the vessels of wrath fitted to destruction. And that he might make known the riches of his glory on the vessel of mercy which He had prepared unto glory".

Complains will rather worsen the situation because it paves way for the devil to take advantage of your situation. We must be strong and courageous to observe to do the will of God according to the word of God and pray that we shall be made to manifest the God's purpose of creation. And do away completely with unnecessary complains and accusations against God. Only by meditating and implementing God's word in our lives, that we shall make our way prosperous and shall have good success. Complains are enemy to your success and even to your health because it brings jealousy, envy, hatred, wickedness, murdering, etc. These are demons, when allowed to operate in one's life will lead to destruction. Our appearance on earth is so important to God that God does not take off his eyes from us. There is a purpose for every human being on earth to accomplish. God did not send us to this world for fancy sake, Jesus said to his mother, when she said, why have you made us look for you all over the district? Jesus said, "Look for me! don't you know that I have my father's business to perform (Luke 2:49)." We have been sent to the world by our Father to execute and accomplish a particular mission and when we fail to accomplish that mission, we shall be guilty of our act in the world. For example, someone is sent by his government to America to study and come back to account for, and take up a responsibility. But when he came to America, he abandoned his purpose, and took up a job and entered in the dollar harvest, so what he has to become, he could not, when he returns to his country, definitely he will be thrown into prison and his life will be miserable. As a human being in the world you should ask yourself, from where did I come to the world, to where will I return and what is my purpose on earth. The bible says God sent us to the world to do his will but we have taken to our own way which had made God to separate from us but God the son came down to bridge our relationship with the Father that through Jesus Christ we shall surely see the father by our obedience.

So God searched through the world families and placed you in a suitable family, through whom you will be led to the world to assume the responsibilities of the Father for His glory. God did not create us for fancy sake, but for a purpose. Human beings think we are brought to the world by the knowledge of man, or by the strength of man or by the wisdom of man. Our first appearance in the womb we never looked like a human being neither a substance but God who is able to do all continued to turned us in the womb till we came to resemble a human being. Our God who is able to do all, continued to be turning this child in the womb till it was time for the child to be delivered to the world. That's not the end. The Lord God continued to protect the child keeping him growing. No doctor or human being can tell how man continue to grow but God who is always able does it and we became men. God is an intelligent God, all knowing, all seeing and powerful. Before He created man, He saw that, the earth was dried and man could not carry on the responsibilities, so He waited and made the earth fruitful by causing rain to moisturize the earth, then man was assigned to continue with the rest of the physical creations, not to the glory of man but to the glory of God. So the bible says God cause rain to fall on the surface of the earth to make his plans complete as read from: Gen. 2:6 "But there went up a mist from the earth and watered the whole face of the ground". So God after searching through all the kingdoms of the earth and putting you in a particular kingdom entrusted power and his responsibilities to man. Every human being in this world was sent by God for a purpose and a mission, and each has his training to receive to acquire a specific profession for the plan of God. You are the one God sent to the world to study medicine so that through you God will provide medicine for AIDS [acquired immune deficiency syndrome] a destructive weapon of Satan, which in human sense, caused by the infection with HIV [human immune-deficiency Virus], to stop its destruction of human race but because you took to your own way, you were not able to achieve that profession and the disease AIDS killed and destroyed millions of human beings. The blood of those who have been taken by AIDS and killed will be required of this person who did not achieved his plan of God. That's the judgment. You are the one God sent to the world to be a great engineer to invent a device to prevent accident on the road but you had abandoned that mission. All lives of those wrongfully killed in accidents which could have been prevented by your device which you are the inventor will be required of you. As a pastor, you have one million souls to save but could not achieve that mission, the blood of those lives will be required of you. God needs to save only one big soul with you so that He, God, can use that soul to save millions of souls but you refused to be a pastor, the blood of those millions to be saved will be required of you. If you are a minister of health, minister of transport, minister of agriculture etc. and people died because of your poor administration, all those blood will be require of you in the day of judgment, where you will have no opportunity to come back to correct your mistakes, so now that you have this precious chance to live as human beings, take this opportunity to give your best to this world. So far as you are a human being, you owe your contribution to this world. You ride in a car, you live in a house, you use furniture, machines, factories etc. these are people's contribution. The world is now waiting for your contribution to improve the lives of others. Search through the bible and know your responsibility. You are medical doctor to save life to the glory of God, find out. You are an architect to design complex and beautiful buildings, search for. You are a mechanical engineer to make sophisticated machines to the glory of God, find out. God is going to judge us for abandoning our responsibilities. You are a priest to correct the minds of the people to the glorify God, and not to amass wealth, find out. Because when God gets angry even the righteous will be in trouble. The story of Jonah in the bible, the book of Jonah.

What happens after God has placed us in the womb of our mothers? Many of us know that Satan snatched the dominion and subdued the first man and destroyed him before God. He pushed man into problems, hardship, confusion, financial crisis and things which were not in the destiny of man. Satan not being satisfied is always aggressive and continues to attack who ever God brings to the world to carry out his responsibilities for the glory of God.

You know that Satan is always against God and finds means to destroy all good things from God because of his PRIDE. Satan will say I will not let you work for God, come and work for me if you really want to live in this world because I am the ruler of this world and that's true, Satan is ruling the world. The god of the world. 2Cor. 4:4 "In whom the god of this world hath blinded the minds of them which believed not, lest the light of the glorious gospel of Christ, who is the image of the invisible God, should shine unto them". John. 12:31. "Now is the judgment of the world. Now shall the prince of the world be cast out". And John. 14: 30 "Here after I will not talk much with you for the prince of this world cometh and hath nothing in me". Jesus himself confirmed it that Satan rules the world. Satan after Jesus had chased him out of the earth hides under the sea and sends his agents to carry on with his mission to destroy lives. Isaiah 27: 1. So immediately God finds a suitable family and places man in the womb of the woman by the word of the Angel, Satan will also send his agents to approach the family and talk to them to misdirect the child's glory which God has given to him. This is the message normally from Satan by his agents; 'You are pregnant, you should seek for protection, you know this child must be a great man or woman.' Satan believes that God has created everybody to be great and special, the bible confirms it and Satan will refer as he did to Jesus from Psalm 91 in Luke 4: 10-11 and was defeated. Seeking for protection means accepting his offer. The wiles Satan used on Adam and Eve, still holds against this modern generation. We forget that the child was put into the womb by God and the weapon to protect the child is the word of God and our righteousness and prayer. After this couple has surrender to Satan, he begins to laugh at them and becomes happy because this family has surrendered to certain circumstances. And if this family should seek for that protection, if they do, the glory of this child, the power of this child and the dominion God has given to this child for the glory of God is stolen from this child. The child becomes defenseless spiritually, his godly understanding is taken from him. Satan has a well organized deceptive world administration which he uses to blindfold and take people captive. He always imitates what God does and produce its counterfeit. Let us listen to the voice of God and let His word influence us as Mary and Joseph did. Luke. 1:30-31 "And the angel said unto her, Fear not, Mary : for thou hast found favor with God. And behold, thou shall conceive in thy womb, and bring forth a son, and shall call his name Jesus". Matt. 1:20-21 "But while he (Joseph) thought on these things, behold, the angel of the Lord appeared unto him in a dream, saying, Joseph, thou son of David, fear not to take unto thee Mary thy wife; for that which is conceived in her is of the Holy Ghost". God sent an angel to appear unto Mary and also in a dream unto Joseph. Satan also do send his agents to carry out his deceit, to give dreams to families which belong to others, so we have to be careful. Job. 9 : 24. says "The earth is given unto the hand of the wicked : he covers the faces of the judges (the rightful owners) thereof ; if not, where, and who is he?" The mistakes Adam and Eve did is still being repeated by us unconsciously. So humanity need the Plan of Deconfinement which makes an environment plays an important role, the garden of Eden was healthy and peaceful environment for the first man and the woman, but when they were kicked out, they landed in an environment which made them come under curse and in bondage, a mistake which caused them a life time and has affected the whole human race. So now with the mercy and compassion in the power of salvation, it is so significant to set yourself free from an environment which is pushing you down and start working on a plan of release because Satan through deception has already cause destruction of the destinies of most people. You are born into families in which not even one person is prosperous. So when you are born into a community where there is no one to look on, no one to copy, no one to learn from, no one to admire, that person has become a just product to that community, just occupying a space in the community. There is no motivation, when such a person sees even something nice or beautiful, he or she cannot even admire it. The only hope for such a person is Jesus Christ who did not come as a king but lived among the poor to taste their poverty and for this reason, only Jesus can liberate this poor because he was out there, and knows how to handle the situation of poverty Luke 2:7. So with the help of Jesus, there is a time in life when one do make decision to change lifestyle or to continue like that to be poor, even a mad man has a period of awareness. This is the time to say, you did not have that favor to have much opportunity, but with Christ you have to make a decision, and something has to be changed in your life.

There are rivers in life and bridges must be built to make it easy to cross those rivers. Through someone you entered into your situation, so through someone you will come out of that situation. Nehemiah had no profession and made a plan to come out of that situation to rebuild Jerusalem. There were people who are comfortable in their situation. Nehemiah had the mindset to be successful and prosper. Therefore he decided and apply the following:

1. A deconfinement plan - a plan for freedom.
2. A rediscovering your purpose - plan to seek.
3. A recovery plan - a preservation plan.
4. A plan of restoration - saving plan.

The environment from which you were brought up made you a captive, but now there is an ability to become a doctor, an engineer, an accountant, a pilot, etc. Now you have to make a deconfinement plan and rediscover your purpose, then rescue and restore. You have been told you are a captive but now you are out of captivity, so rediscover and also restore to go back to Judah and Jerusalem to rebuild. You are a property owner, a pilot, an engineer, a medical doctor. Bear in mind everything originated from the spirit. You are now yourself. Enter into the spirit. Your success is in your own hand.

A man of the country of Ghana called Tetteh Quarshie learned black smithing from the Catholic vocational missionary board and having no hope to start his workshop, travelled to Fernando Po (Equatorial Guinea) in 1970, he made a deconfinement plan, rediscovered his purpose by returning in 1976 to Ghana with few cocoa seed, arrived in his country and went to Akwapim Mampong where he learned the blacksmithing, and obtained a farm land and entered into cocoa farming, which made his nation Ghana the first leading producer of cocoa. He made recovery plan and a restoration plan. He died in December 22, 1892, at the age of fifty years. Tetteh Quarshie was a black smith by profession, moved out into slavery by environmental captivity, after six years he decided to move out of that captivity back to his country, like Nehemiah did, so was Tetteh Quarshie. What are you also doing with what you have in your hand? Tetteh Quarshie acted by faith with six cocoa seed, you can also act with the same faith with what you have in Christ.

You have never built in your life, start making a plan of escape. You are incaptivity because of the circumstance you live in. There is a level which should not be missed, awaiting for you to determine to move out of your circumstance to your next level. "Have faith and trust in God, for nothing is difficult for God." The talent is already in you and once you realize the talent, the next thing is to develop it and use it. If this talent stays ideal for far too long, it will become the devil's workshop. Christianity is not for excitement, neither for fancy. Christianity is a love relationship with God and faith in Christ, which enables one to learn to function the earth as desired by God, with the requisite knowledge delivered unto Satan by Adam, which Christ has redeemed it back to His followers. Remember that change will lead to development and development will emanates prosperity. Let us live on the word of God, live on righteousness, pray ceaselessly, draw near to God so that God will also draw near to us, and we shall know why we are in the world, and our children will be great men and women. God is an intelligent God, who created the earth out of nothing, then out of the earth He created Man, and out of the man He created Woman. And out of the man and the woman He had created, comes the present human beings and the present civilization, the developments and sophisticated technologies. Therefore God had also created us to this world to behave as His likeness, since he created us in His likeness and image;

1. to create jobs out of nothing.
2. to create better living conditions out of nothing.

Why then many of the world population are poor? No one was born with money, all was taken out of the earth. You could also be the richest man from today. May God the giver, bless any person who will own one of this book for spiritual understanding of life to the glory of God.

MARRIAGE (THE REAL UNION)

MEMORY VERSE: Gen. 2:18. 24. "And the Lord God said, it is not good that the man should be alone; I will make him an help meet for him. Therefore shall a man leave his father and his mother and shall cleave unto his wife and they shall be one flesh."

DEFINITION OF MARRIAGE:- Marriage is a concept where by two opposite sex are united whose unification is ordained by God and approved by the native constitution. It is the birth of a new life of a man and a woman from different homes with different characters, seeking to combine the two characters for a unique character. This unification is unto procreation and trusting one another in unconditional love.1Cor. 7:39 The wife is bound by the law as long as her husband liveth; but if the husband be dead she is at liberty to be married to whom she will; only in the Lord. As Christians we have to see marriage as a ministry unto God. In such consideration each of the couple will know that they have a duty to perform and to fulfill unto God and not unto man. Lack of this understanding has cause so much divorce in marriages.

INSTITUTION OF THE LAW OF MARRIAGE :- Marriage was originally instituted by God. God Himself saw that it was not good for man to be alone so He made a helper meet for the man. She is not a servant or slave, but a helper, who is a contributor. Beating a woman means beating yourself, for she is the rib (part) of a man. Genesis 2:18, 21-24. "And the Lord God said, It is not good that the man should be alone; I will make him an help meet for him. And the Lord God caused a deep sleep to fall upon Adam, and he slept: and He took one of his ribs and He closed up the flesh instead thereof; And the rib which the Lord God had taken from the man, made he a woman, and brought her unto the man. And Adam said this is the bone of my bone and the flesh of my flesh: she shall be called woman, because she was taken out of man: Therefore shall a man leave his father and mother, and shall cleave unto his wife: and they shall be one flesh." NB. God spoke and Adam was put to deep sleep. The opening of the rib is the cutting of the rib and closing it up, that is putting stitches to seal it. The same way doctors will chloroform the patient and put him or her into a deep sleep, cut and remove whatever they have to and put stitches to close it up. So God is the inventor of every medical procedure and surgery.

But all was done with His word and not knives and laser kits. Because in Him are all the rays and waves, the electromagnetic waves and rays are in His word. So the word from the lips of a righteous man has the potential to heal and work miracles. Mark 10:6-8 "And He answered and said unto them, Have ye not read that He which made them at the beginning made them male and female. And said, for this cause shall a man leave father and mother and shall cleave to his wife and they twain shall be one flesh. Wherefore they are no more twain, but one flesh. What therefore God hath joined together, let no man put asunder." So marriage is God's divine plan, which should not be interrupted with human ideology. It is solely between a man and a woman, a male and a female, and it makes sense in human criteria and not human ideology and legacy.

PURPOSE OF MARRIAGE : For the woman to be the helper to the man, Genesis 2:18 and to produce their kind (to multiply) and be fruitful, Genesis 1:28; and for the man to provide for the wife with all her needs. Originally woman take care of the household, put the house in order, take care of the children in the house. The man is to work and bring food, clothing and provide accommodation for the family. (Exo. 21:10 If he takes another wife, he should not diminish her food, her clothing, and her marriage rights.) So the portion of the man is to work hard to cater for her, and the marriage rights which is the purification of the bed. Genesis 3:17-19 "And unto Adam He said, because thou has hearkened unto the voice of thy wife and has eaten of the tree of which I commended thee, saying thou shall not eat of it: curse is the ground for thy sake: In sorrow shall thou eat of it all the days of thy life. Thorns (illness and sickness) also and thistle(the struggle and difficulties in life) shall it bring forth to thee: and thou shall eat the herb of the field. In the sweat of thy face shall thou eat bread, till thou return unto the ground: for out of it was thou taken, for dust thou art and unto dust shall thou return." The Lord gave work to man and child bearing to woman but civilization and modern technology empowered by human right demand that the wife is equally as husband and have the right to work for her own estates.

FUNCTION OF MARRIAGE :- To cleave unto one another, binding themselves to each other, respecting the marriage bed or keeping the marriage bed undefiled, no cheating on one another. Respect your position in the marriage eg. the man as the head of the family, 1Cor. 11:3 "But I will have you know that the head of every man is Christ; and the head of the woman is the man; and the head of Christ is God". 1Peter 3:5-7; "For after this manner in the old time the holy women also who trusted in God, adorned themselves, being in subjection unto their own husbands. Even as Sarah obeyed Abraham, calling him lord: whose daughter ye are, as long as ye do well and are not afraid, with any amazement. Likewise ye husbands, dwell with them according to knowledge, giving honor unto the wife, as unto the weaker vessels, and as being heirs together of the grace of life; that your prayer be not hindered". The wife administers the house, in otherwise the administrator of the house. Marriage will not function when the two are not bound together and they do not know their position in the marriage. As it is said in Matt. 19:5-6. "And said, For this cause shall a man leave father and mother and shall cleave to his wife and they twain shall be one flesh. Wherefore they are no more twain but one flesh. What therefore God hath join together let not man put asunder". 1Cor. 7:10-11. "And unto the married I command, yet not I, but the Lord, let not the wife depart from her husband. But even if she depart, let her remain unmarried or be reconciled to her husband: and let not the husband put away his wife". 1Cor. 7:27. "Art thou bound unto a wife, seek not to be loosed; Art thou loosed from a wife, seek not a wife". Rom. 7:2 "For the woman which hath a husband is bound by the law to her husband so long as he liveth, but if the husband be dead she is loosed from the law of her husband". (Q : what if the wife should kill the husband and marry another?) A. That will be terrible evil and unacceptable, In Num. 35:33 says. When you kill a person, you pollute the land, and bring curse upon the land and the only way to clean up the mess is by the blood of the murderer.) Also Num. 35:30(31-33) "Whoever kills a person, the murderer shall be put to death on the testimony of witnesses; but one witness is not sufficient testimony against a person for the death penalty." Rom. 7:3. says "So then if while her husband lives she be married to another man, she shall be called an adulteress, but if her husband be dead, she is free from that law; so that she is no adulteress though she be married to another man". Matt. 5:32. "But I say unto you, That whosoever shall put away his wife, saving for the cause of fornication, causeth her to commit adultery; and whosoever shall marry her that is divorced committed adultery." Luke 16:18. "Whosoever, put away his wife, and marry another commit adultery: and whosoever marries her that is put away from her husband commits adultery." It is the will of God that every man gets his wife and every woman also gets her husband, therefore divorce is not the will of God and Jesus made it point blank. It is a straight forward saying. Sexuality was designed by God to couples and sex is given between a man and a woman who are legally married or in marriage covenant. The rest are fornication and adultery. Sex is God's sanctified gift to couples to make children and not for pleasure. Even among married couples, when sex become or be for pleasure, it leads to addiction and becomes sin. We do not eat food for pleasure but we eat food for a purpose, to nourish the body, to give energy and strength. When eating food becomes pleasure, after sometime, it will lead to addiction and become sin. Sex is the same thing when it be for pleasure unto addiction, it damages the brain and cause weakness in thinking capacity. It also make the body look absurd, and is a terrible sin. 1Cor. 3:16-17 "Do you not know that you are the temple of God, and that the Spirit of God dwells in you. If anyone defile the temple of God, God will destroy him. For the temple of God is Holy; which temple you are." Matt. 10:28 "And do not fear those who kill the body but cannot kill the soul. But rather fear those Him who is able to destroy both soul and body in hell." When sex be for pleasure, both soul and body are destroyed. What you are reading are words and words are SPIRIT, they are powerful, move fast and sharp to change your life for better from worse. Those who take sex for pleasure unto addiction, lose their glory to prosper because the glory is given by the Father and once we take things for granted, we are disconnected and His glory is also disconnected. There are people who take sex for pleasure and hobby. No matter how much given to them, they never get satisfied. These people achieve nothing in this world. Many at times, the other partner escapes.

PRECIOUS VIRGIN:- Prov. 31:10 "Who can find a virtuous woman? for her price is far above rubies." As a virgin woman, you are so precious in the sight of God and God sees you as His daughter and expect you to prove yourself expensive in the eyes of men for the glory of God. So do not give yourself to men to use you as study material, we are studying ourselves, I have to study him and he also have to study me. This mindset is unacceptable before God and as a virgin woman, it must be over your dead body. Let men come to seek your hand for marriage through your parent, and God is happy to see that happens, because your parents represent

God in your marriage. Don't let men see you in the street and straight away begin to abuse you and dump you along the way. Most women never succeeded in dating, let us study ourselves is not a vivid ground for marriage. They end up in serious poverty and having complications of spiritual marriages and become single mothers for life because of the spiritual marriage.

CHILD TRAINING. Child training has nothing to do with bearing children. You can have children and might not know how to bring them up. Feeding kids and sending them to school every morning is not the only training for children, it does not constitute the best future of children. But teaching them to do things for themselves and helping them to behave and speak with intellect and dignity towards and in public is what is desirable of trained children. Prov. 6:22. "says train up a child the way he should go and when he is old he will not depart from it." So children need direction from parents and one thing we have to know is, it takes the involvement of the community to raise up the children. The direction of the parents only is not enough because the parents will not be able to see everything the children do.

COMMUNITY INVOLVEMENT IN THE LIFE OF YOUR CHILDREN :-The community is the catalytic factor in the life of the child. The parents attitude towards the community is essential. Prov. 3:11-12. "My son despise not the chastening of the Lord neither be weary of this correction. Even as a father, the son in whom he delight". The Lord represents the community, so parents should not be mad, when the community correct the child. Prov. 19:18 says, "Chasten the son while there is hope and let not thy soul spare for his crying". Most parents train their children with leniency and fear which will end up in destroying the child's life or future and the child will blame the parents when he is old, simple because he lacked certain qualities which the parent did not impart to him, because of leniency, eg." He will stop when he is old or it will take time for him to stop." Meanwhile no effort was made to correct the child from the wrong direction. Especially when the community is involve, the parents could even make it a police case as child abuse which could be wrong. Eph. 6:1-3. "Children obey your parents in the Lord for this is right, honor thy father and thy mother which is the first commandment with promise. And ye fathers provoke not your children to wrath but bring them up in the nurture and admonishing of the Lord."

THE PART OF EACH PARENT IN THE CHILDREN'S LIFE:- It is the duty of the parents to help the children to grow with certain qualities and never depart from it. The children after the parents had brought them up, it is authentic the children will have to respect the parents as the scripture says. It is the right thing for them to do and as the fifth of the commandments which promise them full capacity to live their full days on earth, if they observe and obey their parents, Deut. 6:7 says, "And thou shall teach them delightly unto the children and shall talk of them when thou sits in thine house and when thou walk in the way and when thou lies down and when thou rise up." The father's protection spiritually and physically becomes a hedge of the child that no one harms him. He also provides for the family table and give direction to the future of the child's life. He corrects the child when he is going the wrong way or path. The mother contribute love towards the child. Therefore when parents themselves do not understand their marriage and are always at loggerhead, it is likely the marriage will not stand and the future of the child or the children will be jeopardize. When parents do not know why they are married and what they are doing, then the marriage will end up in pain and bitterness and will destroy their children's well being or future. This is the more reason why couples must receive marriage counseling before their marriage vows, which is pre-marital counseling.

MARRIAGE COUNSELING 1 :-

1.) Husbands must love their wives and wives must submit to their husbands. This is a formula for marriage, because the bible is full of formula for life. One and one equals two, so if one and one becomes six, then an outrageous situation has occurred. The formula is love and submission equals success, so if there is no love, there can't be submission and the marriage cannot be successful. Beating your wife means beating yourself because she is the rib (part) of the man. The wife is not a servant or slave, but a helper. Being weaker vessel does not make one a servant. She takes all the administrative responsibilities in the house. The wife is not designed to compete with the husband but these modern days the situation has changed, all are going out there to struggle. That was not the plan of God. Eph. 5:28-31. "So husband ought to love their wives as their own bodies; he who loves his wife loves himself. For no one ever hated his own flesh, but nourishes and cherishes it, just as the Lord does the church. For we are members of his body, of His flesh and of His bones. For this reason a man shall leave his father and mother and be join to his wife and the two shall become one flesh."

2.) Do not compare your past relationship with the present, either by the husband nor the wife if any of them ever had. Do not let such words be heard from your mouth. Focus ahead and not turn back;. 1Cor. 9:24-26. Apostle Paul is saying those who run proceed onward, if we want the price. Therefore if we want our marriages to succeed then we should only focus ahead and forget the past.

3.) Stop any negative comments about yourselves (wife and husband) comparing husband or wife to friends and condemning your own marriage which is very precious in life. Apostle Paul is saying corrupt communication concerning our marriages will physically and spiritually damage our marriage but speak that which will put life into our marriages. We should also do away with every bitterness so that it will not aggravate the Holy Spirit who is our helper to hinder answer to our prayers, Rom. 6:12-16.

4.) The wife is not a servant or slave but a helper. Some teachers portray marriage and classify the wife as a helpmate, I do disagree with them because a helpmate has no full legal right or status eg. A driver mate has no right with the drive, he always take instruction from the driver and has no right to do certain things, on his own. Likewise roommate is not a tenant, therefore has no full right like a tenant. Therefore considerations which a tenant may receive, a roommate may not. In like manna helpmate is under subjection and not a contributor. The Holy Ghost is a helper and not a helpmate and has authority. The wife helps the husband in his decision making and has authority, if she refuses to help nothing is achieved, because behind every successful man is a virtuous wife. She stands behind the husband to succeed in all that he undertakes, encourage the husband when he is discouraged. The wife does not take instruction from the husband to perform or know her duties in the house. So on behalf of the wives I reject the word helpmate in Jesus name. Helpmate is slavery and not be used in a civilized countries or democratic countries. Helpmate is referred to in underdeveloped countries or developing countries where women are oppressed and not in developed countries. Gen.2:18, Eph. 5:28.

5.) Avoid cheats (adultery). The bible says any man or woman who commit adultery or cheats has no understanding about marriage (the reason why he or she marries). So before you marry, you should be taught to have a clear understanding of marriage else marriage is a blessing but lack of understanding can turn it to be curse for the couple. Prov.6:32-33 "Whoever commits adultery with a woman lack understanding. He who does so, destroy his own soul. Wounds and dishonor he will get. And his reproach will not be wiped away." Hebr. 13:4 "Marriage is honorable in all, and the bed undefiled but for fornicators and adulterers, God will judge." Prov. 18:22 "He who finds a wife finds a good thing. And obtains favor from the Lord." (1Cor 6:13, 16, 18-20.) Learning the ethics of marriage before the wedding is called pre-marital counseling. It is an academic lectures or lessons given to new couples wishing to marry. It is important to every young couple heading towards marriage and this is simply always before the marriage, which is given by an expect or qualified pastor of a church before the couple is joined together. This should have a maximum duration of three months to six months, depending upon the instruction (appointed periods) of the expect or a minimum duration of six weeks. It is advisable that married couples go for counseling called post-marital counseling, every two or three years after their wedding for at least one week and this will depend upon the couple to decide. This will make their marriage successful and whenever there is misunderstanding they can quickly identify the source of the misunderstanding. They can also see their counselor. With counseling, the marriage is more secured because raising ones academic standard in marriage makes one understand the pros and cons of marriage which helps the couple to be committed to one another. Post-marital counseling helps couples to mend and repair the broken pillars and walls or the collapsing foundation of the marriage. Post-marital counseling is strength to every marriage.

6.) 6.) Appreciate your wives effort to promote happiness in the house. Honor your wives. Husbands should dwell with their wives according to knowledge, behave wisely and give the wives honor, so that there will not be any hindrance against your prayers. Be one mind together. Give them surprises and send them out to treat them, let the wives be part of you. 1Pet. 3:1, 8. "Likewise ye wives, be in subjection to your own husbands; that if any obey not the word they also may without the word be won by the conversation of the wives. Finally be ye all of one mind, having compassion one of another, love as brethren, be pitiful, be courteous." Apostle Peter is saying eg. when an illiterate is married to a literate, either the illiterate will conform to live a life style as the literate or the literate will conform to live a lifestyle of an illiterate. One will definitely be conformed or influenced to live the lifestyle of the other. So a husband or a wife who does not obey the word of God is easily influenced.

7.) Wives honor husbands.1Pet.3:5-7. The wife must look on the first Christian women and live with their husbands. Those women were willed to live holy and they trusted God, meaning they gave their everything to the service of God, (money, strength, beauty etc.) and they subjected themselves to their husbands. Even Sarah went as far as calling her husband Abraham "Lord." The bible says the wives are the daughter of Sarah therefore the wives should imitate Sarah.

8.) Do not render evil for evil, because the husband fail to fulfill her demands, she will refuse to talk to the husband, to have mutual relation with him. 1Pet. 3:9; 1Cor. 1:3-5; 1Cor. 7: 5. As Christians we do not have to pay one another evil for evil, or bitterness with bitterness but do things that will bless one another. This bitterness situation will result in stress, leading to high blood pressure and complicating to diabetes and even stroke and finally premature death. If a couple desires to break their marriage by rebellion, death will take advantage to separate them. We have to know that we have been called for a mission to inherit, especially a well prepared blessing, let go all bitterness, outrage, anger, clamor and evil speeches, and completely put away in marriages these behaviors, and be as Christians or responsible citizens for world peace.

9.) Encourage one another. Rom. 14:19. "Let us follow after things that make for peace and things which bring encouragement to both couple. Two are better than one because they have a good reward for their labor. If one fall then one will lift up his fellow; But woe to him that is alone when he falls he had not another to help him up. If one prevails against him the two shall withstand him, for a twofold cord is not quickly broken."

10.) Divorce is ruled out of marriage (in Mala. 2:14) and according to the Christian doctrine except death separate the couple, even that, if the wife or the husband is capable, he or she can decide not to marry and live the rest of her or his life alone, cleaving unto things of God. Luke 2:36. Fornication and adultery is the only violation which can be used as basis for divorce. Even that if the husband or the wife loves her or him, nothing prevent them from continuing with their marriage. 1Cor. 7:10-11 ; 1Cor. 7:39; Rom. 7:2-3 ; Matt. 5:31-32; Matt. 19:3-9; Matt. 22:28-32; Eph. 4:29-30. God hates divorce Mala. 3:16.

QUALIFICATION FOR DIVORCE :- The things that can permit divorce are :

1. **Sexual immorality in marriage:-** Matt. 19:9 "I say to you whoever divorce his wife, <u>Except for sexual Immorality (corruption, wickedness, dishonesty), and marries another, commits adultery; and whoever marries her who is divorced commits adultery.</u>" This means if a husband or a wife seek for divorce for lust and be married to another man or woman, this is adultery and idolatry. Idolatry could also be anything that a person sets his or her heart to cleave more than God. This is both physical and spiritual. For physical adultery the husband or the wife can decide to keep the marriage. If my wife is disturbing my relationship with God, do

I continue to hold onto her to completely cause me to fall? God forbid. Matt. 18:15-17.

1Kings 11:8-10 God was angry with Solomon. Matt. 5:30 "If your right hand disturbs, cut it off, better you enter into heaven with one hand than enter into hell with two hands."

Matt. 5:28 But I say to you, whoever looks at a woman to lust for her has already committed adultery with her in his heart. Matt 19:10 His disciples said to Him, if such is the case of the man with his wife, it is better not to marry.

2. **Spiritual adultery:-** Matt. 5:30 And if your right hand causes you to sin, cut it off and cast it from you; for it is more profitable for you that one of your members perish, than for your whole body to be cast into hell. If any of the couple is visiting idols or shrines or witchcrafts and all efforts proved denied, which can lead to drunkenness, adultery, threats, and killing, that is a point of contact for the devil to destroy the whole family. He comes to steal, kill and destroy.

3. **Unacceptable behavior:-**Uncontrollable anger, violence person and continuous disgraceful behavior. A trouble maker, animal behavior, attacking everybody unto external families and relatives, and lack of simple understanding. Matt. 18:15-17 "Moreover if your brother sin against you, go and tell him his fault between him and you alone. If he hears you, you have gained your brother. But if he will not hear, take with you one or two more, that by the mouth of two or three witnesses every word may be established. And if he refuses to hear them, tell it to the church. But if he refuses even to hear the church, let him be to you like a heathen and a tax collector(publican), no understanding, no forgiveness, a heathen." It can call for separation.

Love within marriage is a blessing but love besides marriage is adultery and curse. Adultery is an abandoning of sexual purification. Sex is God's ordained acceptable grant. It was established for a man and a woman legally married as husband and wife or in marriage covenant. Outside this every sexual act is adultery. Sex is wedding blessing, given by God. Love relationship outside the marriage leads to satanic worship and satanic protection and invites demon into the marriage and this situation grieves the Holy Spirit. All these can be the bases for divorce. These could have serious effect on both partner's relationship with God. If fasting and prayer (deliverance) could not solve it and the situation escalates in grieve, hatred, and violence leading to death threats, because she or he love to be in that situation, it may demand separation. But know that in Mala. 2:13-16 The Lord hates divorce for it brings violence. In all these peace begins with one person. If one of them should lay down his or her life for the family to seek for deliverance, which is the Christian's final solution. God our Father Himself will intervene and peace will prevail. Understand this that marriage is unconditional love.

PRE-MARITAL COUNSELING:- This comes before the wedding. This type of counseling enlightens the couple of what they are about to accomplish. It is the birth of a new life of a couple from different homes.

POST MARITAL COUNSELING:- The couple must receive counseling every five years maximum duration and two years as minimum duration but could decide to receive counseling once every year depending on the couple. The marriage becomes more secured because it raises the couple's academic standard in the marriage and makes them understand the marriage both spiritually and physically, which helps them to be committed and responsible. Post marital counseling help to mend and repair the broken pillars or foundation of the marriage. It is the strength of the marriage and the strength and well being of the children, the main foundation of the life and the future of the children.

BIIBLE QUOTATIONS : Prov. 29:17, 13:24, 3:11-12, 22:6, 19:18, 6:23, 10:1-3, 23:19-21, 4:10,20, 7:1, Deut. 6:7, 5:16, 8:5, Eph. 6:1-4, Colo. 3:20-21, Exo. 20:12, Lev. 19:3, 1Kings 2:1-4.

MARRIAGE COUNSELING 2

DAY 1

WRONG PURPOSE : If outward attraction is the basis of the marriage, anything can break the marriage, meaning marriage that depend on conditional love is a curse. It has already failed. Marriage must depend on unconditional love. Conditional love means, beauty, prosperity, money, education, help, etc. But marriage must be without exchange.

Prov. 18:22 "Whosoever finds a wife, finds a good thing and obtains favor from the Lord." Meaning the Lord has given the wife to the husband. She is the love of God, given as a gift to the husband. Bear in mind, gift is always precious and must be handled with care. It is the monument of love.

Prov. 19:14 "House and riches are the inheritance of the fathers, and a prudent wife is from the Lord." God has given wife to the husband to take care of and has judgment to it.

Prov. 12:4 "A virtuous woman is a crown to her husband but she that maketh shame is as rottenness in his bones." Marriage is a blessing from the Lord but can easily become a curse and bitter, if abused.

Eph. 5:22-23 "Husbands love your wives."

DAY 2

WOMAN TO MARRY : Prov. 31:10-39. Ask yourself, do I fit into that criteria of this chapter, criteria as wife or husband. Am I ready to marry? We do not just jump into marriage, because your friends are married or just because you have to marry or out of desperation. If you will just marry, you will just divorce. Marriage must be with a purpose and a vision and each must be a support to the husband or the wife. Behind every successful husband, there is a virtuous wife and the glory of a wife is her husband, she satisfies her husband even at the risk of her life whilst the husband is always there and ready to protect and defend the wife.

DAY 3

PRIDE: When each partner feels he or she is superior to the other and looks down on the other, such behavior may lead to confusion and instability in the marriage and can cause divorce; such situation may be caused by lack of knowledge, parental capacities, partner weakness and unfaithfulness. 1Sam. 25:14-36.

DAY 4

RELIGION : Spiritual abilities and capabilities may incarcerate or incriminate. Their spiritual capabilities may not be the same but their spiritual mind may be leveraged. It depend on the partners to learn to understand their faith. Understanding faith is different from being a faith believer. One can be a faith believer and not understand the faith. That is a serious and terrible situation.1Cor. 7:12-17.

DAY 5

INSULTS : The most dangerous behavior in marriage, Prov. 18:21; James 3:2-12. It takes only days for insults and pride to cause divorce. Insults can create such a situation as unbearable and must not be allowed. Eph. 5:18 "And be not drunk with wine, wherein is excess; but be filled with the spirit." Only 2% of alcohol is needed in the body constantly and that is obtainable from the food we eat. Consumption of physical alcohol is an excess to the body that can harm the body. Therefore you don't need wine or whisky or grapa or shnap or beer in excess. Alcohol does not fall under the category of essential nutrients which produce the right amount of alcohol needed for the right functioning of the body. The essential nutrients, that the body needs are carbohydrates, protein, fat, vitamins, minerals, and water. Drunkenness is unnecessary and can cause serious situation in marriage. The godly wife is a treasure to behold, a beauty to admire and a woman to be greatly cherished. Adultery or fornication is a sin against God and not against man and comes with terrible curse. That family and their generation will fornicate, bear children and have no husbands or wives and sometimes the woman may not even know the father of the child. That marriage will end with divorce even if the sin is not exposed, spiritually the marriage is broken and brings single parenthood in pain.

Prov. 5:18-19 Let thy fountain be blessed and rejoice with the wife of thy youth. Let her be as the loving hind and pleasant roe; let her breasts satisfy thee at all times: and be thou ravished always with her love.

QUESTION:
Why would a husband or a wife cheats?

ANSWER:

1. Love – lack of love, a stressful marriage- misunderstanding and confusion. Eph. 5:25; Col 3:19

2. Denial - 1Cor. 7:5 Defraud ye not one another, except it be with consent for a time, thatye may give yourselves to fasting and prayer; and come together again, that Satan tempt you not for your incontinency.

3. The grace of God - Pray for God's grace, (lack of God's grace is a hindrance) praying together and for one another. Rom. 5:1-2, 5-6.

4. Neatness: - Lack of neatness can be a hindrance. Attract one another. 1John 2:16.

5. Lust - Sometimes, not that the husband or the wife does not love the other but they do that out of lust (pray seriously against lust, for lust is an unclean spirit). Jude 16; Rom. 13:14.

6. Unacceptable behavior:- Uncontrollable anger, violence, unreasonable talks not considering the damage it shall cause. Continuous disgraceful behavior and can put both parties under stress. Rom. 1:29-30

HEAVEN (YOUR NEXT DESTINATION).

The Universe contains the heavens and it is beyond description. It is great, whose advancement is infinite. It is about infinity in area and cannot be compared to just a universe. Heaven is a place God has prepared unto those who love him and believe in Christ, those who are righteous. Gen. 17:1 When Abram was ninety-nine years old, The Lord appeared to Abram and said to him," I AM THE ALMIGHTY GOD; WALK BEFORE ME AND BE PERFECT." One must be perfect to be righteous and one must be righteous to be holy and once one becomes holy, he becomes the true image of the invisible God.

The breakdown:-

100% Perfection = Righteousness

100% Righteousness = Holiness (Jesus needs only 2% of righteousness in you to connect you to himself)

100% Holiness = The True Image of The Invisible God.

Perfect means being careful with few mistakes. Righteous here means very, very careful and very hard to make mistake. Holy means one with no mistakes. As human being with flesh and blood and cares of this world, you cannot be holy, because only Christ is holy, and your little righteousness will connect you to Christ. Gen. 15:6 "Abram believed God and was credited to him as righteous." Rom. 4:3,9,22; Gala. 3:6. Because he believed God, he was very, very careful and tried to avoid mistakes. Holy means you think of the welfare of every human being. You do not have bitterness, hatred, anger, evil thoughts against anybody. You love every human being, every creature, every work of the hand of God and care for their health and have the desire to help all. As a servant of God or a child of God it is your responsibility to love what God loves and hate what God hates, and believe in Jesus Christ. When the poor are hungry and cry, God is angry saying, what are my pastors doing and what are Christians doing and my politicians, what is wrong with them? But when the poor are satisfied, God is at peace. John 14:1 "Let not your heart be troubled, ye believe in God, believe also in me." Because, that God you believe, is the One talking to you. Jesus Christ is God, if he is not God, he wouldn't have commanded the wind to humble itself before him, and the wind obeyed. If he is not God he wouldn't have asked the hurricane to be obedient before him, and the storm obeyed. If he is not God he wouldn't have asked death to come out of Lazarus who had died four days and buried, and death, Satan's greatest weapon against humanity, the spirit of separation, pain and sorrow, obeyed and came out of Lazarus and Lazarus lived. He Is The Living God. The scripture says in the beginning, the spirit of God was moving upon the face of the waters and He came to the physical realm and walked physically on the face of the water. If he is not God, the sea would not have obeyed and hold him in suspense on the surface of the water. He is God, in Hebrews 1: 5-8. "For which of the angels did He ever say; You are my Son, Today I have gotten You? And again I will be to Him a Father and He shall be to Me a Son? But when He again brings the first fruit to the world, He says; Let all the angels of God worship Him. And of the angels, He says: Who make His angels spirits And His ministers a flaming fire/ But to the Son, He says: YOUR THRONE, O GOD, IS FOREVER AND EVER; A SCEPTER OF RIGHTEOUSNESS IS THE SCEPTER OF YOUR KINGDOM"(Ps.45:6-7).

WORDS ARE OBJECTS :-

Apostle Thomas who saw the youthful life of Jesus Christ was the only disciple who testified of the infancy miracles of Jesus written in the Non Canonical which is not in the New Testament, known as The Infancy Gospel Of Jesus Christ, which says that, I Thomas an Israelite, judged it necessary to make known to our brethren among the Gentiles the actions and miracles of Jesus Christ in His childhood, which our Lord and God Jesus Christ did after His birth in Bethlehem in our country, at which I myself was astonished; the beginning of which was as follows. When the boy Jesus was five years old and there has been a shower of rain that was now over, Jesus was playing with other Hebrew boys by a running stream, and the water run over the banks and stood in the little lakes; but the water instantly became clear and readily obeyed Him after He had touched the water. He took from the bank of the stream some soft clay and formed out of it twelve sparrow; and there were other boys playing with Him. But a certain Jew seeing the things which He was doing, namely of His forming of clay into figures of sparrows on the Sabbath day, went away and told his father Joseph, behold your boy is playing by the river side, and has taken clay and formed it into twelve sparrows, and profane the Sabbath. Joseph came to the place where He was and when he saw Him, called Him and said, Why do you that which is not lawful to do on the Sabbath day? Then Jesus clapping together the two palms of His hands, called to the sparrows, and said to them: "Go, fly away, and while you live remember Me." So the sparrows fled away, making great noise. The Jews seeing this, were astonished and went and told their chief of the community, what a strange miracle they had seen, done by Jesus.

Again when the boy Jesus was playing at the ford of a stream, He then made soft clay and shaped it into sparrow and said to the clay bird, "Be Off, Fly Away, and remember Me, you who are now alive." And the sparrow took off and fly away with noise.

The Quran also quotes this, Quran 3:49 says, "I create for you out of clay the likeness of a bird, then I breathed into it and it became a living bird with God's permission." This is Jesus in the Quran, even His miracle birth is written in the Quran and why people do not believe and accept Him as the messiah. Quran 43:57-63 And the Son of Mary was presented as an example, immediately your people laughed aloud. And they said, are our gods better, or is He? They did not present the comparison except for argument. But, they are a people prone to dispute. Jesus was not but a servant upon whom we bestowed favor, and we made him an example for the children of Israel. And if we willed, we could have made of you angels succeeding on the earth. And indeed, Jesus will be knowledge of the hour, so be not in doubt of it, and follow Me. This is a straight path. With these in the Quran why people do not believe and accept Him as messiah.

It is also said in the, Quran 5:110, "And Allah said: O Jesus, Son of Mary, remember My favor to thee and to thy mother, When I strengthened thee with the Holy Spirit; Thou spoke to people in the cradle and in old age, and when I thought thee the Book and the Wisdom and the Torah and Gospel, and when Thou did determine out of clay a thing like the form of bird by My permission, then Thou did breathe into it and it became a bird by my permission; and thou did heal the blind, and the leprous by My permission; and when thou did raise the dead by My permission; and when I withheld the Children of Israel from thee when thou comes to them with clear arguments, but those of them who disbelieved said: This is nothing but clear enchantment." Jesus spoke to the three wise men two days after His birth, in the cradle, which in the history of the world, He is the only one of its kind.

Quran 21:91. And We made her (Mary) and her Son (Jesus) a sign for the world.

Quran 2:87. And We gave unto Jesus Son of Mary, clear Miracles.

The Father Himself gave Him the Miracles because He is the Only True Holy Son of God, and the Father has made Him God over the universe. The Non Canonical and the Quran all bear witness of Him and the miracles He performed.

Again, when Jesus was seven years old, He was on a certain day with other boys, each was creating some shape with clay, like asses, oxen, birds and other figures. Each boasting of his work and endeavored to show greatness over the rest. Then the Lord Jesus said to the rest of the boys, I will command these figures which I have made to walk and immediately they moved and when He commanded them to return, they returned. What prevents Him to be God? He is God. The Father has made Him God over us. The bible testifies that He did many miracle which were not recorded in the bible which the world could not contain them. The following bible verses confirm this:

John 20:30-31 And truly Jesus did many other signs in the presence of His disciples, which are not written in this Book; but these are written that you may believe that Jesus is the CHRIST, the Son of God, and that believing you may have Life in His name.

John 21:25 And there are also many other things that Jesus did, which if they were written one by one, I supposed that even the world itself could not contain the book that would be written. Amen.

Jesus was using miracles to explain to humanity the life in heaven. In heaven language and thoughts are objects. Once you desire to be there, you are already there. In heaven words are not words as we experience on earth, you say and wait for hours or days to see on earth but in heaven they are objects and realities. Once you say cup, cup is right in front of you. In heaven whatever you call appears, it is real, you do not walk but you appear, you do not leave but you vanish. Once you enter into heaven you do not see it as spiritual place where people are flying and walking in the air, but a physical place. In heaven it is so real as the earth is real to us. So Jesus said to His disciples in Matt. 17:20-21, (Luke 17:6) "Because of your unbelief, for assuredly, I say to you, if you have faith as a mustard seed, you will say to this mountain, move from here to there and it will move, and nothing will be impossible for you. However, this kind does not go out except by prayer and fasting." In heaven one does not call the name God, the only name you will hear is THE CREATOR, "ELOHIM" which is Hebrew. Life in heaven is the opposite of the life on earth. In heaven the only time you eat is at the Lord's super. On earth you fast occasionally but in heaven you eat occasionally. In heaven the people are LIVING SOULS but on earth people are living beings. To be able to command things to be real as in Gen. 1:8-12 and 14-21, know that, everything was commanded and God created man in His image. So God has already given us this grace and potential to command things to be real. All that He needs from us is to connect to Him by fasting and prayer. By doing so we will have His spirit to serve Him. We will listen to His voice, and obey to do His will. God never spoke and it delayed, likewise no angel speaks and it delays. John 3:27,31 "A man can receive nothing except it be given him from heaven. He that cometh from above is above all: he that is of the earth is earthly and speaks of the earth: he that comes from heaven is above all." So miracles are from heaven where words are objects and don't delay. Once we are connected to heaven, the spirit of God comes upon us and our words become objects, we speak a word and we instantly see the word in object or reality. Words are invisible on earth but in heaven words are visible. Every prayerful Christian will connect to heaven, because God gives the prayerful believer the Holy Spirit's timely prophetic gifts eg. dreams and visions, which are available to all believers. Acts 2:17 "And it shall come to pass in the last days, said God, That I will pour out My Spirit on all flesh, Your sons and your daughters shall prophesy, Your young men shall see visions, Your old men shall dream dreams, And on My menservants and maidservants, I will pour out My Spirit in those days, And they shall prophesy."

Once we receive the Spirit, the kingdom of God has come upon us. We speak a word and we see it right there. We declare and it comes to pass, we decree and we see it. We are not the first to experience this, it's been in existence since the beginning of creation. All these are followed by miracles, signs and wonders, performed by God through those connected to heaven who receive signals from paradise.

Luke 23 : 42-43 "Lord remember me when you come into Your kingdom." Because he saw the grace on the face of Jesus. "And Jesus said unto him, Verily I say unto you, today you will be with Me in Paradise." Jesus knew what He was talking about. There is paradise in heaven, a heavenly kingdom within heaven where only the righteous dwell and worshiped by celestial beings and the twenty four elders who submit report of the activities on earth. And these twenty-four with the arch-angel are allowed to work in the chambers of the apocalypse, a huge establishment, where all the information about the earth and man since the beginning of creation till now is kept, how many people have been in the world and how many have died and the record of each life and planet in the universe. It's the DATA processing department and archives. Whatever administration and technologies we have on earth is an imitation from heaven. That is why Jesus rebuke Satan when he asked Jesus to throw himself on the ground before him, so that he can give him the world administration to possess. 2Pet. 3:13 Nevertheless we, according to His promise, look for New Heaven and a New Earth in which righteousness dwell.

We create sicknesses with our tongue, ask the doctors and scientists who gave names to the diseases and hurricanes, where do they get the names and how do they create the names and from where do they obtain the names? Anything that does not exists does not have name. Every accepted created name comes to stay with mankind and become part of our community. All is brought about by the tongue. The tongue is dangerous, powerful, sharp and fast and can cause horrific damage and at the same time good for blessing. You cannot live in a community without a name, you must have a name to be part of the community. Therefore with the tongue disaster, diseases and sicknesses become part of the community. It's better to avoid creating horrific names and evil words to keep our community and our world safe.

John 13:19. "Now I tell you before it comes that when it comes to pass ye may believe that I am He." You have to believe now and not when it has come to pass, it will be late, when Jesus had already taken his throne for judgment, to tell Jesus now I believe. Apostle Thomas saw the infancy of Jesus and all the miracles He performed, but did not believe Jesus when he was told Jesus has risen and lost the great blessing because Jesus blessed those who had not seen him and believed. John 20:28-29 And

Thomas answered and said to Him, "My Lord and My God!" Jesus said to him, "Thomas, because you have seen Me, you have believed. Blessed are those who have not seen and yet have believed." The same applies to Heaven, people don't believe there is Heaven which the Father had prepared through Jesus Christ for those who have faith in Christ, that's those who love God through Jesus. Anyone who does not believe in Christ, there is no life eternal for him, because only in Christ Jesus you can find eternal life, therefore, there is no heaven for the Christ infidels. Without the Lord Jesus Christ we will not see the father. It's only by Jesus we will see the father.

Jesus said in John 14:2-3, 8-9. "In my father's house are many mansions; if it were not so I would have told you. I go to prepare a place for you. And if I go to prepare a place for you, I will come again, and receive you unto myself; that where I am, there you may be also." Jesus is saying that we do not have the kind of righteousness which is equivalent to HOLINESS to open the heaven gates. The heaven gates are opened only by holiness and only Jesus Christ can open it but with our little righteousness connected to His Holiness (which means He will recommend and co-sign for us with His holiness, since He co-sign for us to be created) we will be able to enter into heaven and will see the face of His Father whom no one had ever seen. Philip said unto Jesus in John 14:8, "Lord show us the Father and it suffices us. Jesus said unto him, I have been so long with you and yet has thou not known me, Philip? He that hath seen me hath seen the Father: and how saith thou then, show us the Father?" So in Jesus is the Father, in Jesus is the Holy Ghost, in Jesus is the Godhead bodily found. That is the hope of a Christian. All Christians have this in mind. Two thousand years and over since Jesus left, he has not finished the place he was going to prepare for his followers, how complex and beautiful the place is. We cannot compare the earth to the beauty in heaven. This project is almost completed, it's only left with the finishing touches. Very soon Christ will come with the reward for those who served him according to his WILL. Brother and sister, if you have not taken Christ, look for a Christ church, that's a bible teaching church and go to accept Christ so that you don't regret, and that you will have a place in God when Jesus Christ returns with his reward.

Hebrews 11:16. "But now they desire a better country, that is, an heavenly: wherefore God is not ashamed to be called their God: for he had prepared for them a city." God is pleased to call us His people and to us our God, we lost this grace but by the love of God and the grace of our Lord Jesus Christ we have been restored and today we can be proud to be called God's people. Eph. 2:19. "Now, therefore, you are no longer strangers and foreigners, but fellow citizens with the saints and members of the household of God" - meaning we were born into an unknown kingdom and we were strangers, foreigners and aliens to the kingdom of God but after accepting Christ we are born again and no more strangers, foreigners and aliens in the kingdom of God. We were lost but now no. We did not have God but now, Yes, we have God through Our Lord and Savior Jesus Christ.

Hosea 11:9 For I am GOD and not MAN. The HOLY ONE in the mist of thee. The holy one means whatever He had said He is able to do. Something no man can do. He has promise us heaven, He will surely do, it's a wonderful paradise and heaven. The things that are impossible with man are possible with God. There are every evidence and instances in the bible that proves the existence of heaven.

DECRIPTION OF HEAVEN

Heaven is a destination unreachable to the ordinary, reserved for those who walk with God blameless in Jesus Christ. For this Jesus said, John 7:3 You will seek Me and not find Me, and where I go you cannot come.

Rev. 21:16 "And the city lieth four square, and the breadth is as long as the length: And he measured the city with the reed, twelve thousand heavenly furlongs. The length and the breadth and the height of it are equal." 21:17. "And he measure the wall thereof, an hundred and forty and four cubits, according to the measure of a man, that is, of the angel."

A normal human form in heaven is beyond description as compared to earthly human beings. The bible says the angels which deserted their habitation who were the sons of God saw the daughters of men that they were fair and they took them wives of all which they chose and bare them children which were giants and mighty men, in that they were also become flesh, because they became human, they were stripped off their heavenly appearance, and even the little heavenly energy left in them the bible says they were giants. So you can see how huge and fearful Angels can be. Rev. 10:2 "He (the angel) had a little book opened in his hand. And he set his right foot on the sea and his left foot on the land." One can imagine someone who has one foot on the land and the other foot on the sea, how huge an angel can be, left alone the <u>TRINITY</u>. Also 1Chron. 21:16 "David lifted up his eyes and saw the angel of Lord standing between heaven and the earth, having in his hand a drawn sword stretched out over Jerusalem. So David and the elders, clothed in sackcloth, fell on their faces." As soon as angels are sent to the earth, they transform and take the normal earthly human form. Matt. 17:2-8.1Kings 8:27-28. "But will God indeed dwell on the earth? Behold the Heaven and Heaven of Heavens cannot contain thee; How much less this house that I have built! Yet regard the prayer of your servant and his supplication. O Lord my God, and listen to the cry and the prayer which Your servant is praying before You today." Yet have thou respect unto the prayer of thy servant and to his supplication, O Lord my God to hearken unto the cry and to the prayer which thy servant prays before thee today". So one furlong in heaven is thousand and thousand by thousand furlongs on earth. The bible says, one day is with the Lord as thousand years and a thousand years as one day. 2 Pet. 3:8. What we have to understand is thousand years on the earth is one day in heaven and one day in heaven is three hundred and sixty-five thousand earthly days. So your boastful hundred years on earth is just two and half hours in heaven. When we look at the mosquito, its longest lifespan is three to four or five days, but the mosquito knows it has lived long a lifespan on earth. Even so our heavenly two and half hours seemed too long for us on the earth. James 4:14 "Whereas ye know not what shall be on the morrow, for what is your life? It is even a vapor, that appears for a little time, then vanishes away." So you could see you are just little passing being before the angels. But the angels are compare to love us because the father which is the creator loves us.

Rev. 21:18. "And the buildings of the wall of it was of jasper, and the city was pure gold, like unto clear glass. Jasper is one of the wonderful precious stones with very high world demand, more difficult to come by, you can imagine the cost of an ounce of this stone, more precious than gold." It is this mineral which is used in the construction of houses in heaven. Gold in heaven is just a common stone. The whole roads and streets in heaven is made of gold and the ground also made of gold. As we do not value the soil of the earth we walk on it, we urine on it and do all sort of filthy things on it, so gold is very common, the heavenly beings look on and walk on it. If gold of a size like the football is released from heaven to New York City downtown-Manhattan or in the Bronx or downtown Brooklyn, millions of people will die from the gun and that piece of gold will belonged to no body, whilst in heaven people walk over it. That which the dog will see and bark the cat will close its eyes, it's nothing for the cat. So the Christian is glorified.

Rev. 21:19-20 And the foundations of the wall of the city were garnished with all manner of precious stones, The first foundation was jasper; the second sapphire; the third chalcedony; the fourth an emerald; the fifth sardonyx; the sixth sardius; the seventh chrysolyte; the eight beryl; the ninth topaz; the tenth chrysoprasus; the eleventh a jacinth; the twelfth an amethyst. This is describing the procedure of construction in heaven. The buildings have twelve stages of foundation, each step of the foundation is made of different material, unshakable and untouchable, so one can imagine how strong the buildings will be. These stones are precious stone mixed with the gold for the foundations of the buildings in heaven and the whole wall of the twelve cities. The area of the city is of indefinite measure to the area of the universe. The timber in heaven is diamond. So all the furniture are made of diamond. The whole ground of heaven is gold. The foundation of the buildings being excavated is gold. Gold has no value to the hosts of heaven, it's value is only on the earth. From the time of Adam we have not been able to finish developing the earth, Only small part of the earth is developed which is less than half the area of the earth, and to completely develop the earth will take another twelve thousand years, that's from Adam to present [that's Adam to Noah to Abraham to Moses to David to Jesus to Obama, every 2000 years God sends someone for such identical purpose or sign but Jesus' was superior to all, demonstrating His deity. How then do we expect Jesus to finish that great work of heaven which He promised in John 14, which is indefinite to the universe in two thousand years but He is God. Christ is doing something extraordinary for Christians. God is not man therefore God does not do what man can do, and this makes Him God. I hope everybody will have the desire to be there, and Christians will have the patience and waiting spirit from God.

It's a fantastic and awesome place. People still doubt the existence of Heaven but there are some people who have been taken to heaven and reincarnated. Enoch, was taken to heaven Gen. 5:24 and came as Moses, Elijah was taken to heaven 2Kings 2:11 and came as John the Baptist, and Jesus the son of God the incarnate of God, was taken to heaven Acts 1:9 and will come as the judge Acts 17:31, lion of Judah. As Moses was on the mountains, the Sinai and people complained he was not returning but finally he returned to the people so Jesus has tarry for too long, yet He will return to us. Jesus is doing a great work and is going to take extra more years. But those who will continue to wait on Him will be saved. Heaven is a great place, our ultimate or final destination. Every human must have the desire to be there and you will never regret. You will see that this earth is not a place for you and regret for being on earth but no human being can go to heaven without passing through this earth, that's not possible. One of the two crucified who were on the cross with Christ said to Jesus in : Luke 23:42-43 "Lord remember me when You come into Your kingdom." Because he saw grace of heaven on the face of Jesus. "And Jesus said unto him, Verily I say unto thee, Today shall thou be with Me in Paradise." Jesus knew what he was talking about, it is His mandate to meet the righteous in Paradise. There is PARADISE before heaven, a heavenly kingdom before heaven, where only the righteous wait and dwell to receive protocol and worshiped by celestial beings. It is a place where those who enter are given the tree of life to eat for eternal or everlasting life before they proceed to heaven. No one will enter into heaven without first receiving eternal life (Rev. 2:7). From paradise those pure who were slain for the sake of the Lord Jesus Christ and his work will enter into VALHALLA (a place of honor, glory and happiness, for souls who will receive the crown) but all the righteous will enter into ELYSIUM (the final home of the souls who were pure) where they will see the twenty four elders before the THRONE of the living God who receive and submit report of the activities on earth. These twenty-four with some archangel are allowed to enter the chambers of the apocalypse, a huge establishment, where all the information (past and present and future revelations) about the universe, earth and man since the beginning of creation till now are kept, how many people have been on the earth, their life on earth and how many have died and the record of each life, dead and alive and every planets, every animal, every bird and every natural activities (hurricanes, volcanoes, tornados etc.) in the universe and planets. It's the DATA processing department and ARCHIVE. Whatever administration and technologies we have on earth is an imitation from heaven. That is why Jesus rebuke Satan when he asked Jesus to throw himself on the ground before him, so that he can give him the world administration to possess. There is a new earth and a new heaven for those who believe in God through CHRIST. 2Pet. 3:13 "Nevertheless we, according to his promise, look for New Heaven and a New Earth in which righteousness dwell." This is heaven, is the hope of a follower of Christ. But you who do not believe in Christ, what is your hope, the Christian has another hope also in the grave. In Matt. 28:20 Christ said "I am with you always even unto the end of the world." When the Christian is dead, so far as the world has not come to the end, the judgment day has not yet come, the angels of God are with the believer in God through Christ even in the grave till he or she (the soul) is raised the third day and preserved for forty days in wait for the observation of his final welfare on earth, then after the forty days the angels of God will lead him to Paradise, where he will be with Jesus. For this promise to be yours, if you have not receive Christ Jesus as your Lord and savior, do so now. We see this clearly in Gen. 28: 12 "Then he {Jacob} dreamed and behold, a ladder was set up on the earth, and it's top reached to heaven; and there the Angels of God were ascending and descending on it." When Jacob slept, he was as dead, because when one sleeps, he cannot tell what goes on around him, meaning we die every day and are raised by God every morning and renewed our strength every morning. So when a Christian dies, he is asleep as Jacob slept and Angels of God ascending and descending. That's exactly what happens in the grave, because we believe in Jesus Christ. But one fascinating thing is that, the grave or the tomb of the Christian is converted to be like the inside of a mansion where angels are seen ascending and descending twenty-four-seven and because of the angels there is always light in his grave or tomb, till he or she is received up into Paradise. This is one course of the Christian salvation promise. When Lazarus was dead and laid in the tomb [John 11:43-44], Jesus commanded him to come out, and He also commanded the people to loose him which means Lazarus was bound with linen according to the tradition and culture of the Israelites. How was he able to come and stand at the gate of the tomb? This shows that there were angels with him in the tomb who brought him to the gate by the command of Jesus. And the people loosed him and came to live again among the living. Likewise, you will also have angels with you in your grave and you will never be alone. So as righteous souls, we are mandated to enter into heaven, receive protocol in PARADIS, even so the unrighteous souls from HADES who will be received in hell will also receive hurling and terrible protocol into SHEOL(a dark dreary horrible, disorderly place where no one goes and comes back). Whoever goes there is held captive for hell. It's a place of darkness with molten fire enclosed with darkness and PARADISE is above with unreachable distance. This distance between paradise and sheol is unreachable by human but in spirit it takes seconds. Unrighteous souls are hurled into sheol, awaiting entry to hell, so there is no help from otherwise. Do not wait till tomorrow for tomorrow may not be for you. Sheol is not a place a human being who have experience life on earth should be there, yet people chose to experience sheol. As it is being described to you, protect yourself and refuse to be a captive of sheol. Just lift up your hands and read this prayer below loudly and be saved.

PRAYER OF REDEMPTION

Thank you father God, for your wonderful love towards me. Even though I rebelled against you and took to my own way, you did not abandoned me but took good care of me, I am still alive. Thank you for your mighty power and mercy towards me. The bible says! "For God so love the world that he gave his only begotten son, that whosoever believes in him shall not perish, but have everlasting life." Father God you are the only TRUE HOLY LIVING GOD. I repent, Lord, I repent. Lord Jesus, I do not know how to express my thanks to you: because you laid down your life for my sake and poured out your blood to purchase me, at a very expensive price. Father, Lord Jesus, today I lift up my hands to receive you as my Lord and Savior. Forgive me all my sins and receive me unto yourself. Lord of host I thank you. I will worship you for the rest

OCCUPY TILL I COME (RAPTURE)

The bible says in John 10:34 "we are gods" meaning we are copies of God, connecting God. So once we are disconnected from God, we cannot function. It's like GPS applications, billions of sub-applications or living applications has been taken from the main or mother application so when the sub-applications are disconnected from the main application, all the down loaded applications or the sub-applications will malfunction or not function. So you as a human being, who is a little god who does not believe in the Main God, means that individual is disconnected from God who is his source of life.

Jesus promised us that He was going to prepare a place for us and when He go and prepare the place for us, He will come again and receive us unto Himself, and where He is, there we shall also be. John 14:1-12. Jesus is building a new heaven and a new earth for His followers which are Christians. He has finished building the place. Now He has to complete the battle between the dark world (the Erebus) and heaven, concerning the physical world. He has to take out the dark world to combine our earthly world and the heavenly world. This is the war Jesus and the Angels are fighting now. Luke 19:12-13 A certain noble man went into a far country to receive unto himself a kingdom and to return. And he called his ten servants (Jesus said, ten servants, he was referring to the disciples, because Judas was out who committed suicide and the other John, whom He gave him special assignment to take care of His mother, who died naturally, son behold thy mother, John 19:26-27, so the disciples were left with ten of them,) and delivered them ten pounds and said unto them, "Occupy Till I Come." He was talking about a spiritual war on both sides against the Erebus kingdom. That is why He said, "occupy on the physical side till I come" meaning Christians have to fight back and speak back. We should not allow the devil and his kingdom to take Christians for granted. We don't have to let Satan and his kingdom think that they can just come and say whatever they want to say and get away with it. We don't have to sit back and allow Satan and his kingdom to be free on this earth with the fight they have set in motion. God created the heaven and the earth. Satan was in heaven and was casted out of heaven unto the earth. Jesus came to the earth and took him out of the earth. So now Satan had formed his world between heaven and earth which he calls no man's land, waging a war to destroy the earth by every means and heaven is also waging a serious war to protect the earth and to remove that formed dark world of wickedness. So We Christians have to fight back because Jesus said, "OCCUPY TILL I COME" which means there is serious war in place against Satan and his angels (the devils, the witches, the wizards, the demons), and they are loosing on the other side, but our occupying in the human world is loosing because we are being pushed out of the human world into the substantiating dark world so we are expanding the human world which is delaying the second coming of our Lord and Savior Jesus Christ. So Christians are making Jesus feel so bitter because we are not doing His will, we are not occupying till He comes as He commanded us. This physical world that we see, there is another world behind it which is a spiritual world we don't see with our eyes. This world behind this our physical world (EREBUS) is the dark world, full of evil activities and whatever they do is destruction. And behind this dark world is the "DIVINE WORLD" which wants the inhabitants of the physical world to occupy the physical world so that the divine world will take out the dark world behind the physical world, and when the dark world is taken out, then our Lord Jesus Christ will appear to us physically, and that is the finally appearance of the Lord.

TERRESTRIAL WORLD:- Greek word giinos, meaning, relating to the earth and the Latin word terra meaning earth. So the terrestrial world means our physical earth which is the only planet with life, the best God can give mankind.

CELESTIAL WORLD:- Derived from Latin caelestia, meaning heavenly from caelum meaning heaven. The Greek which is ouranos meaning the sphere of spiritual activities or above the sky, the divine ouranos.

EREBUS WORLD:- Greek word Epepog, meaning deep darkness, a place of darkness above the underworld, the hades. Erebus world is a world of darkness behind our physical world. It is a spiritual world know by those God has given the grace to see. It is a place of evil and destruction. It is the place where all evil on earth come from. And the inhabitants of this world are always waging war with the inhabitants of the terrestrial world (the earth). The reason for this war is that, God created the earth and created man and all living things on earth, but when Satan was casted out of heaven, he landed on the earth, because that is the place of life and he made his world on earth and seized the earth and became the ruler. Rev. 12:7-13. The Lord Jesus

Christ came and drove him out from the earth and he has made his world behind this physical world the terrestrial world and always making everything possible to destroy the inhabitants of the terrestrial world that's our world. But behind the Erebus world is the celestial world, a divine and Holy World which protects the creations of the terrestrial world. In otherwise there is war between the celestial world and the Erebus world which does not permits the Erebus world to have complete access to destroy the terrestrial world. 1Cor. 15:40 "There are also celestial bodies and terrestrial bodies: but the glory of the celestial is one and the glory of the terrestrial is another." Now Satan himself is not in the battle because he has been locked up by Jesus, so now the battle is between the angels of Satan (the devil, witches, wizards and demons in the world) and the followers of the Lord Jesus Christ, that's Christians. Our Lord Jesus, when He had locked up Satan has entangled the physical side of the battle to Christians and said I am going to the celestial kingdom and from there I will take over the Erebus world unto the terrestrial world to create a new earth because physical thing cannot overcome spiritual things, it takes the grace of God. Eph. 2:14 "For He is our peace who hath made both one and hath broken down the middle wall of partition between us." Christ has not yet appeared because Christians are not yet in good standing in the fight, and their occupation on earth is very weak because they do not see there is war. For Christians to be able to occupy needs righteousness, fasting, prayer and the reading of the scripture to overcome Satan. Occupy till I come means four things, righteousness, fasting, praying (deliverance) and reading of the word of God. For this Apostle Paul said in 1Tim. 4:13-14 "Till I come," give attendance to reading, to exhortation, to doctrine. Neglect not the gift that is in you, which was given thee by prophesy, with the laying on of the hands of the presbytery." This is what it means by occupy till I come and Christians are not occupying, even pastors, the so called men of God are not occupying, but rather they are helping Satan to delay the second and final coming of our Lord Jesus Christ. Christians have become the reinforcement to the kingdom of Satan (the kingdom of Erebus). Satan is strategic and has entangled Christians with worldly cares. 2Tim. 2:4 "No man that wars entangles himself with the affairs of this life; that he may pleased him who hath chosen him to be a soldier." So Satan has a strategic administration and plan to cripple Christians with financial hardship, corruption and all kinds of inheritance. In 2Pet. 3:13 "Nevertheless we, according to His promise, look for New Heaven and New Earth, wherein dwelleth righteousness." Are Christians practicing righteousness, that is the most powerful and strongest weapon against Satan. Satan is destroying the world so that God will not be interested, and this is one thing Christians have to know. But our God is a faithful God. Whatever He has said to do, He will do it. Rev. 21:1 "And I saw a new heaven and a new earth: for the first heaven and the first earth were passed away; and there was no more sea." The first heaven and the first earth which comprise of the divine world, the dark world and the human world (the earth) will pass away because no matter how hard the dark world will fight, their kingdom, their world, the world of wickedness will be eliminated and Jesus will combined this our world, the physical world and the divine world which will be the manifestation of the new heaven; and as soon as the new heaven and the earth are combined. Once this is achieved, the rapture will take place, where the saints will be raptured and the Erebus world will be destroyed and joined to the terrestrial world, which will be stretched out to form the celestial world, and there we shall see the new heaven and the new earth physically as we are, and will be filled with the holiness of the Lord. Satan knows this and he is working hard to make Christians ignorant of God's word. Therefore believers must also work hard, so we shall have the living heaven which is the heaven that can be seen afterward. So the physical world will be covered by the world of heaven which will become the New Heaven. The lifestyle of some Christians has been hindrance against the coming of our Lord Jesus Christ ; corruption, fornication, idolatry, lying evil mindset etc. The life of Christians has strengthen the Satanic kingdom to make it difficult for the Lord to come. Isaiah 66:22 "For as the new heavens and the new earth, which I will make shall remain before me, saith the Lord, so shall your seed and your name remain." There is going to be a new heaven and a new earth, and those who will dwell on this new earth and new heaven will be the righteous people: a righteous person is the one who is moved with fear to do the commandment of God. Because all the activities of the New Earth is righteousness. The new earth and the new heaven will be revealed when our Lord and Savior Jesus Christ come, the second time. When the angels came down after Satan and he over powered them (Gen. 6:2), he knew that anything can happen and another battalion could come after him. So he occupied the extension of the world behind the physical world and blocking the divine world from the physical world to make the battle difficult, but

Jesus had driven him out of the physical world and his hands are weakening in this physical world. A war is being wage in both sides of the Erebus world behind this physical world. Jesus is gradually winning this war. He started with twelve disciples and now has 2.7 billion followers. Again once the dark kingdom is taken out and the Divine kingdom and the Earth kingdom are put together, then the rapture will take place.

RAPTURE :- MEMORY VERSES:- Matt. 24:35 Heaven and earth will pass away, but my word will by no means pass away. Matt. 24:36 But of that day and hour no one knows, not even angels of heaven, But the Father only. Isaiah 10:3 What will you do in the day of punishment and in the desolation which will come from afar? To whom will you flee for help and where will you leave your glory? Rev.14:13 Blessed are the dead who die in the Lord from now on. Yes, says the spirit that they may rest from their labors and their works follow them.

MEANING OF RAPTURE:- Rapture is the snatching of the Christ church in otherwise Christians or Christ congregation or followers of Christ or believers of Christ. In John 14:2-3 Christ gives Christians hope after death, quote "In my Father's house there are many mansions, if it were not so I wouldn't have told you. And if I go and prepare a place for you, I will come again and receive you unto Myself, that where I am there you will be also. This is the assurance of the Christian, so that the Christian is not wasting his or her time, but preparing toward eternity which there is, and is real. The rapture is the departure of the followers of Christ from this earth as the bible has said from time to time as also in 1Thess. 4:16-17 "For the Father Himself will descend from heaven with a shout, with the voice of an archangel, and with the trumpet of God. And the dead in Christ will rise first. Then we who are alive and remain, shall be caught up together with them in the clouds to meet the Lord in the air. And thus we shall always be with the Lord. Therefore comfort one another with these words." The rapture is the day of the Lord, It will come as a thief in the night, the sudden destruction which will come upon people at their time of their marrying- which will be equally like the labor pain upon a pregnant woman and nobody shall escape as said. Matt. 24:19, 43-44 "But woe to those who are pregnant and those who are nursing babies in those days" "But know this that if the master of the house had known what hour the thief would come, he would have watched and not allowed his house to be broken into. Therefore you also be ready, for the son of man is coming at an hour you do not expect." Also in Joel 2:30-32 "And I will show wonders in the heavens and in the earth: Blood of Fire and pillars of Smoke. The Sun shall be turned into Darkness, and the Moon into Blood, Before the coming of the great and terrible day of the LORD. And it shall come to pass, That whoever calls on the name of the LORD, SHALL BE SAVED. For in Mount ZION and in JERUSALEM there shall be deliverance; As the Lord said, Among the remnants whom the Lord calls." Those in the Lord spiritually and committed will not be overtaken as a thief in the night by this destruction, they are aware of it and they are prepared for it. Those of us who have heard of this, let us put on (i) the breast plate of faith (2) the hope of salvation as helmet of love against the rapture being the day of the Lord. This is not judgment but the cleanup for judgment. Judgment is not for the ungodly because the ungodly is already condemned as is said in John 3: 18 "But whoever does not believe in Jesus Christ is condemned already because he has not believed in the name of the only begotten Son of God." Then there rises a question, WHY CHRIST? (1) Because Christ was sacrificed for the sins of the world, therefore it is an obligation for every human being alive to believe in the name of the Son of God, Our Lord and Savior Jesus Christ. (2) Another reason for condemnation is that the world had lived in darkness for far too long but when the light came among them, they still love the darkness and they did not receive the light which is Lord Jesus Christ. (3) Man had borne the image and the characteristics of Satan for far too long and for the love of the things of Satan man refuse to cleave unto immorality but to stay in morality, like unto incorruptible to corruptible. There are some unbelievers who have been living righteous life and those people can have the mercy of God if they will repent and confess the name of Jesus Christ and believe the Son of God just the time.

BEFORE THE RAPTURE :- Impersonation of Christ:- People will deceive others that they are Christ. There will be wars and rumors that the end has come. There will be earthquakes in various places, nation will rise against nation, there will be famine and pestilence. There will be tribulations and killing of Christians and hatred by all nations for Christ sake. Many will be offended, they will betray one another and hate one another. Many false prophets will arise and deceive many. There will be lawlessness and people's love will be cold, people will be discouraged and confused. Those who will endure to the end will be save. The gospel will be preached in all nations as a witness in all nations and the end will come. False Christ and false prophets will do great signs and wonders to deceive even the elect who are the chosen Christians. There will be the Rejection of the Son of Man by this generation, Luke 17:25. There will be more celebrations and reviling and legalization of abominations. Luke 17:26-28.

ACTION OF MANKIND AT THE RAPTURE :- Those in Judah (in the cities) will flee to the mountains, Those on house top (people will run to the roof of the skyscrapers and) will remain there and will not come down. Those in the fields will not be able to come home for clothes. The pregnant and the nursing mothers will be in great affliction because how will they run. We should pray that it is not going to be winter where the earth is covered with snow. Where do we go? Man will go through tribulation which has never happened in the world before. If those days are not shortened all who are not rapture will perish (we have to pray for the mercy of God that we may not follow the false Christ and false prophets and that those days be shortened. Mark 13:20. The prophecy of Noah seemed a dream and the people rejected and went about their business and that prophecy came to pass and people perished. Also the prophecy of Sodom where Lot dwelt, the citizens did all kind of evil and rejected whatever warning given to them and continued with those deeds and the whole city was wiped out with brimstone from heaven. Likewise the prophecy of the Rapture will come at a time we do not expect. Many have refused and rejected the Rapture, so it shall be a surprise to mankind.

THE BEGINNING OF RAPTURE :- (1). The Sun will be darkened and the Moon also will be darkened. Darkness will fill the Earth, the Stars will fall from Heaven. The power of Heaven will be shaken. This will be for some days and not only one day. (2). The Elect will be gathered together from all the four corners of the earth. (3). The parable of the fig tree : when these things come then know that the time is near at the door. Luke 13:6-9, (the churches which do not bear fruit but filled with sin, the Lord will wish to cut them off and Angel have been pleading for them for one more chance.) (4). The world will strongly reject Jesus as the Son of God and His suffering, Luke 17:25. and (5). The gospel will be preached in all nations and the end will come, and it's you and I who will go out to the nations to do the preaching before the end will comes.

CHAPTER TWO

UNDERSTANDING FASTING

Introduction:- Fasting is the greatest of the amour of God delivered to Christians for the well being of the Christian. It is the first and foremost in the life of a believer to seek the face of God. Fasting has been in application not in our modern days but has been in existence time immemorial. It worked for our fathers and it also works for us. Whether you believe it or not, it works. Fasting based upon the word of God and by God's direction. When we set our minds to fast and start the fasting, then a spiritual war had began because we set our minds to understand and humble ourselves before God. The demon behind the problem will fight hard and call for reinforcement to stop the fasting throughout the days of the fasting. Every Christian has an angel who watches on him and protects him or her, the guardian angel will also fight hard and call for reinforcement from heaven for the period of the fasting. If we are able to complete the fasting, we had overcome, a victory has been won. It is our fasting that helps and empowers the angel to fight hard. That is what happen to the prayer of Daniel. Dan. 10:12-13 "Then he said to me, Do not fear, Daniel, for from the first day that you set your heart to understand and to humble yourself before God, your words were heard; and I have come because of your words. But the Prince of Persia, withstood me twenty-one day; and behold Michael one of the chief princes, came to help me, for I had been left alone there with the king of Persia." Matt. 18:10 "Take heed that you do not despise one of these little ones, for I say to you that in heaven their angels always see the face of My Father who is in heaven." This is the form of an angel who fights on our behalf. Rev.10:1-2 "I saw still another mighty angel coming

97

down from heaven, clothed with a cloud. A rainbow was on his head, his face was like the sun, and his feet like pillars of fire. He had a little book in his hand. And he set his right foot on the sea and his left foot on the land." Someone with his right foot on the sea and left foot on the land, just guess how huge and fearful he could be. He sees every corner of the earth and if such a person is with you what will you fear. This is the mighty power behind a Christian.

Memory Verse :- Esther 4:16 Go, gather all the Jews who are present in Shushan {abundant lilies, the capital of Elam (eternity) the son of Shem and the grandson of Noah} and fast for me neither eat nor drink for three days night and day. My maids and I will fast likewise. And so I will go to the king which is against the law, and if I perish I perish. Mark 9:29 This kind can come forth by nothing but by prayer and fasting.

Points for Fasting:-

1. Fasting is the ceremony in the air against principalities, rulers and powers and agents of spiritual wickedness. It is the highest activity in ones life. It is the basis of ones spiritual life for a new direction. Acts 10:30, 9 - 10.
2. Fasting brings humbleness before God. It is sowing to the spirit to reaping the fruit of the spirit. Psalms 35:13 1Kings 21:27-29
3. Fasting brings righteousness to improve our relationship with God and enable us to communicate with Him and for God to hear us to obtain his mercy and grace. Joel 2:12 Matt. 5:6.
4. Fasting brings the anointing of the Holy Ghost. Acts 13:2-3, Acts 10:9-10. When we have the anointing of God we shall see the mind of God and He will reveal things to us.
5. Fasting is the magnetic weapon for every Christian. Exodus 34:28-30.
6. We fast to magnetize the demon behind the problem for which we are offering prayer into the arena to be conquered. If you fear fasting you can never have breakthrough. Matt. 4:2-4
7. Fasting means asking the devil to bow before God. eg. authorities are forced by hanger strikers to do their will for them. Dan. 10:2-5 The enemy surrenders and God's hand become great.

8. Fasting should be to the Lords. Zech. 7:5, Luke 2:37, Isaiah 58:3-10, Matt. 6:16-18.

9. Fasting means mourning, when we fast to the Lord, the Lord will take control of the situation, you will be comforted. Matt. 5:4 Blessed are they that mourn for they shall be comforted. Dan. 10:2-3

10. Fasting is part of our spiritual warfare as it was with Jesus. Matt. 4:1-11.

11. Fasting is part of our preparation for the service in the spiritual development as well as defeating Satan. Neh. 1:4.when you fast you are demonstrating your love for God and your readiness to walk with Him

12. Fasting gives us strength and privilege for the tremendous calling of the Lord. Acts 14:23.

13. Fasting opens up to the spiritual world (for identification of good and bad). Ester 4:1-7.

14. Fasting facilitate the infusion of spiritual energy and life. 1 Kings 19:8-9.

15. Fasting presents the body as a vehicle for prayer. Exo. 34:28, 33:11

16. Fasting in itself offer prayer to God. 2Sam. 12:16

17. Fasting drains away unbelief and opens up more spiritual insight.

18. Fasting alert the spirit to be more aware of the world forces of darkness and spiritual forces of wickedness.

19. Fasting expose us to God, giving God the appeal and commission to change us to what he wills and to use us in a more dynamic way. Isaiah 58:5-10 Fasting also expose the gift of God in us.

20. Fasting works in lifting our prayer to God. Mark 9:29.This kind can come forth by nothing but by prayer and fasting.

21. Fasting opens the door of positive spiritual power in the Holy Ghost. Matt. 4:2-11.

22. Fasting acknowledges the true source of life. And helps us to have dominion over our physical body to enter into the spiritual realm.

23. Fasting releases revelations of Jesus and power in peoples lives. Acts 10:9-10.

24. Fasting brings spiritual issues to surface and purges the body of the poisons. eg. hatred, wickedness, murder, idolism, adultery, witchcraft, fornication, etc. Acts 9:9.

DEFINITION:- Fasting means waiting on the Lord in the new testament and in the old testament, it means mourning which also means abstaining from food and drinks, sex, etc. Fasting is casual and not permanent abstinence, therefore children of God should not fear to fast. Fasting becomes necessary when everything has failed, strength, wisdom, effort, knowledge, family, friends, nation, etc. concerning our success besetting sin, fear, problems, demonic attacks, wars and besiege. Is. 40:28-29. We should not fast by motivation of self interest and self seeking because God hates that. Fasting and praying should be God initiated and ordained if it is to be effective, ministering unto the Lord yields good results.

Personal Benefit :- Fasting is more of a tonic than medicine. In times past fasting formed part of the medical profession. Under the physical condition it is very good as a cleanser. It helps the mind or the brain to have it's proper realization deserved for all future activities. Your body begins to renew in the fullness of it's beauty after fasting. Emotions or senses- become less burden which reflects in the face by the peace of God, in your heart. Phil. 4:6-7. As a result this good health is experienced, Dan. 1:15 and also Is. 58:8-9. with pure conscience towards God (righteousness), God rewards the individual (Matt. 6:17-18; Lk. 4:2).

Major Purpose Of Biblical Fasting:- In whatever fasting you project yourself, the supreme intention should be the central focus. eg. To change God's mind Jonah 3:5-10; To be heard of on high to glorify God Ezra 8:21-23; To free the captives Is. 58:6; To deliver the oppressed Is. 49:24-25; For revelation Dan. 9:2-3; To avoid flesh pots of Egypt; the Israelites complaining of hanger. Ex. 16:3; Eve deceived Gen. 3:6; Noah was intoxicated and resulted in cursing Ham his son Gen. 9:20-21; Israelites spoke against God Num. 21:5, Num. 11:4-5, 2 Pet. 2:18-20; Consequences 1 Cor. 10:7-10; To cleanse the body 1 Cor. 9:27. (consequences: to minimize too much eating and the desire for too much sex) Jer. 5:7. Avoid the negligence against God. Deut. 32:15-19; solution Rom. 13:14 and For good health and healing. Dan. 1:15, Isa.58:8.

The Three Kinds of Fasting: There three kinds of fasting in use. **Absolute, Normal, and Partial.** The selection of the kind of fasting depends on the type of situation to be handled. People pay some men of God to fast for them. Even though it might work, the member is only helping the Levitt to strengthen his relationship with God and that member will never have intimate relationship with God. Know that hiring someone to bring you to God does not work always, it might work sometimes and sometimes it might not work but the Levitt reap the benefit.

Absolute :- This kind of fasting is devoid of any food or drink for whatsoever. And the maximum duration according to medical advice is three days in order to maintain normal health. This is normally done in most dangerous and critical situations in the life of a child of God and the answer is obvious because God is faithful. The people involved mostly dwell on supernatural plain or are ministered to by the angels. In fasting we are healed of infirmities. Depending on the seriousness of the problem you can fast for three days straight without food and water and after that you will even feel more healthier followed by miracles. Esther 4:16. This could be done by any normal human being. But there are situations where some people fast for straight seven days dry or even fourteen straight dry days. There are instances where people fast for straight thirty [30] or forty [40] day and night without food or water. Moses did it Exodus 24:18 and Exodus 34:28. Elijah went without food for forty days 1Kings 19:8, Jesus the Son of God set us an example by fasting for forty. Luke 4:2. In fasting for thirty days or forty day dry the person is elevated and some even visit paradise and come with testimonies. Some also receive unimaginable gifts for the glory of God. Such fasting is very difficult but will depend upon the readiness of our heart. When Jesus was about to go to the cross He said Father My heart is ready. If the heart is ready for God, all will be possible. The scripture said those who will endure, to the end they will be saved. I have not seen any one who fasted for forty days without food or water but I have seen people who fasted for straight seven days dry and fourteen days straight dry. Even a close family member of mine, fasted for seven days straight dry without food nor water. I am witness. You should be encouraged that this will be followed by a major miracle.

Normal :- In this type fasting we normally restrict ourselves to fluid. It is regularly twelve hour or twenty-four hour fasting on daily basis, and it is normally wise to consume enough of fluid or water to suffice and solicit cleansing and tone- up of the whole bodily system, and this is good because it has the effect of flushing out your kidneys and generally cleaning out the body. Counting on the thirst from the fasting and taking large quantities of fluid to your satisfaction does not make your fasting normal and may not yield the result you may be expecting, this can even cause discomfort and will surely jeopardize your mission of fast. Another thing to aim at is sufficient exercise to bring out the accumulated sweat and impurities from the blood stream, if the aim is to benefit the physical body, for blood being the magnetic agent in the body's purification system. Under every spiritual operation, even mental or whatever project at hand, fasting is very indispensable agent. To be specific, Pure water, fruit juice, water with little lemon and honey are kind of purifying agents but it is wise to take just tea or coffee since both are very strong stimulants for more physical benefits at the end. Most believers take it from7:00pm to 6:00pm a twenty three hour duration tested to be very effective. It could be three days, seven days, fourteen day, twenty-one days, thirty days or forty days depending on the situation and your tendency to cope with.

Partial :- In this type of fasting you eat something in between within the twelve hours but you do not eat much. Daniel 10:2-3 and 1Cor. 8:8. By eating something does not mean you can eat at any time or the way you want but you should have a systematic procedure which may have a fixed continuous time interval. This will show that you are fasting eg. At 10.00am you can take a cup of tea with slice of bread and at 3:00 pm a cup of coffee or tea and at 7:00pm you can take a small bowl of soup or vegetable soup not necessary this but you can also depend on fruits. Usually this situation is granted for sick people who are eager to break up their sicknesses and have their liberty. You can also take a cup of water with the food. It all depend upon the capacity and the faith of intention of the believer.

Uncomfortable Reaction :- People who do not fast often face uncomfortable situations and normally experience some type of physical reactions in the initial stages of the fasting. It's basically because of our chronic habits or our eating life style. The most popular unpleasant physical reactions are headaches, very severe dizziness and sometimes stomach pain. This is because you are liberating your body to do a lot of clean-up screening which is needed to be done. Where hunger is so severe, you have to lay down to rest and pray by taking the amour of God in resistance against the tricks of the devil. Use the shield of faith to quench all his flaming darts and wiles. Also with the sword of the spirit declare victory of the Lord over the enemy. Use it as is written in Matt. 4:4 on the devil by Our Lord Jesus Christ. Elderly people must also be careful when they fast, they may experience physical reaction, more especially when they break the fast. Under no circumstance should a believer break a fast with cold foods. Do not drink or eat cold foods and then eat or drink hot or warm food or drink over it. You will experience very serious uncomfortable situation. Why? The stomach and the intestines are already contracted and once the cold liquid gets in, they over contract and squeeze or cramp, and as a result causing stomach pain. Now when a hot or warm food or liquid is placed over the cold food, there will be instant expansion of the cold food or drink and can cause severe stomach pain and can end the fasting. Always break the fast with some warm drink or food or foods or under normal atmospheric temperature not in winter.

Preparing to Fast and During Fasting :- Positive faith based on the promised reward. Refusing to fast is refusing to receive the promise reward. Have no hidden desire. Recognize your spiritual objectives not self-centered but pleasing God. In fasting you have to put disciplinary measures to yield obedience in your fasting in order to have control. Whatever spiritual operation you undertake, the first thing to do is to fast. Do not forget whilst fasting to take bath often with consecrated water (pray on the water and the soap) or even herbalated water (hyssop, sage, mint, basil etc.), and anoint your body Matt. 6:16-18, do not look pale this will attract the angelic host, Angels are allies in collaboration, given by the Holy Spirit, in order to achieve a successful mission. Elijah was fed by an angel of God. They have God's name in them. Before undertaking any spiritual activities or operation, unless you have been instructed you should fast for three days and set your mind on the desired intention with prayers, mourning afternoon and evening.

Conclusion: The constant practice of fasting and prayers will make the angel with you effective and attract other angels to be your friends, and draw you closer to the omnipotent and nothing will be hidden from you. A good and pleasing fasting before God will also help you bridge the gap between the higher consciousness and the brain level to achieve telepathic conveyance and receptive mind or spirit of discernment. Continuous fasting and prayer will attract an angelic corporate partner, which is the controller of the nine gifts. All things will be exposed to you, either interpretation of dreams, miracles, healing, protection, learning, fortune, prosperity and breakthrough, Good health, Righteousness, Glory to the Lord, Answered prayer, Refreshing, Continual guidance, Satisfaction, Restoration, work of endurance. All these is achieved with a God ordained fasting. No hindrance will stand your way.

PRAYER.

Prayer is a two way communication with God. It is a wish hoped for, the picture of one's desire believed to receive, the thought of one's imagination. It is a spiritual communication, the spiritual pipe through which the power of God flows. Prayer is the only way to communication with God, besides this there is no other way. It is the ceremony in the air, it's one of the highest activities in one's life. It is the basis of one's life and a life giver, and can't be done anyhow, it has a process and principle. Therefore to refuse to pray to God means to seize to the talk to God who gives life. Prayer is a right for every human being to communicate with God. There is no other way to reach God. The one offering prayer sends request unto God and God in turn also gives unto the one in prayer. Prayer superimposes the will of God in one's life because it goes to the root of the problem. Only prayer can change the decision of God. Prayer is words, and words are spirit, powerful, move very fast and sharper than two edged sword, and wherever they land either blessing or curse follows. When we say word against any object or a curse against any object, they will come to pass, why, because when we say things, things are listening, they are ready to perform the word. When words are sent out, they need to fulfill the desire before they come back. Isaiah 55:11. Christ is word, and since prayer is words, when a Christian prays, it is assumed that he is invoking Christ, and when prayer becomes Christ, God cannot rest. When prayer depends on God's Spirit, it goes way far beyond that we think. In prayer we talk to someone we do not see but we trust that He hears us and answer because He is always God. It is not our faith in Him that makes Him God because He existed before creation. He does not needs us to be alive but we need Him to be alive. Prayer is the only way to tire down the work of Satan in one's life. It does not cause faith to work but faith cause prayer to work. Therefore any prayer obstacle is a problem of doubt, doubting the integrity of the word and the ability of God to stand behind his promise in his word [Christ] who lives in us. It is not just prayer that gets result, but it is your spiritual connection with God the father, learning his wisdom, drawing on his strength, being filled with his meekness and spirit in his love that brings result to our prayer. We have to believe that prayer works because once the words are spoken, and come in contact with the atmosphere, they are converted into spirit, which means we have released spirit to perform the thought of our imagination because it came out of a spirit being in a living being.

PURPOSE: We are bound to pray because it sets man apart from all other existence on earth. God made man with eternity of their hearts to pray. Eccl. 3:11 "He has made everything beautiful in its time. Also He has put eternity in their hearts, except that no one can find out the work that God does from beginning to the end." And Jesus said "Blessed are the poor in spirit for theirs is the kingdom of heaven." in otherwise, Jesus is saying "blessed are those who are conscious of their spiritual needs (those who pray) for they will occupy the kingdom of heaven, hence, prayer helps us to reach out to the spiritual realm, helping us to live righteous life leading to eternal life, bringing and filling our lives with happiness. We pray whenever we have the need of help from God our Father or we need wisdom or answer to a particular problem that seem beyond human scope or capacity or knowledge. We also pray when we need our heavenly father's comfort, when we are stressed out or when we know we have lost all hope in life, physically and spiritually. We also pray to our Heavenly Father for our mistakes and wrong doings and for forgiveness of our transgressions.

FOCUS: We pray to the father of our Lord Jesus Christ, that was the instruction Jesus gave to us. John 14:13,14 "And whatever you ask in My name, that I will do, that the Father may be glorified in the son. If you ask anything in My name I will do it." By the words of Jesus we have to pray to the Father in his name and He will ask the Father to give us what we ask for or intercede for us from the Father so that we will glorify the Father for granting our prayers. Praying to the Father means recognizing that He is the creator and above all, and responds to every problem and every situation. Jesus himself set us an example when He was about to be crucified. He came with the disciples to Gethsemane and there He prayed to the Father, "Matt. 26:39 He went a little farther and fell on His face and prayed, O My Father, If it is possible let this cup pass from Me, nevertheless not as I Will but as You Will" Again the second time Matt. 26:42. He went away and prayed, saying "O My Father, if this cup cannot pass away from Me unless I drink it, Your Will be done." Our prayer must also be the will of the Father as Jesus had shown us the example, Let it be your will and not Mine. What is the will of the Father? The will of the Father is asking for something that pleases the Father as to obey and carry out the instruction of the Father, and to contribute to the welfare of humanity and world peace. It is not to ask anything from the Father to go and live high and boasting. This is not the will of the Father. We are also to pray as a church (group), in fellowship or as individual. The change of time has also changed the direction of prayer in these modern times. Elijah, Elisha and the prophets prayed directly to God the Father, without passing through nobody but these days of the New Testament known as the time of grace, unless we believe in Jesus Christ and let Him be our point of contact, our prayer will not reach the Father and will not be granted {John 14:13-15}. Jesus also has made it plain to us that prayer could be carried out anywhere, at church service, our study meetings and even on our way to work and in our work place if it's possible. That is the worship in spirit. John 4:20-24 "Our fathers worshiped on this mountain, and you Jews say that in Jerusalem is the place where one ought to worship." Jesus said to her, "Woman believe Me, the hour is coming when you will neither on this mountain, nor in Jerusalem, worship the Father. You worship what you do not know; we know what we worship, for salvation is of the Jews. But the hour is coming and now is when the true worshipers will worship the Father in spirit and in truth; for the Father is seeking such to worship Him. God is spirit, and those who worship Him must worship in spirit and truth."

PRESENTATION: There is so much argument going on among Christians and especially people who are confused about what posture they have to obtain in prayers. Prayer must be conducted in a suitable and comfortable posture. There is no obligation to sit down or to stand upright or to be walking around or fall on your face, whichever is more comfortable must be your posture and not to be under obligation of distress to interrupt your concentration and meditation. Effective prayer is always achieved out of concentration and meditation. Effective prayer must comprise of Exaltation, Worship, Praise, Obedience, Forgive and forget, destruction of the work of the enemies, protection and intercession. As Jesus laid down in Matt.6:9-13 and is the greatest prayer in life.

REPEATED MINISTRATION. In certain cases prayer must be repeated several times before it could yield result, that is known as repeated ministration. Such ministration pertain to deliverance and prayer request, where there is a powerful spirit behind the situation, or a situation God has permitted it, repeated ministration will be necessary:-

1. Elisha asked Naaman to wash seven times to receive healing. 2Kings 5:10,14. The bible says in 2Kings 5:18 By Naaman the Lord had given victory to Syria, but he did not give glory to God but rather to Rimmon and worship this god so the leprosy was by God, like that of Miriam.

2. Elijah prayed seven times before the rain was released 1Kings 18:42-45. Ahab made the people to forsake the commandment of the Lord and followed Baal, because he was married to Jezebel, 1Kings 18:18 her father was Ethbaal, king of Zidon and Tyre, and high priest of Baal of the Phoenicians. 1Kings 16:31 and that was the cause of the drought by God.

3. Elijah prayed for a dead boy, he had to stretch himself upon the child three times. 1Kings 17:21-22. The mother of the child was a native of Zidon, idol worshipers, who captured other nations and take them captive and sell them and this made them rich. 1Kings 17:9

4. The priests blew the trumpets seven times as they went round the wall seven times at the command of Joshua coupled with the shout and the wall of Jericho fell down flat. Joshua 6:16,20. Because Jericho was a hindrance to the reality of God's promise to the Israelites of the Promise land. Deut. 11: 24-25

5. Jesus had to minister the second touch before the blind man could see properly. This means until the situation is overcome we must not cease to pray over the situation. Mark 8:22-25.

TWO TYPES OF PRAYER:

1. Defensive Prayer (prayer of mercy) - asking for God's protection and open doors. Matt. 6:9-13, Psalm 30:9-10

2. Offensive Prayer (prayer of chastisement) - prayer that will close the doors and put our enemies into trouble and confinement, and destroy their evil plans towards us. Psalm 68:1-2 and Luke 4:35. Psalm 109.

THE FIVE METHODS OF PRAYER:

1. Silence Prayer : Helps us to meditate for God to reveal His mind and give us direction for whatever plans He has for us and we have. Silence prayer is a gift and not everybody has that gift.

2. Vocal Prayer:- It is helpful to pray aloud sometimes because it stops your mind from wondering from one thing to another. Satan tries every means to take away our prayer life or make our prayer ineffective by means of distracting our concentration and meditation, giving us ungodly thinking and pictures, bringing temptations into our lives, and putting fear into our hearts and bringing discouragement and defeat. Vocal prayer remove stress and take away depression, its a healer.

3. Individual :- where one enters into his closet or a solitary place to have intimacy with God. Mark 1:35.We do the praying and God our Father does the work. The more people pray the more we engage God our Father into work. God has completed with all the creation, therefore when we do not pray, our Father God have nothing to do. God likes always to engage Himself at work, that is why He said in Luke 18:1 "men always ought to pray and not lose heart." and also in Thess. 5:17 He said : "pray without ceasing." Also Eph. 6:18 says "praying always with all prayer and supplication in the spirit, being watchful to this end with all perseverance and supplication for all the saints." We engage God our Father to feed us, cloth us, shelter us, and prosper us. He will have much instruction for the heavenly host.

4. Corporate:- prayer by believers (more than one) in agreement. Jesus said, If two agree on earth concerning anything that they ask, it will be done for them by his Father. Matt. 18:18-20. When one is sick and visits the doctor, the patient believes that the doctor can cure him, and the doctor also believes and trust that he is ordained for that purpose and that through him God will heal the patient, the two do come into agreement in prayer unknowingly and for that reason, healing will take place in the life of the patient and definitely healing takes place. It is not the power in the medicine that heals but the power of the faith agreement.

The medicine comes in because we are human and we need a physical sign and the medicine is just the physical sign but not the healer. It's just catalyst to their faith. It is the faith agreement in God that heals. This has nothing to do with the Christian, is a principle of application. Christianity comes in when the doctor passes specified judgment, and by faith in God that judgment is abolished and made dream comes true.

5. Intercessory :- Prayer of intercession can be either corporate or incorporate. It is the most powerful among all the prayer methods, Acts 12:5 Peter was imprisoned to be executed, but the church assembled in a room and prayed day and night for him and an angel rescued him from the jail. Peter learned from Jesus Christ and when Jesus was gone, Peter became the leader, so if he was killed the church would completely collapsed. So the members acted and God also acted, so there was two actions joined to form a great explosion that brought Peter out of Jail. Here, God said YES, and acted immediately. Peter was a good student of Jesus Christ, outspoken and dynamic and learned leadership from Jesus.

GOD'S ANSWER TO PRAYER:

The following are the three responses of God to prayer:

1. Wait - God can say it's not time to give you the request but at appropriate time He will do it. It might not help you at that time, which is to your advantage. John 2:3-4.

2. Yes - When God sees the urgency of our request and sees that we need it and it will help us He responds immediately. Luke 7:6. Jesus said yes because it related to human life and based upon the centurion's faith revealing the deity of Jesus Christ and power of God.

3. No - God can say no when there is danger to the request, when it is for money and fame. Acts 8:18-22. Simon wanted to exchange money for the Holy Spirit for personal fame. eg. if a son asks his father for a car but he has no driving license, which father will

grant such prayer, even we as human as we are, t is a sign of death blinking and a sign of imprisonment.

OUR CONFIDENCE IN GOD TO PRAYER:

1. Nothing is too hard for our God Jer. 32;17; Gen. 18:14.
2. He is faithful and lives up to His promise. Gen. 12:2-3: Gen. 24:1; 1John 5:13-15
3. He loves us and wants to give us hope and better future. Jer. 29:11=14
4. He has committed Himself to grant our prayer. Jer. 33:3; Luke 11:9-10; John 14:11-15
5. Through the Lord's mercies we are not consumed, because His compassion fails not. Lam. 3:22.

`THE EFFECT OF DEFFICIENCY IN PRAYER

1. It is sin not to pray - 1Sam. 12:23 - That is the reason why prayer is a right for the Christian to pray and not a privilege because right cannot be revoke but privilege can be revoke. Without it we will loose God's presence and anointing with us.
2. If we do not pray we deny relationship with God and the spirit of God upon us is quenched and His promise will be broken. 1Thess. 5:17-19, John 14:13-14, James 4:2-3 It is just that sometimes we do not know what to pray for but when we do God works it out for us. Roman 8:26 Likewise the spirit helps in our weaknesses. For we do not know what we should pray for as we ought, but the Spirit Himself makes intercession for us with groaning which cannot be uttered.
3. Consistency in Prayer :- Prayer must be consistent and we must select specific times for prayer. The consistency of prayer is necessary for the maintenance of the spirit and the soul. It is also necessary for our daily achievements. Prayer must be a lifestyle, like taking bath, two times daily and eating three times daily for the good health and strength, and the maintenance of the

body. Even so the SOUL and the SPIRIT demand prayer, four times daily, morning, afternoon, evening and midnight, which is the four watches, for their maintenance. In this way the guide or the Angel with you, is always present. The worse of all should be morning and evening. Because prayer is the channel through which the power of the anointing flows and faith is the channel for prayer. Prayer is a spiritual exercise and must be consistent and be a custom. And when this spiritual exercise become custom or culture, miracles and wonders happen and things are revealed continually. It becomes the gate way for prophetic ministry. Luke 4:16 and Acts 17:2 It was the custom of Jesus and Paul to be in the Synagogue every Sabbath and every day.

THE SIX REASONS TO PRAYER.

1. Prayer makes one turn from his wicked ways and bring the full blessing of God - 2Chr. 7:14.
2. Prayer enable one to have silence moments with the Lord to reveal Himself. Matt.6:6
3. Prayer brings love and increases faith in the Lord. - John 15:17, John 14: 13-14; Matt. 21:22
4. Praying with lifting up holy hands touches the heart of God. - 1Tim. 2:8
5. Prayer can close and open opportunities. - 1Kings 17:1; 1Kings 18 :42-46.
6. Prayer makes the righteous who do not keep silence not forsaken. - Isaiah 62:6-7; Psalm 37:25

SOME OF THE NAMES OF GOD IN PRAYER.

These are some of the old testament names used in prayer but the new testament says we should pray in the name of Jesus Christ. It is a privilege to use these names in prayer but is not a right to prayer. These names do not answer prayers but make prayer strong. The name of Jesus Christ is a right because is the key for an answer to prayer.

1. El-Roi - Omniscient God [God that sees and knows - Gen. 16:13-14].
2. Elohim sabaoth - Omnipotent God [God of Host - Jer. 15:16; Psalm 84:8]. The creator. Jam.5:4.
3. Emmanu-El - God with us [Isaiah 7:14]. God made flesh
4. El-Gibor - The mighty Living God [Isaiah 42:13, 9:6; Gen. 17:1].
5. El- Shammah - Omnipresent God [God who is everywhere- Gen. 28:16, Eze. 48:35].
6. El- Jireh - God the Provider [Gen. 22:14].
7. El- Raah - God our Shepherd [Ps. 23:11].
8. El- Rapha - God the Healer [Exo. 15:26].
9. El- Tsidkenu - God our Righteousness [Jer. 33:16].
10. El- Hosenu - God our Maker [Ps. 95:6].
11. El- Shalom - God our Peace [Judges 6:24].
12. Yahweh Zawah- Jehovah Lord the knowledge in the wisdom [Prov. 4:7, 8:12]
13. Yahweh Ethny - Jehovah Lord our Salvation [Ps 68:20, Ps 1:2].
14. El- Dam - God the Merciful.
15. Yahweh Nissi - God the Protector, Our Banner {Exo. 17:15].
16. El-Ethny - God our salvation Ps. 68:20, 62:1-2.
17. El-Shaddai - Almighty God. Gen. 17:1
18. Yahweh - Jehovah Exo. 3:14 I am that I am.
19. Adonai - Master Ps. 69:6, Matt. 23:8
20. El-O'lam - Everlasting God Gen.21:33
21. El-Mekaddeskum - God the sanctifier Exo. 31:13
22. El-Shaphat - The Judge Judges 11:27
23. El-Elyon - Lord the most high God Gen. 14:18

SATANIC INFLUENCE AGAINST PRAYER: (actions :- prayer is rejected or will not be honored.)

God had laid down certain pre-requisites for prayer in our lives. With these, prayer is of no avail. It can become an abomination and God cannot answer it. These are:-

1. Known sin. Isaiah. 59:2-3: Psalm 66:18;
2. Willful disobedience to God's word. Prov. 28:9; Zech. 7:11-13;
3. Selfish motivation. James 4:3; Matt. 6:5

4. Lack of genuine faith. Mark 5:36; James 1:6-8; Hebr. 11:6;
5. Idols in the heart. Jer. 11:9-14; Eze. 8:15-18; 14:1-3;
6. Unforgiving Spirit. Matt. 5:23-24; 6;21-25; Mark 11:25-26;
7. Hypocrisy [self praising, boasting]. 2Chro. 25:19. Matt. 6:5; Prov. 8:15; Mala. 1:6-10; Job 27:8-9;
8. Prideful attitude. Mala. 1:6-10, Job. 27:8-9; Matt.6:5;
9. Refusing home visitation and relationship. 1Peter 2:17;
10. Tithe evasion. Mala. 3:10-12;
11. Refusing charity to the needy. Prov. 21:13, John 3:16, Rom 5:8;
12. Forsaking the Lord and his ways. Jer. 14:10-12;
13. Discouragement. Job. 1:9-10;
14. Evil thoughts. Gen. 37:18-20.

SATANIC INFLUENCE IN PRAYER : (results:- prayer does not even depart)
1. Fear (false, evidence, appearing, rear) 2. spiritual marriage. 3.Stealing (thief). 4. cheating. 5. jealousy. 6. Hatred. 7. Bitterness. 8.Tempt. 9. Defrauding. Failure comes with disappointment, leading to disgrace, which comes with fear and lead to sickness. If a Christian is not praying the right way, then he might have one of these seriously in control of his life, he needs help. Sam. 1 - Hannah was in this position of jealousy, hatred, bitterness, fear, cheating, until she change her mind and repented. If the person could even pray, he or she will pray anyhow in that situation.

When our prayers are not answered by God, our Father; there must be a purpose for that. As human we only see what is outside our prayers. How beautiful it can be for us, what we think we shall be when the prayer is answered. But God sees what is inside the stomach of that prayer, the troubles inside the prayer, the destruction, the death etc. inside the prayer. And for this reason God will not answer that prayer or delay the answer to that prayer or convert that prayer into life for you to live again. As human we see the external view of our prayer but God sees the internal view of our prayer. He only answers when we are at the safest side. Dan. 11:32 "But the people who know their God shall be strong and carry out great exploits." We have people who live on earth and those who live in the world. The earth belongs to God and the world belongs to Satan. It is difficult to live in the world and serve God but it is possible to live on the earth to serve God, but the World is on the Earth. It is personal decision and choice.

QUALITIES FOR A SUCCESSFUL PRAYER

1. Faith - total believe in CHRIST.
2. Broken Hearted - total repentance. Discarding bitterness and forgiving others.
3. Righteousness - ask for forgiveness of sin and be someone whose sins are forgiven. God fearing and someone charitable and does not jumps into conclusion confess sins.
4. Worship - One with humility, a peace maker.

God gives the prayerful believer the Holy Spirit's timely Prophetic gifts eg. Dreams and vision, which are available to all believers. Acts 2:17. A believer's life begins with prayer and grows in prayer, which is the right of coming to God's throne in faith as a Christian.

QUIZ
1. What is prayer?

    Prayer is a wish hoped for and a way to communicate with God.
2. Is prayer a privilege or right?

    It is a right, that's why God has committed Himself to answer your prayer and has no choice to deny your prayer except that it may endanger the one's life. It's like the citizenship, it is a right to everyone born in that country and could not be revoked. If prayer does not based on the will of God, that prayer right will diminished with time.
3. What are the two kinds of prayer in use?

    (a) Defensive prayer (b) Offensive Prayer
4. Give the five method of prayers:-

    (a) Silence (b) Vocal Prayer (c) intercessory (d) corporate (e) individual.
5. Why do we have to pray in Jesus name?

    Because Jesus is the point of contact for our prayers. (a) John 14:6 I am the way, the truth and the life. No one can come to the father unless by me. (b) John 6: 29 This is the work of God that you believe in Him whom He sent.

6. What give us confidence that our prayer to God will be answered if we based on His will?

(a) Nothing is too hard for our God. Jer. 32:17.

(b) He is faithful and always lives up to His promise. 1John 5:13-15.

(c) He loves us and wants to give us hope and better future. Jer 29:11-14 (d) by His mercies we are not consumed. Lam. 3:22.

(e) He has committed Himself to answer our prayers. Jer 33:3, Luke 11:9-10, John 14:11-15.

7. What are the qualities for a successful prayer? Or What does one have to do for his or her prayer to be answered?

(a) Have faith - (total believe in God with your mind, your heart and substance.)

(b) Have the spirit of worship psalm 95:6-7 spirit of humility that's humbleness and obedience (c) Be righteous – able to confess and ask for forgiveness of sin – some one whose sins are forgiven Isaiah 43:25 and full of good works Acts 9:36.

(d) Broken Hearted : be able to discard bitterness and forgive others. Heb. 12:14-15

8. What is God's response to prayer-?

(a) Yes - Luke 7:6 (b) No - Acts 8:18-22 (c) Wait.

THE ANOINTING OF GOD.

MEMORY VERSE:- Acts 2:2-4.   Exodus 30:22-25.

What is this anointing? It is the result of the physical display of the presence of God upon us, the awareness of His presence. That is the significance of the expression of unseen creator which dwell in unapproachable light, identifying Himself that He had come in the mist of His people, in the manifestation of His love. This manifestation of His love, always proves of His power and the miracles of His might. God gives his anointing for a purpose. The anointing is to set one apart and empower God's elect for the mission He intend to achieve. The setting apart of kings, priests, prophets. etc. the anointing makes this purpose of God extra-ordinary. God passes through the elect to say what He wants to tell his people and also to perform his miracle among His children. Anointing is the physical aspect of the Spirit of God or the Holy Ghost.

THERE ARE TWO KINDS OF ANOINTING:

1. Physical Anointing:- Involve in ministering with oil from the olive, Judges 9:8-9.
2. Spiritual Anointing:- Involve basically with the Holy Ghost, Acts 2:4

PHYSICAL ANOINTING FROM GOD:- The old and the new testament all talk about anointing as well. But the old testament is more of physical anointing with oil specially prepared of the authority and direction of God [to Moses, not human decision], for the anointing of God's elected people and things of divinity in the house of God. Exodus 30:22-30. God instructed Moses to prepare the holy anointing oil for the anointing of his elect and the altar and things of God and tabernacle. Leviticus 8:10-12 Moses through him the anointing oil was made and spirit of God came upon those elect (Aaron and his sons). 1Samuel 10:1 Samuel poured vial of oil on the head of Saul for the Lords anointing as the king to the Lord's children. 1Samuel 10:10-12 The spirit of the Lord came upon Saul after the anointing and he prophesized among the prophets. 1Samuel 16:13 David anointed by Samuel due to instruction of God, with a horn of oil. 1Kings 19:15-17 Hazael, Jehu and Elisha appointed to be anointed by Elijah according to Gods command. 1Kings 1:39 Solomon anointed by Zodak as instructed with a horn of anointing oil. 2Kings 11:12 Joash anointed king. 2Kings 23-30 Jehoahaz anointed as king. From the old testament we see the anointing of priest, prophets, and kings which was a physical anointing with oil made according to instructions God gave to Moses and the prophets. This anointing with oil was sanctification which sets apart and fill the person with the Spirit of God for the Lords service. If the person disobeyed God, then he is no longer under that anointing. 1Samuel 16:14 But the spirit of God departed from Saul.

SPIRITUAL ANOINTING:- This is the anointing of the new testament which is given to those called to God by his grace. We no longer live under the law, but under the grace of God. Jesus could not commence his ministry until the anointing came upon Him, the Holy Spirit has to come upon Him and whenever the Holy Spirit comes upon us we see a physical sign. Matt. 3:16-17 Jesus was baptized and the Holy Spirit came upon Him. Luke 4:18-19 (Isaiah 61:1-2). We need the anointing of God to preach the word of God. The spirit of the Lord is upon me (this took place during the baptism, hence we receive this anointing in baptism, either water baptism or Holy Spirit baptism).

1. 1.Because He has anointed me to preach the gospel to the poor- meaning all must hear the gospel and no partiality.
2. He has sent me to heal the broken hearted, give hope to the hopeless.
3. To preach deliverance to the captive. the preaching must deliver the captive.
4. And recover of sight to the blind. The blind must receive his sight.
5. To set at liberty those who are oppressed. The oppressed will have his freedom.
6. And to preach the acceptable year of the Lord. The period of grace and peace.

Without the anointing, none of these we can do. Our Lord and Savior Jesus Christ is saying we must be elected by God and be anointed for his purpose, so that we shall be able to perform that duty of which we are elected. Acts 1:4-8. But the election comes when we freely open our heart to receive the gift of this grace.

In times pass:-

1. It was the rich and the great men, and the Elders who hear the scripture, but this time of grace all are receiving and hearing the gospel

2. The priest took instruction from God and communicated only with the kings, the rich and the elders to take counsel and one must be from the priesthood genealogy to be a priest, a prophet etc. John 11:46-54, but in this time of grace ordinary people are made elders and pastors.

3. In the old testament, those with curse died with it, they had no hope, but in this new testament era we have hope. Luke 13:11-16, the woman with infirmity received healing, Mark 5:2-19 the madman with his dwelling among the tombs regained himself to once again live among the living. The impotent man from birth raised to walk on his feet. Acts 3:1-9 and 4:9. all these are examples of the hope Jesus Christ has granted us, through the anointing.

4. The blind had no hope, but in this new testament era he has. Mark 10:46-57. Bartimaeus, the blind man received his sight.

5. The poor was always poor, they had no hope for the future. But by Jesus Christ, those who believed in Him have hope for a better future. 2Cor. 8:9 "For ye know the grace of our Lord Jesus Christ that, though he was rich, yet for your sake he became poor, that ye through His poverty might be rich." Christ has already taken care of your poverty, so you are not poor anymore. Jeremiah said in Jer. 29:11 "For I know the thought I think toward you, saith the Lord, thoughts of peace, and not evil, to give you an expected end." Bad future could be change to a good future;

a. By the grace of Christ, b. By the mercy of Christ, c. By the power of Christ, d. By the anointing of the Holy Spirit, Acts 4:7-14 and 2-4. Acts 2:29-41. e. By the blood of Jesus Christ. *The Holy Ghost anointing comes by spending time with God, by prayer and fasting and the reading of the word of God.*

We can change dreadful situations and turn the whole thing from anti-clockwise to clockwise. Without the anointing of the Holy Ghost and the power of the blood of Jesus Christ none of these we can do, so Christ is saying we must be elected by God and be anointed for his purpose, so that we shall be able to perform that duty of which we are elected. John 20:22; Acts 4:31. Where there is the anointing of God there is the Holy Spirit, the Holy Spirit is the anointing so when the anointing come upon us the Holy Spirit himself has come upon us. Acts 2:2-4. Therefore a Ministry without the Holy Spirit is like soup without salt, the ministry might not be for Christ. John 16:7, 15:26-27. Luke 4:32. "And they were astonished at his teaching for his word was with authority." When we preach and teach the word of God with authority which come from the Holy Spirit:

1. demons cry 2. demons scatter 3. demons tremble

Luke 4:40-44 1. Jesus did these miracles due to the anointing upon him. 2. The anointing of God which is the presence of the Holy Spirit is an essential requisite manifestation to every ministry of Jesus Christ.

1John 2:20 "But ye have an anointing from the Holy one, and ye know all things." - It is the anointing of God that reveals things in the spiritual realm to us. 1John 2:27 "But the anointing which ye have received from him abide in you and you do not need that anyone teaches you; but as the same anointing teaches you concerning all things and is true and is not a lie and just as it has taught you, you shall abide in him."

When we have the presence of the Holy Spirit upon us, we have supernatural knowledge. Without the anointing we shall not be able to learn things of the spirit and through the anointing we know the gifts of the Holy Spirit which are;

1. The gift of the word of wisdom.
2. The gift of the word of knowledge
3. The gift of faith.
4. The gift of healing.
5. The gift of the working of miracles.
6. The gift of prophecy.
7. The gift of discernment.
8. The gift of kinds of tongues.
9. The gift of interpretation of tongues.

It is the anointing through which the Holy Spirit opens to us all the scriptures and teaches us from the scripture concerning all things. 1Cor. 14:1-5.

The promise is for every Christian? Mark 16:16-18. "He that believeth and is baptized shall be saved, but he that believeth not shall be damned. And these signs shall follow them that believe. In my name shall they cast out devils, they shall speak with new tongues, they shall take up serpents, and if they drink any deadly thing, it shall not hurt them, they shall lay hands on the sick and they shall recover." We have to understand that these will not follow the believer, without the spirit which is the baptism of the Holy Spirit. The bible says he that believeth and is baptized, and a Christian must be baptized in Christ and made acceptable to Christ, these signs shall follow him, at least one of these gifts must be seen with him which is anointing of God.

How do we come to know this anointing? First of all, we must understand the scriptural background of the anointing. All the anointing God made upon his elected people, kings, priest, and prophets through his servants was to set apart those elected people for Gods assignment and the manifestation attached. The setting apart is the identification of the anointing.

What about the believer? We live under the new testament or new covenant and we have been called by God's grace for a purpose and without the anointing that purpose cannot be achieved, so the believer also needs the anointing.2Cor. 1:21. "Now he who establishes us with you in Christ and has anointed us is God." We are clearly told that God has both established us and anointed us (set us apart in Christ for his purpose) (1John 2:20).

How is this establishment and anointing happened? Jesus said that unless one is born again he cannot see the kingdom of God (John 3:3). For a man to enter into the kingdom of God he must be born of water (water baptism) and of the spirit of God [the holy spirit baptism] which is a second birth after our birth by our mothers which is the physical birth. It is the 2nd birth that brings the Holy Spirit upon us who lead us into the kingdom of God and by this we clearly see the establishment and the anointing.

How many times can we receive the anointing? We can receive the anointing as many times possible, meaning charging the anointing. The apostles were filled 3 times:

1. Jesus breathed on them (John20:22).
2. They were filled (Acts 2:4).
3. They were filled again (Acts 4:31).

TRANSFER OF ANOINTING THROUGH CLOTHES AND GARMENTS. The believe in the transfer of anointing and healing power through clothing and garments are clearly written in the holy bible. People who do not believe, to them it is stupidity and absolutely craziness and they will have no part in this blessing, and wonderful supernatural powers. 1. 1Kings 19:19 2. Acts 19:11-12 3. Matt. 14:36 4. Mark 5:27-28, 2Kings 2:13-15.

TRANSFER OF ANOINTING THROUGH LAYING ON OF HANDS. That is the primary application of the impartation of the supernatural powers of anointing by a man of God to another person who has faith in God. Anyone who believes that by the contact of the hands of the man of God, to his body upon a revelation and word of God will bring about the transfer of the anointing of God, will surely receive it, according to the capacity of his faith.

1. 2Tim. 1:6 2. Deut. 34:9 3. Acts. 13:3 4. 2Tim. 1:14 5.Heb. 6:5-7

TRANSFER OF ANOINTING THROUGH ANOINTING OIL. Jesus himself instructed the disciples to anoint with oil. Anointing oil has wonderful power in it, if only people will believe this power. Saul was anointed by Samuel and the spirit of God came upon him. 1Sam. 10:1. David was anointed by Samuel and the spirit of God came upon him. 1Sam. 16:12-13. The anointing oil is made of olive oil. This oil has great potential for healing which is necessary to look for. Judges 9:8-9 "The trees once went forth to anoint a king over them. And they said to the olive tree, reign over us! But the olive tree said to them, should I cease giving my oil, with which they honor God and men, and go to sway over trees." Even olive tree value the gift of God and cherishes it to be more precious than any other thing, but human beings value the gift of men than the gift from God.

1. Mark 6:13 2. Jam. 5:14 3. Lev. 21:12

FAITH IN THE MAN OF GOD. God has elected certain people to represent Him. He use these people to reveal His thoughts, and also speak through them to the world or His people. One cannot have faith in God without believing the man of God. These are apostles, pastors, prophets, evangelists, etc. Luke 7:7-10 2Kings 2:13-15 Mark 5:22-23, 28-29 Acts. 9:38-40 Acts 8:15-17 2Kings 4:1-6 2Kings 5:1-13 Luke 4:25-27. Having faith in the man of God is the sign of believing in God. The man of God represent God in the Church, therefore believing in the priest or the pastor, the prophet, the evangelist, the bible teacher, the apostle, the bishop is having faith in God. How can one have faith in God when he does not believe the priest or the pastor. These are the people God use to manifest Himself, so if the church don't believe in them, the church of course don't believe in God either. God is found in the church and through the priest God is found. 2Chron. 20:20 "So they rose early in the morning and went to the wilderness of Tekoa and as they went out. Jehoshaphat stood and said, Hear me O Judah and you inhabitants of Jerusalem, Believe in the Lord your God and you shall be established, Believe in His prophet and you shall prosper."

THE FIVE FOLD MINISTRY:- [1Cor. 12:28, 9-10; Eph. 4:11]

These leaderships become frustrating without the anointing of God, and must be a calling from God. This is the reason why people use other means to satisfy the calling, which is very sad because it is an abuse and degrading against the power of God. These are the leaderships :-

1. The Apostle is church planter.
2. Prophet is a visionary and a seer.
3. The Evangelist is a miracle worker a soul winner.
4. The Pastor is a healer and a shepherd of the church.
5. The Teacher is a bible Scholar and feeds the church.

THE WIND OF THE HOLY SPIRIT. The Holy Spirit can blow as wind over people to receive the anointing of God for His purpose. John 20:22. "And when He had said this, He breathed on them, and said unto them, RECEIVE YE THE HOLY GHOST." Acts 2:2. "And suddenly there came a sound from heaven as of a rushing mighty wind, and it filled all the house where they were sitting."

ANOINTING FOR FINANCIAL PROSPERITY :- Anointing must not make one poor because if anointing can raise up the dead people, why the same anointing can't make one rich. The only thing is to know the kind of anointing to make one financially sufficient.

There are five specific types of anointing for financial prosperity. These were the five talent the Lord Jesus spoke about in Matt. 25:14-30. These are :-

1. TUWSHIYYAH — Sound wisdom anointing. H8454 - tuwshiyyah - Job 11:6 - the secret of wisdom.
2. UMATZLAKH — Success anointing in the midst of enemies. - H6744 - umatzlakh
3. TSELLAKH — Prosperity anointing. - H6743 - tzallakh
4. HATZLAKH — Elevation anointing. - H6746 - hatzlakh
5. UMATZLEKHIM — Building Wealth anointing - H6745 - umatzlekhin

To be financially prosperous, the first level is sound wisdom or anointed wisdom which gives the wisdom follow by anointing for success. This must be followed by prosperity anointing and the next step is anointing for elevation, follow by anointing for building wealth. Without these prosperity is impossible.

1. TUWSHIYYAH ANOINTING :- is the anointing for sound or efficient wisdom to do business. The bible says in Matt. 25:14 There was a man who was travelling to a far country and gave talents to his three servants. One he gave five talents according to his faith (someone who has not much connection and not a business man), the second he gave two according to his faith (he was smart but did not have much connection). The last, he gave only one talent according to his faith (a smart, highly influential and great amount of connection) and proceeded to his journey. When he returned, he called the three to make account. The one with five talents presented ten talents, the master said to him, a good servant, you will rule a kingdom, but the one with two talents also presented four talents, he said to him good you will also rule half of a kingdom. the last who had one talent said, I know you reap without sowing, so I hid your talent in the earth, here is it. Matt. 25:26-27 His lord answered and said unto him, thou wicked and slothful servant, thou knowest I reap where I sowed not, and gather where I have not strawed. Thou oughtest therefore to have put my money to the exchangers and then at my coming I should have received mine own with usury. The last had the Umatzlekhim (building wealth) anointing but refused to work with and lose the whole

kingdom. This is a hidden knowledge. Why did the master gave them the talents? He wanted them to prosper because they have been a long time with him and had compassion for them.

1Kings 3:7-9. "Now, O Lord My God, You have made Your servant king instead of my father David, but I am a little child; I do not know how to go out and come in. And Your servant is in the midst of Your people whom You have chosen, a great people, too numerous to be numbered or counted. Therefore give to Your servant an understanding heart to judge Your people, that I may descend between good and evil. For who is able to judge this great people of Yours?" King Solomon asked for this Sound Wisdom Anointing and God granted him and he became the wisest and richest man in the world till now.

Colo. 2:3 "In whom are hidden all the treasures of wisdom and knowledge." So only our Lord Jesus Christ can impart to others this Anointing of Sound Wisdom.

2Thess. 3:8 "Neither did we eat any man's bread for nough but wrought with labour and travail night and day that we might not be chargeable to any of you." Apostle Paul had the Tuwshiyyah, the Umatzlah, the Tzelach, the Hatzlah, and the Umatzlehim anointing and worked hard as a business man, operating a tents factory so that he was not a burden to the church and congregation. Likewise, he is advising pastors to do so that they don't become burden to their churches and the congregation. Likewise in Gen. 47:13-26 Joseph had all the five anointing and was made great in the land of Egypt.

Prov. 2:7 "He lay up sound wisdom for the righteous. He is a buckler to those who walk upright." This anointing for wisdom is reserved for those who walk upright in God. It is a gift and a privilege to them.

Phil. 4:19 "My God shall supply all your needs according to His riches in glory by Jesus Christ." It is God who supplies the power and the Tuwshiyyah anointing, gave Jacob the wisdom to use the rod of green poplar and of the almon and chestnut trees, peel the white strip in them and exposed the white which made the flock gave birth to streaked speckled and spotted and made Jacob very rich, exceedingly prosperous, a large flock, female and male servants and camels and donkeys. Gen. 30: 43

Gen. 4: 7 Cain built a city and named it city of Enoch. One must be rich to build a city.

Gen. 13:2 Abraham was very rich.

Gen. 26:14 Isaac was exceedingly rich in the midst of enemies.

Gen. 41:42-44 Joseph was very rich, prominent, and a man of power in a foreign land. He took all the money of the people, all the live stock of the people, all the land of the people and invested their own land with them to work for him.

Mark 15:43 Joseph of Arimathea was a very rich man who gave up his tomb for the burial of Jesus. Matt. 19:22 The rich man who had a great possession and wanted to follow Jesus but because of his wealth could not.

All these were achieved through the power of SOUND ANOINTING, TUSHIYAH. Prov. 2:7; 3:21; 8:14

UMATZLAKH ANOINTING :- The Umatzlakh anointing makes one to succeed in whatever he does. No matter where he will be, he can be a slave, a foreigner, a servant, it matters not what situation he will encounter, he will still be successful. The brothers of Joseph looked at him and saw a dreamer, the merchants looked at him and saw a slave, Potiphar looked at Joseph and saw a servant, the prison officers saw him as prisoner, God looked at Joseph and saw a prime minister of Egypt so the umatzlakh anointing upon Joseph cause the king to share his leadership position with him. Friends may see you as a labourer but with umatzlakh anointing God sees you as a president.

Gen. 26:12-16 "Then Isaac sowed in the land and received in the same year an hundredfold and the Lord blessed him. And the man waxed great and went forward and grew until he became very great. For he had possession of flocks and possession of herds and great store of servants and the Philistines envied him. For all the wells which his father's servants dug in the days of Abraham his father, the Philistines had stopped them, and filled them with earth. And Abimelech said unto Isaac, Go away from us, for thou art much mightier than we."

Isaac went to live in Philistine and for the first place he was a foreigner and the whole country had been hit by drought and all wells were dried, only Isaac, for the sake of the Umatzlakh anointing upon him, his wells never fail to be full of water. He had water in his father Abraham's wells and the Philistines envied him because he came as a family with nothing and in a very short time, he prospered and became prosperous, he was envied more and they filled his wells with soil. He had spiritual water which connected him so when the people closed the wells, Isaac still had water for his business. He had a God, the father of Our Lord Jesus Christ, our most Elder Brother who is our God, the Christian God with him.

TZELLAKH ANOINTING:- This anointing makes one prosper not only financially but prosper in having many servant, children, companies, even a village and in your country your word is respected, you are needed and looked up to. Prov. 10:22 "The blessing of the Lord makes one rich. And He adds no sorrow with it. Gen. 26:13 Isaac began to prosper and continued prospering until he became very prosperous." Because Isaac was blessed by the Lord through the Tzellakh anointing, there was no sickness in his house, no death in his house for a certain grace. He was highly respected. By human administrative standards and scientific administrative standards, Tzellakh does not make sense but it is real and possible. In 2Chronicles 20:20-21 while the enemies came against Israel, in the time of King Jehoshaphat, with guns and dangerous weapons, the Israelites went against them with singing, praising the beauty of the holiness of the Lord. And the enemies turned against themselves and killed and destroyed one other. God does not make sense but He is always right. It was the Tzellakh anointing with which King Solomon anointed the synagogue he built for God in Israel, which made God to take up the battle upon Himself. There is a God who performs miracles. King Solomon never saw wars in his time. People of tzellakh are dangerous in prosperity, tzellakh means to overtake and overflow and when you have tzellakh and people are busy opposing you, you shall overtake and overflow. When the devil knows you have the tzellakh anointing, he will do whatsoever it takes to stop you from reaching where you are going. Tzellakh is to prosper, to advance, to overtake, to overflow, to partake, and to invade. With tzellakh, it does not matter how many people have similar company or product, you shall overtake, you shall invade, you shall partake, you shall advance, and you shall overflow. Tzellakh is a number in Hebrew H6743 which represents prosperity.

HATZLAKH ANOINTING:- Hatzlakh anointing is the anointing that elevates a person. It makes one to be heard of. It makes one popular and advertises him. It creates magnetic fields around the person and his house so that the person is heard of all over the planet earth. Hatzlakh anointing is very powerful and no evil force or demon can go near. Whenever they make attempt they perish. This anointing gives a person a brand name, meaning it changes your name and makes that person a loving person, loves all and loved by all. In Gen. 41:41-44 "And Pharaoh said to Joseph, see I have set you over all the Land of Egypt. Then Pharaoh took his signat ring off his hand and put it on Joseph's hand: and he clothed him with garment of fine linen and put a golden chain around his neck. And he had him ride in the second chariot which he had; and they cried out before him, bow the knee! So he set him over all the land of Egypt." Joseph was lifted beyond imagination and became popular and mighty even more than the king. Without his consent the king did nothing. Joseph was a foreigner and a slave but because of all those powerful anointing upon him, he excelled and excel mightly. These are overflowing anointing and are unstoppable.

UMATZLEKHIM ANOINTING:- This is the anointing for building wealth. This anointing brought Israel to Egypt, made Joseph secure a land for them to dwell in the land of Egypt. So Joseph built a town for his Jewish family and Israel multiplied in the land of Egypt. They also became wealthy in the land of Egypt and were untouchable and greatly feared in the time of Joseph. Joseph who was a slave built great wealth in the midst of an advance country in those days. He prospered and became prosperous. He had the power to repay Potiphar and his wife, as well as his brothers but Umatzlekhim anointing does not work that way. It does not revenge. Jacob said in Gen. 48:16 "The angel that has redeemed me from all evil bless the lads. Let the name of my fathers, Abraham and Isaac and let them grow into a multitude in the midst of the earth." Because of this anointing with Jacob, he always had an angel to defend him and made his words be confirmed. There is a secret in prosperity and there is a hidden secret in Israel. This is a hidden secret of the covenant of the promise land, reserved for the children of God. And as a Christian it is reserved for you also, because the bible says in Gal 3: 29 "And if you are Christ's, then you are Abraham's seed and heir according to promise." This is your qualification to claim these anointing. Seek to receive these anointing, TUWSHIYYAH, UMATZLAH, TZELLAKH, HATZLAKH and UMATZLEKHIM which Jesus described in the parable of the talents. These are the five anointing He spoke about in the parable in Matthew 25:14-30. Jesus spoke in proverbs and we need the help of the advocate He sent, to understand those parables. The best is yet before you and yet to come.

ANGELS OUR CORPORATE PARTNERS.

Angels are God's manifestations who are spirit beings. The corporate partners means they are at our disposal at any time. We are made to understand that every Christian has an angel before God Matt.18:10. "Take heed that you do not despise one of these little ones for I say to you that in heaven their angels always see the face of My father who is in heaven." The word angel was derived from the Greek word angelos which means intermediary, someone who corresponds between two media in otherwise a messenger.

Angels are spirit beings which communicate between man and God. Matt.4:11. One cannot be messenger if he is not trustworthy, therefore an angel is a holy righteous being who protects and saves. Here we see the picture of CHRIST, portrayed as the angel of God, who communicated the plan of God based upon His word and salvation towards mankind. Luke 19:10; Daniel 3:25. Angels are spirit beings which can transfigure depending upon the type of operation assigned to be accomplished. We see so many examples in the bible like, Jacob prevails over the angel Gen. 32:I, 24-30; Some strangers are angels Heb. 13:2: Gen.18:2; Gen. 19:10. Angels are celestial beings (1Cor. 15:40) who can appear with terrestrial resemblance (Gen. 18:2) and for this matter they have the choice of human appearance and even remain human Gen. 6:2.

CHARACTER OF ANGELS

1. Angels can be visible. Gen. 18:1-2,19:1; John 20:12; Exo. 3:2-6
2. Angels are invisible 1Sam. 3:7-10; Gen. 22:11
3. Angels were created by God. Psalm 8:5; Hebr. 1:6-7
4. Angels do not have their own will. Hebr. 1:13
5. Angel are sons of God. Luke 20:36; Gen. 6:2; Job 1:6
6. Angels have extremely high intellect. 2Sam. 14:20; Mark 13:32; 1Peter 1:12
7. Angels Protect human. Daniel 6:22 8. Angels are righteous and holy Luke 8:38
8. Angels have immeasurable strength. Psalm 103:20.
9. Angels do not marry Matt. 22:30

10. Angels are highly righteous. Luke 1:11, 19.
11. Angels have immeasurable strength. Psalm 103:20.
12. Angels are very swiftly. Daniel 9:21.

Angels have different categories of assignment. We have angels whose responsibility is to protect the throne of God in Heaven in otherwise they are termed as the body guards. The same angels (some of them were sent to) guarded the garden of Eden when the rightful owners abused their right and were rejected. They are the most powerful angels and they are the group of CHERUBIM. They carry wings which means they do fly and very fast in operation, Dan. 9:21, no matter how long the distance, it takes second and they are there. Gen. 3:24.

We have a Second fast classification of angels:- who also carry wings and they protect the Throne of God in Heaven. They do not depart from the Throne and always proclaim the holiness of Our Father. These are known and called Seraphim Isaiah .6:1-3. Each of these celestial beings has six wings, three on each side [back of the left and right shoulders] which each pair represent one of these, obedience (worship), peace (praise and adoration) and love(action) and that's their qualification for worship, a highly gifted celestial super worshipers. The second pair of the wings control respect among the angelic host apart from the Cherubim. They impact spirit of humility to all the angels and mankind. This shows that man is not of himself but for God. The last and third pair of the wings make them vanish, a movement more faster than any celestial beings or object in the universe, Dan. 9:21. This tells us how fast they can respond to emergencies. Joshua 5:13-15. Jesus said this is the doings of God and no one can understand it.

The Archangels:- They are the labor force of creation in heaven and they have exceedingly mighty power beyond expression, Psalm 103:20. They also respond in time of war against the adversaries of the nations of God. They also protect all the properties of God. They are eight in number, they are very swift, one can anticipate the imagination of their response. They are 1. Michael 2. Gabriel 3. Lucifer {Assiah replaces Lucifer} 4. Atziluth 5. Briah 6. Yetzirah 7. Raphael (deliverance).

1. Michael:- The leader, warrior and fighter. He is always for victory. He was the corporate partner of Israel's victories Joshua 5:13-15 and leader of Lucifer's rejection from heaven (Rev. 12:7-9).

2. Gabriel:- The messenger for principal communications for highly important classified messages and blessings. Luke 1:26-38.

3. Lucifer:- This name means the son of the morning. We saw this in the creation. This is the angelic name for Satan prior to his fall. He is the fallen archangel. He was the intermediary of the Godhead bodily and the angelic host. He fell due to rebellion and power struggle which ended him all the satanic names as: 1. Satan Job 1:6; Luke 10:12, 4:10: Rev. 12:9 2. Dragon Rev. 12.9; 3. Devil. Rev.12: 9; Eze. 28:14: 4. Accuser Rev. 12:10: 5. The Old Serpent 2Cor. 11:3;. Oppressor Acts 10:38; 7. Liar and murderer John 8:44 7. Prince of the Air Eph. 2:2: 8. Prince of the Darkness Eph. 6:12: 9. Prince of the World John 12:13, 16:11: 10. God of this World 2Cor. 4:4: 11. The thief John 10:10: 12. The Roaring Lion 1Pet. 5:8:13. Corruptor of Mind 14. Beelzebub Matt. 10:25. Every Christian knows the story of his fell and his jealous deeds against man on earth. Lucifer is replaced by Archangel ASSIAH. What happened in heaven also happened on earth. Lucifer was replaced with angel Assiah when he fell, even so Judas Iscariot was replaced with Matthias when he fell. Acts 1:23-26

4. Atziluth:- This is the angel in charge of the sight of creation. A powerful angel with unimaginable strength and divine intelligence. The bible says, and the earth had no form, and the spirit was hovering on the surface of the waters.

5. Briah:- The angel in charge of the world of thrones of the nations in the interest of the inhabitants of the nations when the people cry unto the Lord about the kings. God created the thrones of nation in his care, who prepared the garden of Eden and placed man in it. God's name is in the angel and once you see His angel, you see His visitation. Adam did not pay attention to this voice of the angel.

6. Yetzirah:- This angel is the God's anointing upon the creation and good things of nations and thrones. And God saw that it was good. He is God's help for people of the nations to do the will of God by being obedient.

7. Raphael :- He is the deliverance angel for all children of God, that's, those who believe in Christ, against the spiritual marriages, demon possess libration in all forms. This archangel controls the heart of the inhabitants of nations to obey God.

There are angels known as the Host Of Heaven who are always before the Throne of the God in heaven. They are given among those who believe and are followers of Christ. They show up with the form of Holy white Doves, Intermediaries, Watchers [watching on Christians] and can be visible and invisible. They can even take the form of humans. They are the sign of the appearance of the Holy Spirit. John 1:32-33.

CLASSIFICATION OF ANGELS:- Ezekiel 1:13-19

MALACHIM:- This is the host of angels who maintain universal harmony.

CHERUBIM:- They give strength. They protect and guard creation and they cause increase on earth. These are Angels of justice who carry out God's decisions and they are the chariots around the throne of God. They can take any form to execute God's purpose. The angels of flame of Fire which chastise disobedience against the creator. 1Kings 8:6-7, Ezekiel 10:7-10.

SERAPHIM:- They proclaim the holiness and guard the Throne of God. The highest order of hierarch of Angels. They are Angels of flame with Love (mercy) and light (truth). They constantly sing praises and worship. Isaiah 6:2-3

ELOHIM:- They are the creating Lords of nature and universal life. They maintain prosperity and progress of life. These are Angels with Godhead name EL, the plural is Elohim: Michael, Gabriel, Raphael, Uriel, Zadkiel, Chamuel, Jophiel. They give victory to nations and individuals. The classification of dominion. Dan. 10:13, Rev, 12:7

BENI-ELOHIM:- They calm the inner sense of man. They also control the celestial order. They are the Angels of miracles, blessing and faith. They are known for virtue and grace.

CHASCHMALIM:- The angels of beneficence which enlighten the terrestrial images, they can enlighten even an animal to talk Num. 22:28, even objects, for the glory of God. Jesus made clay birds and commanded them to fly.

ARALIM:- They are the stimulating intelligence for the creation of new ideas and supply energy of thoughts. They give encouragement and boldness.

ISHIM:- They assist in all terrestrial operation.

THE GUARDIAN ANGEL:- There is the Guardian Angels which are the sole corporate partners who work hand in hand with the believer. They are the gift of God to the believer from the Holy Ghost ready to act or intervene at anytime in any operation or danger. We also plan and take decision from the Lord through them. They are intercessors. Matt. 18:10, Luke 9:55.

When were angels created? Was it the day of creation? Was it before creation?

Etymology: Latin - Angelus, Greek - Angellos, Hebrew - Malakh, and all mean messenger. Angels were not mentioned in the physical creation because angels do not belong to the physical creation. They were before creation. For this reason they shouted joyfully when the foundations of the earth were laid. Job 38:4-7. They existed before the physical creation. Angels have the power to enter and exit at will on the earth and can be visible and invisible. They are celestial beings who act as intermediaries, between heaven and earth, God and man. Angels protect and guide human beings and carry on with God's instruction. Angels came into existence with the Lords.

In conclusion angels are our corporate partners to work in agreement with us under the control of the Holy Spirit. So we can ask them for any help or dispatch them to go and perform specific operations based on the will of God, and they will obey and do. Matt. 8:8-9. We are not to worship them but they are to help us and to work with us in whatever we do.

DEMONS

INTRODUTION :- Satan is the god of the dark world, and the god of the darkness.

Under Satan are :- 1. the devil (gods), 2. witches and wizards, 3. demons.

The devil claims glory for Satan, he is the son of Satan. Devil is the one who possesses objects, shrine and rivers and trees to be worshipped, who claim glory for Satan. It is devil which controls the witches and wizards. Because witches and wizards are acquired, they do not live in lifeless entities. Satan possesses citizens with corruption which is the most dangerous weapon to destroy a nation, which has the potential to collapse a nation. Corruption is witchcraft, a powerful evil spirit, that possesses a nation and collapses it, into completely desolation. Any citizen or native who will rise against the witchcraft of corruption will not live for long or take their offer of wealth to live when that person is too strong for them. The greatest network and medium Satan is using to destroy the world is corruption and wants to make sure the whole world is corrupted, that he will own the world, and Christians are at a great war with Satan. Corruption is direct spirit from Satan.

The Devil, the son of Satan, will use the witches and wizards to protect their nation and destroy other nation. Witches and wizards distribute demons according to the desire of devil in the form of adverse situation like: demon of sickness, demon of illness, demon of financial difficulty, demon of court issues, demon of marriage issues, demon of child labor, demon of oppression, demon of child abuse, demon of drug addiction, demon of jobless, demon of stealing, demon of stupidity and foolishness, demon of murder, demon of spiritual marriage, demon of hatred, demon of humiliation and demon of addiction, demon of fornication, demon of prostitution, demon of adultery, demon of masturbation, demon of action limitation, demon of jealousy, demon of selfishness, demon of harlotry (Hosea 4:12) and so on, to torment mankind and all come with disgrace and death. The duty of demons is to make life difficult for mankind, afflict and oppress people which takes many forms and years. All these Satan is the master mind of it, because he is jealous of man for the simple reason that man has the opportunity and favor of God. Because God has given his estate on earth to mankind through Jesus Christ. That is the reason why Satan is doing everything possible to destroy man. He is using so many networks and mediums to capture human race, purposely to destroy them. Satan still does not admits his fault and counts on pride, he feels he is better than man because he has only one category with man, we are all created by God but he is spirit as God and does not admit that anyone can judge him. His time is yet to come. Many at times, people who are possessed by demons, cannot believe until it manifests, some might know but all can be delivered. The witches and wizards do not possess but they are acquired because those humans like to have them on purpose and agenda. The world is at war with the satanic world. Demons are unclean spirits and witches and wizards are evil spirit. One being the higher that is the spirit of witchcrafts and are acquired, and the other being the lesser that is demon, is released to possess based on condition and opportunity. The gods are those which cause human beings to worship them, an abomination and the greatest sin in the universe which make God separates. The gods are direct spirit of Satan. They are cool and collective, they are not aggressive like the witches and wizards. They also claim glory and when they have to cause havoc, it's a big havoc and disaster. Their havoc could take a whole nation and whole nation could come under its power. These are spirits which possess Rivers, Lakes, Idols, Grooves, Statues, Rocks, Mountains, etc. Because they desire human beings to worship them and they drive human beings into materialism and paganism. They normally do not torment because they receive glory from mankind, but when they desire to cause harm, it's a big havoc. Witches and wizards are the smaller and what they do against humanity is, they torment people with demons. Demons are the smallest among the spirits. The harm and the havoc demons cause is the smallest. But what we call the smallest, one can imagine the effect. These cause what we call illness, sickness, confusion, addiction, pride, lies, bloodshed, fornication, adultery, emulation, lasciviousness, madness, cancer, ulcer, high blood pressure, kidney failure, stroke, cardiac arrest (heart attack), diabetes, divorce, spiritual marriage, hardship and the like. The devils known as gods take captive of the witches and wizards to use them. These little evil spirits create panic in mankind. When demons tarry for far too long they will develop and become witches and wizards, which are aggressive and torment the person and use him or her to destroy other innocent human beings. Know that witches and wizards perform evil activities in the life of mankind in the form of situations known as demonic. So demon is an evil situation and is a spirit.

WHAT IS A DEMON? Demon is an unclean spirits. These demons are spirit beings without material or physical body which seek a physical or material body to live in. They do not care whether they live in a person or in an animal, all that they need is to have material body, through which they can express themselves or operate or function or manifest. They can enter into objects when an opportunity is created for them, provided the object or the body can serve their purpose. There are so many doors without security in life and when they are liberal, demons become real, Mark 5:7-13. They enter and they will torment that person. We have been made to understand by the power, knowledge and wisdom of Jesus Christ, that these demons could be cast out. Matt.12:43-45, meaning if we as Christians live to the will of God, then these demons will be nothing before Christians. When we command them under proper authority, they must get loosed, come out and depart (cage them and do not let them have their will). The bible says these signs shall follow those who believe and are baptized, in my name they will cast out demons. Mark 16:17. So as Christians we are empowered to do so because we believe in Jesus Christ and we should not be afraid of demons, neither Satan because Satan was created by God and we are also created by God so Satan is not better than man. The bible says he that is in us is greater than he that is in the world, that's outside us, 1John 4:4. We have Jesus Christ which Satan does not have. Demons can only be cast out by the name of Jesus Christ, (Luke 9:49-50). Without the name of Jesus no demons could be cast out and they will attack. And to be able to cast out demons, you must be a Christian, believe in Jesus Christ and be baptized and live according to the will of Christ. Acts 19:11-17.

CHARACTER OF DEMONS. What we have to know is that the will of demon or demons is to possess a physical body through which they can express their purpose and use the material body to operate the way they want. These demons have knowledge that's why when their attempt fail they take another initiative, they think and they reason. In Mark 1:24. those demons knew that Jesus Christ was the Messiah (the holy one of God). Demons are violence, when they were cast out they went into the lake violently and were choked and because they think and reason, they can plead so the demons in the madman met Jesus and began pleading with Him to permit them to enter into the swines, if he drove them out of the man. Luke 8:27-30. One thing we as Christians must know is that demons have will, that's the desire to do something. In Matt 12:44-45. The demon took decision to go back and when he was back swept the place and garnished and went and took with him other company of seven who are more wicked than himself – that's reinforcement, a strong defense against any intruder or any army and make sure no one can take possession of the place this time. Demons can speak because in the presence of the Holy Ghost they are compelled to speak, tell their story whatever they have done and whatever intention they have also planned. In Matt. 8:28-29 the bible said, "in the country of Gergesenes, there met Jesus two possessed with demons, came out of the tombs with exceeding fierce so that no man might pass by that way and behold they cried out saying (they spoke) what have we to do with thee Jesus, thou son of God? Art thou come thither to torment us before time." They knew they cannot be in those men forever because their time was limited in those men, so these demons will one day come out and continue somewhere else but Jesus did not allow them to go and continue somewhere else but entangled them with His micro waves. Demons do not die but when they have destroyed that body, they exit and seek another physical object and possess it, so that they can continue to function. Only Jesus and the name and the blood of Jesus Christ can kill them. They are very cunning, they have believe and they believe that there is God, someone greater than all powers in the universe, who created all things. James 2:19, so they can capitalize on this since they knew mankind know and believe that there is God. Upon this they invent stories, create panic and cause people to abandon their faith to follow ungodly teachings and hardening their hearts and indulging in all kinds of impurity. 1Tim. 4:1-2, Eph. 4:19. Whenever we do deliverance we have to kill them by telling them to die or perpetually caged, in the name of Jesus which contains the micro waves. Asking them to come out is not enough, is easy for them to possess someone right there. Jesus Christ did not ask the demon to come out and left it, but He said "and have your peace" meaning you can no longer possess anyone any more. They also speak as the Holy Ghost does and make people obscene from meat, stay away from marriage but practice fornication and homosexuality. Demons also enslave people with fear and harassment. In Acts 17:5-9 the demons possessed the people, that's the infidels to rise against those who heard the word and believed and put Jason in custody, enslaving him.

Archbishop Duncan William once said, demons are fallen angels and witches and wizards are Satan's earthly army that work for Satan to carry on satanic agenda on earth concerning humanity. Demons don't fly, they are transported. Angels who have the capacity to transform depending on the assignment at hand. Angels can choose to be spirit or physical beings, even objects, likewise a demon do not transform but possesses a body or an object to harm humanity. There are flying spirits that are rebellious angels and angels fly. So as a believer you have to understand the rankings of Satan and his kingdom. In Matt. 12 :26 Jesus said Satan is not divided because Satan cannot cast out Satan, so you have to understand the subject of demons was introduce by Jesus Christ Himself in the New Testament. In the old testament, demons were not cast out, but were stoned with the person. The prophets did not have the jurisdiction to cast out demons. But it was introduced by Jesus Christ, the Son of God Himself when He came on the scene in the New Testament. He began to command and to expel unclean spirits and unclean spirits are entities without bodies which have the desire to work through bodies. Demons cannot operate without physical body. They need a physical body to identify themselves. They have the emotion to feel according to the bible and they work through the emotion of a physical body. They have intelligence and they have knowledge which are not derived from human source. When the demons met Jesus, they said to Him; Thou Son of God, the Most High, has thou come to destroy us before time. The disciples did not know who Jesus was, but the demons had the intelligence and the information of who Jesus was, and that is what we call familiar spirits. So if someone can tell you something that is true, that does not mean that comes from the Holy Spirit. The demons were telling the truth. You must be able to have deep discernment to know what spirit is speaking. Matt. 8:29, Acts 16:16-18. The damsel was telling the truth but from who? Now the bible makes it clear that we are in a warfare and our warfare and our battle is not with flesh and blood and the enemy has succeeded to get the body of Christ to fight over cares that are not necessary to our eternal salvation.

We fight over everything, we criticize over everything and the one thing that we must do that we are not doing is that we are not dealing with the devil. We wrestle not against flesh and blood but against principalities. When we talk about principalities, we talk about super beings or super powers or cosmic powers, these are high ranking satanic powers. The bible talks about Thrones, it talks about Dominion, Princes and Principalities. When the bible talks about principalities, it is referring to a prince, and when it talks about dominion, it is talking about his administration and authority or the domain of the prince. When it talks about throne, it is talking about his government and operations, and the power means he has authority by which he commands or move things, carries and executes his desires. The body of Christ has to understand that we are involved in a warfare with an enemy we can't see. It does not matter how good you are about the scripture, for the weapons of our warfare are not carnal but they are mighty through God to the demolishing of every stronghold. So there are strongholds and there are unclean spirits. God cannot operate in this human realm without human body and demons also cannot operate without human body. So the battle is over humanity, that is the human body. The battle is over the spirit. The spirit, battles those familiar spirits to protect the soul because the spirit of a Christian has been redeemed (by the works of the Holy Spirit) and the body is redeemed through the unity of the soul and the spirit by Christ. Your soul is been saved by the renewing of your mind, which says, be not conformed to this world as well as be not transformed to this world but be ye transformed by the renewing of your mind, that ye may prove what is the good and acceptable and perfect will of God, Rom. 12:1-2. Now the body shall put on immortality that is the final salvation of the body. 1Cor. 15:53. For this corruptible must put on incorruption and this mortal must put on immortality, and death will have no power over the body, then death is swallowed up in victory, meaning death will be dead and it is the last enemy that shall be destroyed. Up to the coming of Jesus Christ the warfare is upon the body and soul of humanity and believers have to understand the technical symbols and the legal approach and the rules of engagements of the legislative order, so that we will not walk as ignorant believers. Paul said for a messenger of Satan was assigned to buffet and harass me to trouble me. So when you are dealing with the enemy, don't attack the human but declare and decree a divine reversal of the assignment of the messenger to the sender, the master. A witch has demons, which she mentors to wrestle the word: So this demands tactical skills and navigational skills, to move and navigate to tackle the enemies and exert strength over the enemy. Once you overcome the witch, the demons will follow him and run for their life. When you take out the captain who mentors them, the soldiers will be in obedience and they will submit. The demons go into battle for the witch and once you take out the wizard, the demons will surrender.

When Goliath declare war with Israel, the war was between the God of Israel and the god of the Philistines, David knew victory has already been declared over the Philistines, since Dagon fell before the Ark of the Lord. So as soon as Goliath fell, all army of the Philistine fled, because the headman has been taken care of. It is time for Christians to rise up and go for the captain of the kingdom of Satan, who is responsible for the authorities, powers, thrones and dominions. When Jesus went to Gadarenes, He met a madman who was possessed by a legion. The word legion means six thousand soldiers. In those days the Roman legion was made of six thousand soldiers which was equivalent to three thousand horsemen and three thousand footmen. So six thousand demons were in that man. When Jesus said to the man, what is your name? He meant, can I know who you are? And the demon understood it and said, we are legion. Demon doesn't walk, it is transported in multitude. If you are dealing with the demon of captivity know that it comes with demon of oppression and affliction which automatically call for anger, and brings the demon of violence followed by the demon of murder which will take you out of this world. If you deal with the demon of jealousy, you also have to deal with the demon of suspicion and mistrust. No demon moves alone. You need to be sensitive because sometimes when we cast out the horsemen, you must cast out the ground troopers too, they could be in there and you may not know. A Christian cannot be possessed but can be demonized and bewitched. "Apostle Paul said, who bewitched you." So when you see people acting out of character, know that they have been bewitched, they have spell by which they can be cursed because there are curses you bring upon yourself, which curse will affect your generation to the fourth generation, which are self-imposed curses where a person says I wish I die or I cannot take it anymore etc. Prov. 6:2 "Thou art snared with the words of thy mouth, thou art taken with the words of thy mouth." The words you speak are taken against you and taken into captivity by the words of your mouth. The bible says the power of death and life are in the tongue, so whenever you open your mouth to speak, you are under trial because whatever you said can be held against you and all that the enemy wants is to provoke you to curse yourself, because the devil can't curse you but what he does is to frustrate you and create satanic gridlocks and hindrance and prolong the warfare with you, to prolong the battle and delay the manifestation of the answer to your prayer and get you to a point where you get frustrated and begin to speak things which seem legal right and permit the devil to harass you. So when you are angry be careful with what comes out of your mouth. He cannot curse you so he gets you to curse yourself by the things you say. We are dealing with princes, we are dealing with powers and authorities, cosmic powers and enemies, and they are enemies you do not see. You have to understand that Satan is not stupid, he is intelligent, he was trying to drown Jesus before He gets to the other side of Jordan. The horrific storm which was contrary and the disciples cried out of fear. It was Satan which came against the disciple in the form of storm which without Jesus the disciples would have perished. And the disciples called Jesus from sleep and He looked at the sea and said, Wind how can you terrified and threaten my disciples and my assignment, where were you in the created the earth, where were you when I commanded the waters to gather together themselves and they obeyed My voice, Where were you when I spoke and it was so, and immediately the sea obeyed and the storm seized and became still.

1. Demons cannot operate without human body, if they cannot get human bodies then they have to get the bodies of animals. So they operated in the body of the serpent in the garden of Eden because it is illegal for a spirit to operate without a body. Jesus was aware of this because He made that law, that a spirit cannot operate without a living body. So they said to Jesus, send us to the swines, and Jesus granted them their plea and said get out of him and do as you said.

2. They cannot operate out of their territory. They said to Jesus don't send us out of this territory, we love this territory, we have lived in this territory for many years. Demons don't know your mind, they learn and study you, so they said, we have lived in this territory,

we have learn from them, we are one with them, we do influence their thought pattern and behavior and their security system, so do not send us out of this region. We have invested so much in this people, if you take us from this region, you have bankrupt our business. So leave us in this region. Jesus said leave and go into the swines. And because of the fire and anointing and power around Jesus, the two thousand of the six thousand demons that were able to find the two thousand swines fled and possessed the swines while the four thousand of the six thousand demons were trapped in the fire of the Holy Ghost and burnt without ashes, the two thousand out of the six thousand that entered into the two thousand swines run violently into the lake and perished. Once the powerful two thousand were captured the weak four thousand had no strength so they made an attempt to flee and were trapped in the Holy Ghost fire.

Then Jesus said, I am going to raise up a generation of people which I will give them power and authority that will command demons and they have to obey them in My Name. This is the reason why, when the disciples returned, they said to Jesus, even the spirits have submitted to us in Your Name. Demons are territorial, that is, there are demons that control a specific region and don't control other region because the atmospheres are not the same and need the permission and approval of the demons of that particular atmosphere or region to achieve their mission. The also have to be carried to possess. So Christians must begin to pray for deeper understanding and discernment to deal with demons. These days pastors and prophets heal the sick, it is good if it's from God because these pastors and prophets go and acquire power for service and work of God or join occult societies for power to serve God. Is this from God.?Are they not mocking God! God is all the time God else all these people might perished. Because God has said, He is not pleased with the death of a wicked person, so God see them as sheep without shepherd.

The bible says : They shall cast out devils and heal the sick: So you can't heal the sick if you don't cast out the demon which is the root of the sickness. Once the demon is out, the person is healed. Jesus said in Mark 16:17-18 these signs shall follow them that believe, In My name :

1. They shall cast out devils.
2. They shall speak with new tongues.
3. They shall take up serpents.
4. If they drink any deadly poison, it shall not hurt them.
5. They shall lay hands on the sick and they shall recover.

He said first cast out the the demons and then you can lay hands and heal them. Jesus said to the Scribes and the Pharisees, If I by the finger of God cast out devils, then the kingdom of God has come upon you, which means demons and devils have the ability to block the manifestation in people's lives and a greater power is here to destroy their work. In 1Thess. 2:18 Apostle Paul said, Therefore we would have come unto you, even I Paul once and again but Satan hindered us. Demons can't possess the body of a Christian, but they can:

1. oppress 2. harass 3. exert 4. afflict 5. torment 6. frustrate 7. bewitch 8. spell 9. tie 10. hinder a believer.

You have to know how they work to be able to unblock every satanic blockage, to take authority to say; "I break every curse and every bewitchment of the devil over my life, I declare a divine reversal of every demonic conspiracy against my life, back to the sender and his and his kingdom, hundred fold, in Jesus might name."

You have to know how to revoke the powers of principalities. Powers when it comes to your jurisdiction. You have to understand there are legal terminologies and there are rules of engagement when it comes to dealing with the enemy. Whatever God has positioned you is your jurisdiction, and you have the authority to deal with the enemy within that jurisdiction. When there was contention over the body of Moses, know this that, Satan wanted to eliminate Moses before his birth and there was demonic inspired legislation that was put together to make sure that the midwife will kill Moses at the delivery, and the mother was so prophetically inspired that she was willing to risk her life for the preservation of Moses because she knew that Moses was a prophetic seed, and she wouldn't let Moses die. The devil pursued Moses until he was 120 years and even after his death. Moses was the greatest treat to the devil, the devil was so much interested even in the dead body of Moses, and an Angel of God had to come down from heaven to protect and preserve the dead body of Moses. So as a Christian, the devil is highly interested in you, he is interested in your descendants, so crazy about your business, your finances, your peace and your job and it is time to rise up and let the lion in you roar.

The bible says, there is a battle and there is a war over the life of Christians, there is fight over your health, there is struggle over your finances, your marriage, your church, your destiny, your children, your effectiveness and you destiny and it is time for every Christian to raise a counter petition, a standard, a counter motion against every demonic motion. It is time for children of God to stand up and come out violently to object to every demonic and Satanic claims over your life, your children, your family, your business, your health, your spouse in the mighty name of Jesus Christ. It is time for somebody to put his feet down and tell the devil, this is how far you can go, enough is enough. There was dispute over the body of Moses, a conflict over the body of Moses and the bible says that, Michael the minister of defense of heaven could not bring a charge against the devil because Michael was dealing with another prince who is in control of the this world, the reason why Angel Gabriel could not overcome the prince of Persia for 120days was because Angel Gabriel was not the defense minister. Angel Gabriel was the minister of information of heaven, He had the mandate to announce whatever Heaven had proclaimed. Whenever there was a judicial determination or judicial verdict or decision or executive decision of Heaven, It was Angel Gabriel who had the mandate to come to the earth to announce it, concerning the birth of Jesus, the birth of John the Baptist, the battle with the prince of Persia. Angel Gabriel had the anointing and the authority to carry out what he was told. So he comes with the information from the father to man and returns. He was not anointed for war and so for 120 days he was resisting with the prince of Persia and he needed an angelic reinforcement by an angelic defense commander. The bible said even though Satan is defeated and in possession of the jurisdiction on earth, he could not defeat Gabriel on earth, because heaven was within his jurisdiction and Gabriel had the judicial right to deal with Satan and for that, The Father, The Son, and the Holy Ghost did not get involve in the battle. On earth realm Michael could not take Satan up. He could not get him out, so Michael had to refer the war to a Superior authority by saying "the LORD REBUKE YOU" why because he could not take Satan up, for he was operating outside his jurisdiction, for the earth has been given to men and only men could exercise that authority : Psalm 115:16. So only children of men can exercise authority here on earth over the spirits, demons, witches and wizards, but men out of ignorance had left that to angels, but the scripture said a body has thou prepared for me, Heb. 10:5. This means without a body, there is no way God could manifest Himself in earth realm, because God can't operate in the earth without human body; That is why we have to preach the gospel because the more we preach the gospel, the more souls are saved and the more we put Satan out of business. Know this that:

1) demons speak 2). demons have a will 3). demons make decision 4). demons have corresponding power to back their decision 5). demons have self awareness 6). demons compel 7). demons influence 8). demons exert 9). demons afflict 10). demons hinder

In Matt. 12:43-45 the bible says, when an evil spirit leaves a man it goes walking in dry places and when he f0und nobody it says "I will" so demons have will, they speak so they have will, it says I will return to my house from hence I came, "house means body" that is "YOU" a human being. The demon said I will return that is a revenge, or a demonic come back or satanic retaliation, That I will return to my house, the demon called human body a custom made house, because they fell more comfortable in human body than any other object or body. When the demon comes and there is no access, he target your children, the indirect way to get you, is to target your children, by this he could get you because it is the same DNA which is deoxyribonuceic acid - {[(a molecule compose of two chains which coil around each other to form a double helix carrying the genetic instructions used in the growth, development, function and reproduction of all known living organisms and viruses)]}, a self replicating material present in nearly all living organisms as the main constituent of chromosomes. It is the carrier of generic information. And he makes sure that this time, with the reinforcement he can't get out, so he brings with him a stubborn and powerful reinforcement. Abraham said "she is my sister," he was dead and his son Isaac also said the same thing "she is my sister" and it continues. It is trans-generational. If the demons don't get you, they will get your children or your descendants and that's the reason why you have to cover your children or your descendants because the battle is no more over you alone. Somebody has to stand up for your children, you as a father you have to cover your children, you have to fight for your grand children, you have to put out this fight for the next generation, you have to tell the devil, not this time and not these ones, because the battle is no more over you. So the demon goes to the dry place, and demons like dry places, so if you are dry Christian, you have made yourself available for the devil to possess you. Dry Christians, dry churches, dry preachers, talk, teach and no oil to maintain their light. <u>Anointing comes by fasting and praying, reading the word of God and stay away from unrighteousness.</u> It is not the preaching that breaks the yoke, it is the oil that's the anointing and the anointing does not come by preaching, it comes by spending time in the presence of God. When the anointing is upon you, you can fight any spiritual battle, and you will take the battle to house of Satan and not your house. Eph. 3:10 To the intent that unto the principalities and powers in heavenly places might be known by the church, the manifold wisdom God. The manifold wisdom is given to the body of Christ to know the hidden secret of Satan. Apostle Paul said, I know a man whether in the flesh or not I know not, who was cut up into the third heaven, so if there is third then there must be second heaven and according to what Paul said <u>it is time to reason that God is in the third heaven, so that every other heaven is under the third heaven.</u> So Paul is saying the politicians, the military, the scientists don't have the necessary weapon to deal with the enemy but the Church, because they don't have the authority recognized by heaven to deal with Satan. So God said I may make known the intent of the principalities and powers in the heavenly realm through the church. Jesus said, I will build My Church and the gates of hell will not stand a chance. Again Jesus said to peter I will give you the keys of the kingdom of heaven and what thing you bind, will be bound in heaven. Jesus, before He said those words, He said to Peter, who that man say that I am? You have walk with Me, ate with Me, Spoke with Me and have experience the therapeutic power of Mine. You have known that I AM the ELOHIM. And he say, thou art the Christ, the Son of the Living God. Jesus said, then, it's you Peter will I give the keys. So keys are not given to just anybody, keys are given to those who walk in revelation, those who access revelation, those who walk in dominion of God because keys give you access and Jesus did not say key, singular, but He said keys, plural, so you have access to all the twelve gates of heaven and move anything you want to move. He said, once you bind on earth it shall be bound in heaven and whatever you loose on earth shall be loosed in heaven. What this means is, because the Father has found you fit to give you revelation and divine intelligence and advance knowledge, you will know what heaven has bound concerning matters of the earth and you will bind what is bound in heaven, and it shall be bound. you will know what is loosed in heaven concerning matters of the earth and you will loose them on earth and it shall be loosed. So you don't just go round binding and loosing things, but bind and loose by revelation because they are possible to bind and possible to loose according to the rules of engagement.

Restitution - restoring with interest

Restoration - just give back what was taken

Fight back and speak back, Don't allow the devil to take you for granted. Don't let him think that he can just come and say whatever he wants to say and get away with it. Don't let Satan put up a fight and you sit back and let the devil go free. Respond. Whatever the enemy speaks against you, you have to respond because if you don't respond, he will advantage over you.

TEMPTATION is not of God, it is of the devil. Because the bible says, if anyone is tempted, he is not tempted of God. James 1:13. Demons are tricky, they can cause people to lie and sin and bring death unto people, as it happened to Ananiase, Acts 5:1-11, that is enticement, 1Kings 13. They play their wiles on people, and they do not stop tempting because when they rest, Satan will punish them. Matt.26:41 "so we have to watch and pray that we may not enter into temptation. The spirit is willing but the flesh is weak."

DEMONS ARE VERY DECEPTIVE. They deceive some Christians, believers who are baptized and who the Lord's gift has come upon them and give them prideful feeling and deceiving emotion. If we allow ourselves for such emotion to rule our spiritual life, taking the place of the spirit of God in us, that emotion will have impact. Those who worship God worship in spirit. If we allow the spirit of God to rule over our lives, based on the word of God then we will always be able to identify between the spirit of God and demonic spirit. Some believers over react thinking that by so doing, people may believe that they have the spirit of God and put their trust in them. Such believers may feel that they have drawn attention by shaking and jerking of their body and the shivering of their palms and arms and their unprecedented prophecies which sometimes become bored and cause confusion because they give long prophecies which most at times are planned prophecies, which cause trouble in the church. They may also think that they are trying to impress people, especially visitor or new comers, to proof that they have special anointing from the Holy Ghost. These are not from the spirit of God but demonic from the flesh, combining the gift of God with the gift of Satan- the deceiving spirit or spirit of deception.

The spirit of shock is one of the dangerous spirits, it can kill instantly no matter who you are, once it possesses you, reduces your emotions, brings coldness in the body, give you fear and begins to dominate your brain, transmitting the fear to your heart and finally stops the heart. Shock is a demon. Demons do torment humans. Churches claim superiority over other churches, this is demonic influence. If we believe that all churches belong to Jesus Christ then no one has any right to claim superiority. Demons are working seriously and hard for Satan and if Christians should work at that rate, one can imagine what a peace we can bring to the world. Demons can possess any of these persons, a pastors, apostles, evangelist, teachers, prophets, bishops, etc. in short the modern day men of God to do evil. A pastor or an apostle will not like his brother apostle to be equal or do better than him, he will always find a means to cripple the other apostle or the pastor, especially when that apostle is senior and the other apostle is his associate. All these are demonic influences and power. So if such pastor or evangelist or apostle cast out demons, what is he trying to portray or displaying to the church. Oppression, suppression, humiliation, torment are equally the same spirit, they are all demons, Luke 13:14-15, 31-33. Sometimes a pastor will be so sincere to accept another pastor into his ministry and after some time the other pastor will break the church into two and take half of the members away to plant his own church, that's DEMON OF SEPARATION, very powerful, violence and dangerous and easily murders. We can see this by the notion behind the separation, its for money.

TERROR OF DEMONS. Demons join with witches and wizards to

make war among nations by their supernatural strength. War in our time, physical war and spiritual war, is not of God, therefore no one should relate war to be the revelation of God. Who can withstand His anger. He will fight the opponent with natural disasters, the hurricane will slap that nation, Earthquake will swallow the buildings, volcano will melt the earth and there will be no place for mankind. If it's of God, Jesus would have set an example. It is one of Satan's destructive weapon. In Luke 9:54-56 when the apostles wanted to make war, Jesus said, war was not part of my mission, meaning the apostles did not know the kind of fire they were talking about. Basically struggle for power is of Satan, the devil and his witches and wizards and demons fight over power, they fight over position, fight over property and they fight over riches, because they have lost their glory, they have no glory with God and now that is their nature, the only way for Satan to acquire glory. When Jesus came he did not fight over these worldly things because they belong to him. Likewise, you as a child of God, being heir of the creator, owns all these things so a Christian need not to fight over worldly things. When demons possess one emotionally, they make sure that person is completely still, feels rejected, lonely as if he has no help, feels he has failed in life, feels like he cannot do it, who am I, my education is too low for the position. By so doing, affecting the attitude of the person and everything this person does will be wrong and eventually he will not attempt to do anything. He will be doubting whatever he will do, he becomes indecision and procrastination and insecure. Demons can affect the tongue to blasphemy, curse people and speak big lies and gossip about everybody they see and everything they hear. Where one of these spirits is found all these five will be found because they walk together (rejection, fear, blasphemy, lies and gossip). They have no fear, you can be a man of God, they can function in you, if you create an opportunity for them. They need tongue to lie. Demons cause people to become smokers, alcoholics, workaholics, anoxia (children born under alcoholic influence with low amount of oxygen).

CONCLUSION. This is how demons function and operate in and on human beings and now you know how to deal with them. Our environment is full of demons so we should cleave unto the mighty power, Jesus Christ, who will give us his spirit to combat with these demons. Because of our unbelief, but if we have faith like the grain of mustard seed we shall say unto this mountain, remove hence to yonder place and it shall remove and nothing shall be impossible unto us. Matt. 17:20.

BREAKING THE SIN CURSES OF THE PAST

Having been saved: there is more to be done for salvation as Christ like, that's Christian. In your past life the sins you committed, produced curses and those curses are those which possesses you- inscribed in your life. Even though our Lord Jesus Christ has forgiven you all your sins. Jesus has done His part, your sins are forgiven and cancelled meaning Jesus has broken the power of Satan which held you in captivity, but the curses of the sins produced in the past, it's your duty as a Christian, a Christ like, a child of God to work on your deliverance meaning you have to command Satan to come out by:

1. Fasting
2. Reading the Scripture.
3. Prayer -: breaking of the curses - with the blood and name of Jesus, and the power and the anointing of the Holy Spirit. And then in John 8:11 "Jesus said, go and sin no more."

In Zech 3:1-7 "Satan remembered the past of Joshua and used it as legal ground to oppose him. It was the Lord who rebuked him, and liberated Joshua according to his works."

Once you are saved you need to break the curses of the past. If a thief had a cut in the process of stealing and healed, the scar remains, he does not get rid of the scar by being forgiven the crime. Even though the sin of stealing is forgiven the scar will be there until he treats it by applying dermatological creams to remove the scar which is the curses and is not easy to get rid of it. That's what you have to do as a Christian - breaking of the curses. Breaking is very important after being saved. You will call yourself a Christian but because of the sin curses you do not function as a Christian. You are crippled with poverty, crippled with failure and all kinds of oppressions and afflictions, which should not be so with a Christian, a child of God.

Why the curses? Because you have put people in pain and they have spoken curses out of bitterness into your life, these curses had formed the ghost of your life and are highly causing troubles. Curse is a demon holding a person or a living thing captive, based on a legitimate legal grounds.

Foundational curses are the result of the idolatry, wickedness and evil causes of the founding father of the clan and this needs a mighty hand of God to break and excavate the foundation for a complete extermination.

Ancestral curses are the result, when our forefathers prior from our great, great grandparents served idols and did all kinds of wickedness and evil in the sight of God and before man and we had inherited the curses. Once the person is born under that lineage he or she is affected, as in Lam. 5:7.

Generational curses are the result of the rejection of God and sinful deeds that had put people in pain which has become a curse, a spiritual bondage out of bitterness upon fathers to children and children's children, to the third and the fourth generation and even slaves or servants could be under this bondage. Prov. 17:5 "He who mocks the poor reproaches his maker, He who is glad at calamity will not go unpunished." Prov. 18:21 "Death and life are in the power of the tongue, and those who love it will eat the fruit of it" and James 3:6 "The tongue is a fire, a world of iniquity. The tongue is so set among our members that it defiles the whole body, and set on fire the course of nature; and it is set on fire by hell." These curses do not easily come out by salvation. Salvation is one thing and deliverance is also another thing.

Deliverance is the casting out of an unclean spirit tormenting someone against his destiny. Everyone's destiny is good, it is bad when it is altered or did something to change it. In the scripture Matt. 22:25-27, Now there were seven brothers. The first died after he has married, and having no offsprings left his wife to his brother. Likewise the second also, to the third and even to the seventh. Last the woman died also. The woman had spiritual marriage and that was a demon marrying the woman who was the primary husband of the woman whose assignment was to finish that family. This tells us that there was a curse, either foundational, ancestral or generational. When the family was finished the mission was accomplished. This story is not physical but spiritual. You can imagine how demons are transferring from great grand fathers to grand fathers, and from grand fathers to fathers, and from fathers to children, and from children to grand children, and from grand children to great grand children. In similarity, the curse from the bloodline destroy your father's business and took your mother's job, dealth with you and now dealing with your children. These demons dealt with your parents financially and now dealing with you.

Will you allow the demon which is smaller than your thumb to destroy you? Will you allow yourself to die like those brothers? They did not have the technology we have today. Lazarus died in poverty, your fathers also died in poverty. Will you allow yourself to die in poverty? Will you allow yourself to die like a rejected person? Sometimes curse come from different sources. Curses may come from God or from the devil (man). Satanic curses can be removed but godly curses no one can remove it until an anointed man of God intercedes. Jesus Christ died on the Cross so that those who receive Him and believe in His name are saved. The legal grounds of the curse are paid for and broken so by accepting Christ you can renounce those curses. What needs to be done is casting out those demons which are already in possession after your acceptance of Christ, and that is deliverance. This is the more reason why many Christians are suffering and things are not going well with them. We make Christ a liar, that's why when you speak about Christ to people they do not want to hear you, because they do not see your salvation. I have seen Christians being delivered and the curses in them manifest and tell their storey of the past. All is done by the same Christ who gave the same salvation. So after salvation you need to do the :-

1. Breaking of the curse of poverty.
2. Breaking of the curse of barrenness.
3. Breaking of the curse of impotency.
4. Breaking of parental and public curses of Child Abuse, child labor and slavery.
5. Breaking of the ancestral curses.
6. Breaking of the generational curses.
7. Breaking of the curse of rape.
8. Breaking of the curse of humiliation.
9. Breaking of the curse of oppression.
10. Breaking of the curse of sexual weakness.
11. Breaking of the curse of homosexuality that's gay and lesbianism.
12. Breaking of the curse of physical and mental illness, and masturbation.
13. Breaking of the curse of action limitation.
14. Breaking of the curse of CORRUPTION.
15. Breaking of the curse of infirmity.

16. Breaking of the curse of pride, jealousy, selfishness, greed, gluttony, sloth, Envy, Wrath and lust and many more. It is not possible to break all these in one day because they are powerful demons with great force using peoples past to destroy their future.

17. Breaking of the curses of kidney failure, heart failure, lungs, lever, etc. in short the human internal organs failure. Curse is word spoken which becomes spirit and after many years begin to function. An evil word or evil thought out of anger becomes a curse and a curse is a demon. You can imagine how many people have cursed you.

A man drown in a river but the rescue squad saved him. Because he made fun of a disable person, and the disable person told him, "he will perish by water, he will never be the same tomorrow." He took it as joke and did nothing about it, and after many days he drown in a river. He did not die, but he was sick the rest of his life till he died. That was the curse invoked upon him because what the disable person told him was a curse. Curse comes by words and deeds and this shows how powerful are words and our deeds.

In Zech. 3:1-7. Satan remembered the past of Joshua and used it as legal ground to oppose him. It was the Lord who rebuke him and the filthy garment on Joshua was removed. He was a great man of God but there was hindrance in his life which served as legal ground for Satan. This can happen to anybody. Whenever Satan finds a legal grounds in our lives, he uses it and cloths us with filthy garments so we cannot come to the presence of God.

Elisha was a regular person who lived normal life. He was a business man, a farmer, and was rich. And because of the work of God and Israel, he abandoned his business and all his wealth and became the servant of God. He went from Bethel and was met by young people who caused him pain and felt bitter, because they disrespected his office in God and using his situation to mock him, saying" go up you baldhead," Elisha pronounced a word against them and they were mauled by two female bears. 2Kings 2:23-24. Elisha spoke words and it became a curse against them, forty-two of them all died. Words and deeds are very powerful so be careful with your words and your deeds, they could become curse and torment someone, even your family.

"CURSES AND BLESSINGS BY SPOKEN WORD."

2Kings 2:14. Then he took the mantle of Elijah that had fallen from him, and struck the water and said, "Where is the God of Elijah?" and he also had struck the water, it was divided this way and that; and Elisha cross over.

2Kings 2:19-22 "Then the men of the city said to Elisha, Please notice the situation of the city is pleasant, as my lord sees; but the water is bad, and the ground barren. And he said, bring me a bowl, and put salt in it. So they brought it to him. Then he went out to the source of the water, and cast in the salt there, and said, Thus says the Lord: I have healed this water; from it there shall be no more death or barrenness. So the water remained healed to this day, according to the word of Elisha which he spoke."

2Kings 2:23-24 And he went up from hence unto Bethel: and as he was going up by the way, there came forth little children out of the city, and mocked him, and said unto him, go up you bald head; go up you bald head. And he turned back, and look on them, and cursed them in the name of the Lord. And there came forth two she bears out of the wood, and tare forty and two children of them.

WATER CAN REACT TO SPOKEN WORD.

Elisha sent a message through the mantle to the water and the water had no choice but do as the man of God said. Again, Elisha by word action made the water to be healed and was so according to the word spoken. In these two instances, Elisha communicated with the water and because the water has memory and can capture information or has sensory and can react to command and take the form of the instruction or command, it came to pass. There is life in water, and anything that has life has spirit. There is no reaction or capture of information without the spirit. Because words are spirit, they are powerful, fast and very sharp, either to destroy or to do good.

Words when spoken unto water can reduce the structure of the electrons of the water to increase the atomic structure of the water. This allow the hydrogen elements to absolve the sound of the spoken word (the language) which vibrates through the water or the sensory which reduces the oxide and override the oxide. If it's curse the water will take that form. If it's blessing the water will be blessed the same.

"Dr. Masaru Emoto, a Japanese business man and researcher's experiment exploring his belief that water could react to positive thoughts and words, and a polluted water could be cleaned through prayer and the positive visualization which contains photographs of ice crystals and their accompanying experiment."

Because the human body contains sixty percent (60%) of water, curses and blessings could be communicated through the water in the human body and manifests in the life of the person based on "the water and the spoken" word experiment. The body can capture information or react to words spoken against it, this is the reason why spoken curses come to pass. The electrons in the water in the human body could receive the radio waves and the infrared of the sound of the command through the body water that absolve those vibrations which carry gamma rays which are accepted by the heart and transmitted to the brain and contaminate or pollute the entire body system and results in a curse. The diverse could also happen that is blessing and the person will be blessed.

EXPERIMENT:- This is what happened: Water was filled in two plain glasses and labeled "CURSED" and "BLESSED."

1. These words were spoken onto the glass labeled "BLESSED." Whoever drink of thee is blessed. You shall never see destruction. Your beauty shall always prevail. You will reign over waters.
2. These words were spoken onto the glass of water labeled "CURSED." You are ugly and polluted. A servant of servants, you are. No one will drink of thee.
3. The two glasses were stored in the freezer for twelve hours.
4. The glass which was cursed cracked and the surface of the frozen water was very rough.
5. The one which was blessed, the glass was intact and surface of the frozen water was clean and clear.

This concludes that, as Christians we must be very careful with our words we communicate with friends, our family and relatives. As well if you refuse and reject the words spoken against you it will not gain roots, because if you throw a ball against a wall, it rolls back to you, for the wall has rejected and refused it, even so you shall be venerable and not vulnerable. All these power is already in you and needs to be awakened. Christianity is more spiritual than physical and there is power in the name of Jesus Christ.

Question:-

In 1John 5:6-7 says, "This is He who came by water and blood - Jesus Christ; not only by water but by water and blood. And it is the spirit who bears witness, because the spirit is truth. For there are three that bear in heaven: THE FATHER, THE WORD and THE HOLY SPIRIT; and these three are ONE. And there are three that bear witness on EARTH; THE SPIRIT, THE WATER and THE BLOOD; and these three agree as ONE."

Someone may ask what about Jesus, He was flesh and blood like us, a human. So he had 60% water in His body and blood as the scripture says, so what we feel and what we go through, He experienced the same, so He should have been vulnerable to spoken words?

Listen, because Jesus was TRUE LIGHT, HOLY and made Himself WORD (spirit) and venerable and not a living being, spoken words (spirit) could not affect Him, likewise you cannot bless Him. But if He had lived the sinful life that we live, He could be affected. Consider the other side of Him, He was God and a spirit who was a living Soul on earth. Because we are human, we are vulnerable due to sin.

BREAKING simply means destroying the works of Satan (curses) in your life. That is to tear in pieces, in otherwise destroying the legal grounds and all the networks and the media, which Satan is using against you. It is also known as deliverance. Deliverance in the Christian faith is the casting out of unclean spirits tormenting a person against his or her destiny. Our ordained destiny is good. It becomes bad when it is altered or something is done to change it. When someone curses you, be careful it could be legal ground for Satan to capitalize on it and altar your destiny. Refuse and reject it and break it, if possible reverse it. The following scriptures teaches us how to battle the enemy and break every curse in our lives.

1John. 3:8. "He that committed sin is of the devil. For the devil sinneth from the beginning, for this purpose the son of God was manifested that he might destroy the works of the devil."

So we are empowered to destroy the works of the devil by the name of Jesus Christ. We do destroy the plans of the devil in our lives with the following four weapons

1.) 1). Binding:-Matt. 18:18 Assuredly, I say to you, whatever you bind on earth will be bound in heaven and whatever you loose on earth will be loosed in heaven. Matt. 16: 19 I will give you the keys of the kingdom of heaven, and whatever you bind on earth will be bound in heaven, and whatever you loose on earth will be loosed in heaven.

2.) 2). The blood and the name of Jesus Christ:- It is the blood and the name which does the miracle. It cleanses and destroys every works of Satan. Rev. 12:11 They overcame him with the blood of the Lamb and by the word of their testimony.

3.) 3). Bombing-shooting, stoning:- Deut21:21, Joshua7:25 Then all the men of his city shall stone him to death with stone so you shall put the evil from among you, and all Israel shall hear and fear. Joshua 7:25 And Joshua said, "why have you troubled us? The Lord will trouble you today." So all Israel stoned him with stones; and they burn them with fire after they had stone them with stones.

4.) 4). Fire of the Holy Ghost:- 2Kings 1:10-12, So Elijah answered and said to the captain of fifty, If I am a man of God, then let fire come down from heaven and consume you and your fifty men. And fire came from heaven and consumed him and the fifty......; 1Kings 18:38, Then the fire of the Lord fell and consumed the burnt sacrifice, and the wood and the stones and the dust, and it licked up the water in the trench. 2Kings 6:17. And Elisha prayed and said, "Lord I pray, open his eyes that he may see." Then the Lord opened the eyes of the young man and he saw. And behold, the mountains was full of horses and chariots of fire all round Elisha. Luke 13:10-17. This woman was in the church sitting on the power in her as a child of God and yet crippled, she was in possession of the power to command the devil to leave but did not know how to use these weapons. eg. So many countries have all the mineral resources, but yet in poverty, why? Hosea 4:6, Isaiah 5:13

Luke 9:54-55. The disciples realized the power in them and were going to abuse it instead of using the power to perform miracles. So Jesus got mad with them and said even though you know that you have power, you do not have the knowledge of the kind of power you have. Knowledge is an essential factor in the life of every normal human being and in the growth of every economy. Therefore Jesus expected them to have the knowledge of humor, and not to destroy because that was not his mission in the world. NB.- Because they are poor in knowledge they cannot develop. You need knowledge to develop. Once you receive knowledge you can develop and as you develop you will acquire the riches of the land. Have you forgotten what Jesus did? He took your poverty that you shall be rich (2Cor.2:9). John 14:20. I am in my father, and ye in me and I in you. So the Holy Spirit, Christ, God the father and all angels are with you. If someone knows he hasn't what you have, he will do everything possible to cause you to loose the power you are blessed with, so he can possess it. When the priest heard the people said, what a power, they began to accuse the Lord Jesus for haven healed on the Sabbath. People will accuse you and speak evil of you just because they do not have the potentials and the gifts you are blessed with. So In Luke 13:10-17 They used the Sabbath as a yard stick against the Lord, not because he has done wrong, but it was because they were with the woman all her life and they did not have that knowledge that the woman was being tormented by Satan and also because they were not able to do what Jesus was capable to do. God does not want deformity, things that are deformed (Mala. 1:7-8) so beware and attack the devil and break the deformity. Poverty is a disease. It's deformity, a curse. There're two characteristics in the bible (Abraham, and Lazarus) God said I am the God of Abraham, Isaac and Jacob. God did not say I am the God of Lazarus. But God raised him from the dead. Poverty is not from God, God is full of unlimited riches and resources. There is no poverty in God but He loves the poor and desires to change their status.

Phil. 4:13. I can do all things through Christ which strengthens me. Prayer, fasting, righteousness, and the Holy Ghost fire are the weapons. Jer. 51:20-24. We have the weapon to break all the plans and deeds of Satan. Like Illness, poverty, spiritual marriages, marriage breakdown, all form of deformity. What do you do with the power you now possess? The Lord Christ Jesus has invested power in you. It is a sin not to use this power so now begin to use this power and enjoy that investment that the Lord has made in you. The power is yours to utilize it. Curse causes dilapidation, it causes desolation, when we refuse to obey God, we attract curse. Galatians 3:10 For as many as are of the works of the law are under the curse, for it is written, curse is everyone who does not continue in all things which are written in the book of the law, to do them. Again: Malachi 3:9 "You are curse with a curse, for you have robbed Me, even this whole nation." there is no sin that man will commit and freely walk away. All come with a curse.

1. Abraham lied; Gen. 12:13, Gen. 20:2 and the effect affected his descendants. They became slaves in Egypt, foreigners in a foreign land for four hundred years. Gen. 15:13-14 "Then He said to Abraham: Know certainly that your descendants will be strangers in a land that is not theirs and will serve them and they will afflict them for four hundred years. That nation that they serve, I will judge afterwards they shall come out with great possession." Slavery is a curse. So the curse came upon Abraham's descendants for four hundred years. His father practiced syncretism and he experienced the curse of impotency. He was credited righteous but could not give birth to a child. Because his father Terah practiced syncretism which was the greatest abomination to God which also affected Isaac, Rebecca had it difficult to give birth to children. Likewise Jacob's wife Rachel but because Abraham severely dealt with it, the span reduced, Isaac was not hundred years before his wife gave birth but his father was. Likewise Jacob was not hundred years, but, because Rachel was idol worshiper she died young. It went on and on, Joseph had to be sold to become a slave before he was blessed and finally the whole Israel went into slavery but they were blessed when they were delivered as God said to Abraham. Gen. 20:12 "But indeed she is truly my sister. She is the daughter of my father but not the daughter of my mother and she became my wife." Because the senior brother of Abram, Haran, died before his father, so Terah his father took Haran's children, Lot, Milcah and Iscah and raised them together with Abram and Nahor, whom Terah gave as wives. Iscah's name was very much idolatry, meaning "beautiful to look at" given by her father Haran because Haran was deeply into idolism. Terah change the name

from Iscah to Sarai meaning "princess" because she was beautiful to look at. All these names were trouble names and "Abram" also was trouble name because it means "Exalted father" which means pride, equal to God. Both of them had trouble names which was blocking their blessing of having a child. Those names were the gifts of Satan which took almost their lifetime. Pride is the gift of Satan. "Beautiful to look at" Iscah, "princess" Sarai and "Exalted father" Abram, were all prideful names and was tormenting and blocking their blessing. Do not become superior over the community you live, that intention leads to death. Abram being the friend of God whom God loved so much, God then had to intervene and intercede. So Sarai's name was changed to Sarah, mother of nations and kings. Abram's name was also change to Abraham, father of nations, because they love that.

Gen. 17:5 No longer shall your name be called Abram but your name shall be called Abra(h)am - Ya(h)we(h) - YHWH, for I have made you a father of nations.

Gen. 17:15 Then God said to Abraham, as for Sarai your wife, you shall not call her name Sarai but Sara(h) - Ya(h)we(h) - YHWH shall be her name, mother of nations and kings.

So God had to remove the generational curse behind their names and add His name in alphabet (H) to their names before they were able to have a child-son, and because they doubted and laughed at the word of God, the prophecy, it cause delayance from one year to thirteen years. God gave the name Isaac meaning laughter for a remembrance of their unbelief and warning to mankind.

2. Isaac also lied; Gen. 26:7 and the Philistines had to opposed him when he prospered and move from one place to another, terrible distraction of his prosperity. Gen. 26: 12-21 "Isaac sowed in the land and reaped in the same year a hundred fold and the Lord blessed him. He began to prosper and continued prospering and became very prosperous. He had possession of flocks and great number of servants. The Philistines had stopped up all the wells which his father's servants dug in the days of Abraham his father and they had filled with earth." Being opposed is a curse, is the

spirit or the curse of opposition, because it distract your progress and can render you poor- curse of poverty.

3. Jacob lied to claim the birthright and ended him in the house of his uncle, Laban, while running for his life. Gen. 27:18-30 "Jacob said to his father I am Esau your firstborn. I have done just as you told me. Please arise. sit and eat of my game that your soul may bless me." Jacob had to run for his life spirit of distress and fear and affliction and oppression were all after Jacob and became homeless, a curse which has to be dealt with but God love him because he was obedient to God. Even when he returned, he has to be empowered by God before he could face his brother. God had to change the name of Jacob to Israel so that his brother, Esau who vow to kill him, when he met him saw him not as Jacob but as Israel and for that reason Esau could not kill him because he was seeing Israel and not Jacob, Gen. 32:30 "I have seen God face to face and my life is preserved."

4. Joseph felt superior to his brothers because his mother was the legitimate wife (the wife his father wanted and the rest were impose on him) of Jacob his father. Bilhah and Zilphah were maids who became wives. For this Joseph was proud. Gen. 37:2-4 Pride comes with a curse. He posed as supervisor over his brothers and was reporting them and nearly lost his life, he was sold and sent to Egypt. Gen. 37:2 "This is the history of Jacob. Joseph being seventeen years old was feeding the flock with his brothers. And the lad was with the sons of Bilhah and the sons of Zilphah his father's wives and Joseph brought report of them to his father." He was causing a sin that could cause division in the family which may result in chaos, he was sold and taken to a foreign land. Being a stranger in a foreign land is a curse but may also come with a blessing. Some curse end with blessing, depending on the person's relationship with God. Joseph was prayerful and lived a righteous life that connected him to God, so God was with him.

5. King David committed the worse crime by committing adultery with Bathsheba and finally killed the husband Uriah, 2Sam. 11:15, and married her. And King David's own son, Absalom rose against him and nearly killed him. King David, the great warrior at that

time had to run for his life. 2Sam. 11:4-5" David sent messengers and took Bathsheba and she came to him and he laid with her for she was cleansed from her impurity and she returned to her house. And the woman conceived, so she sent and told David and said I am with child." But King David was obedient to God. 1King 15:5 "King David did what was right in the eyes of the Lord and had not turn aside from anything that He commanded him all his life, except in the matter of Uriah the Hittite." The curse put David in a threatening situation to run for his life and abandoned his throne and his glory by his own son, Absalom. This shows how many people will abandon their riches when they see death and how threatening curse is. He was prayerful and worshipper.

6. Moses killed an Egyptian and run for his life. God worked miracles with him and did marvelous works with him but at the end he did not step foot on the promise land, only with his eyes he saw. Exo. 2:12 (11-14) "So he looked this way and that way and when he saw no one, he killed the Egyptian and hid him in the sand." To punish or to kill a person is the decision of God so if it becomes a human decision, it is sin and that was what Moses did. So Moses became homeless and a stranger in a foreign land but ended with a blessing as a great man of God. On the other side of his blessing, Moses was very old and did not have the strength to lead the people anymore and God needed a young dynamic person so He elected Joshua to lead the people but the presence of Moses would be a hindrance. With Moses the people will not heed to the words of Joshua, so Moses had to stay back and not set foot on the promise land and also to avoid him to be an idol to be worshipped by the people. So he was taken care of by the angels and buried by the angels when he died.

7. King Solomon suffered from the generational curse of womanizing because his father was, 1Kings 11:1-4. Because of this generational curse King Solomon deviated from the way of his God, the God of Israel and worshipped idols and shrines through women. 1Kings11:6-7 "Solomon did evil in the sight of the Lord, and did not fully follow the Lord, as did his father David. Then Solomon built a high place for Che'mosh, the abomination of Mo'ab, on the

hill that is east of Jerusalem, and for Mo'lech the abomination of the people of Am'mon." The house of Solomon lost their glory, the kingdom was taken from his descendants and they became ordinary people, that is the curse. Solomon love God and love idols like his great great grandfather, Terah the father of Abraham, for his name is still remembered.

8. Saul was cursed by God and was troubled by a distressing spirit. 1Sam. 16:14, 18:10-11 Saul requested for hundred souls for her daughter from David and David gave 200 souls (18:25-27). Saul was cursed and became so violence and took a javelin and tried to pin David to the wall. Saul and all his children died sad death. 1Sam. 15:1-3; 1Sam. 15:10-29 Saul was rebellious and did not accept his fault

In conclusion, sin is sin, great or small are equally the same, they are all sin and all come with curse, which take different form. Therefore man must be careful of sin and do everything possible to avoid sin. The curse may not manifest in the youthful age, and that is the most painful era of life. It may even go as far as the descendants, whereby they may not be able to trace the root of the curse. These people were descendants of Abraham, and they still enjoyed life and the glory because of the covenant God made with Abraham, but they were prayerful and break those curses in their lives. Our Lord Jesus Christ has given us the weapon and showed us how to break these curses and destroy the legal grounds being used by Satan against the children of the Living God. The weapon is breaking of the curses and commanding and declaring total destruction of them. One thing we have to know is curse is a spirit and should not be allowed to live. All these people, even though they went through terrible situations they never abandoned their God so at the end they were blessed. By the grace of Jesus Christ we now know how to deal with these curses, so far as we believe in Jesus Christ and we are obedient to Him.

CHAPTER THREE

SIN

The word sin when abbreviated means

S = Severe I = Instruction N = Neglected

So from the abbreviation we derive the word REBELLION, which is translated to mean SIN, Rebellion means strictly neglect and resist instruction. Hence to sin means to rebel or neglect severe instruction. Adam and Eve were not the first persons to sin. It was the devil who first sinned with a sizeable percentage of the angelic host. Adam and Eve were caused to sin by the word they heard and believed, that's how sin come about. We inherited sin from Adam and Eve as well as they also inherited it from Satan. It may have been contradicting if God must be creating sinful humans. We are created by God and are all children of God, but we are all not His people. Being God's people is different from being His children. The people of God obey Him and do His will but not all children obey Him. We become sinners from the very first time we sinned as matured humans, meaning we inherited the nature to sin. Therefore we are not born with sin but assumed the continuation to sin. A child is not imputed with his sin but an adult is. We therefore have the choice to refuse to sin. It is the choice of man to choose to sin or not. Sin also means corrupt, and corruption is not man's nature but an acquired situation by a natural tendency of negligence to sin. Corruption is the rotten state of a material or object and may mean that it was acquired which moved from a good state to a bad state. This is how sin look like. Sin was originally not part of human dignity or philosophy. Gen. 1:26 "Let us make man in our image in our likeness and let them have dominion over the fish of the sea, over the bird of the air, and over the cattle, over all the earth and over every creeping thing that creeps on earth." So the decision of God creating man was a perfect decision to create a perfect man who had no bleach or impediment Eccl. 7:29 "Truly this only have I found that God made man upright but they have sought out many schemes." The bible also says in Prov. 14:12 "There is a way that seems right to a man but the end is the way of death". And it says also "because of these things, the wrath of God is coming upon the sons of disobedience." Colo. 3:6.

Hence, sin is the breaking of God's law or failure to obey the commandments of God. In otherwise it's the rejection of God and His commandments, and to live a way contrarily to God's principle. That's what Adam and Eve did, thinking they were now civilized.

MEMORY VERSE:- 1John 3:8 "He who sins is of the devil, for the devil has sinned from the beginning. For this purpose the son of God was manifested that He might destroy the works of the devil."

There are two major sins in life

1. THE REJECTION OF JESUS CHRIST
2. THE WORSHIP OF IDOLS

THE REJECTION OF JESUS CHRIST :- From creation to date we know that Adam and his wife Eve made a horrible mistake which brought condemnation unto them which has affected the whole race of mankind. And God needed someone to intercede and there was none. Eze.22:30 "So I sought for a man among them who will make a wall and stand in the gap before Me on behalf of the land, that I should not destroy it; but I found none." So Christ who is the surety, the co-signer has to be delivered for that sacrifice for the remission of the sins of the world, unto salvation, as the bible says, Hebr. 7:22 "by so much more Jesus has become a surety of a better covenant." Jesus guaranteed every man on earth to be created and He is held responsible for every mistake man did and make. Again in John 1:9 "That was the TRUE LIGHT which gives light to every man coming into the world." Jesus is the One who selected you out of the multitude and granted your coming into the world and empowered you with the Light to come down into the world with a mission. And how then people refuse to accept to believe in Him? It's like ones children refusing to accept him as their father. Such behavior results in sin and comes with a curse.

THE TWO TREASURES OF CHRIST TO MANKIND:

1. The blood of Christ which has the power to cleans us, that's the remission of sin.
2. Lev. 17:11. "For the life of the flesh is in the blood, and I have given it to you upon the altar to make atonement for your souls, for it is the blood that make the atonement for the soul."
3. The body of Christ which has the power to save, that has given us salvation.
4. John 6:50-51. This is the bread which comes down from heaven, that one may eat of it and not die. I am the living the living bread which came down from heaven. If anyone eats of this bread, he will live forever; and the bread that I shall give is My flesh, which I shall give for the life of the world.

This means without remission of sin there will be no salvation. It is the blood of Jesus Christ that brings about the salvation.

Heb. 9:22 "And according to the law almost all things are purified with blood, and without shedding of blood there is no remission." verse 20 And this is the blood of the covenant which God commanded you.

Hebr. 10:28-30, 31 "Anyone who has rejected Moses law dies without mercy on the testimony of two or three witnesses. Of how much worse punishment do you suppose, will he, be thought worthy who has trampled the Son of God under foot, counted the blood of the covenant by which he was sanctified a common thing and insulted the Spirit of grace (the Holy Spirit). It is a fearful thing to fall into the hands of the living God." The only time for man to receive Christ for salvation is when one is human, having physical body, that is the vessel Christ can use. Christ can only enter into the flesh and once a person dies, Jesus cannot enter into the Spirit because spirit cannot possess spirit. Spirit can only possess physical body. So having the physical body is an advantage to receive Christ and that is the purpose of being born with a physical body. So once a person dies there is no salvation for such individual because this person had grace period of time to accept Christ, from the day he was born to the time he lost the physical body, which is the vessel Christ needs to use to save the soul. Jesus cannot have intimate relationship with this person when the flesh is lost without Him. Once Christ is rejected, the target of the purpose in life is missed and the glory of God is also missed because the scripture says in Rom. 3:23 "For all have sinned and fall short of the glory of God." We have already dropped out of the glory, so the more we sin, the far we are driven from the glory of God. There is enough glory for man to occupy but sin has covered it and made it impossible for man. You have been born and you are alive, others were miscarriaged, others were also aborted but God did everything to keep you alive. You are alive not because you want to be alive but because God wants you to be alive for His own glory. 2Cor. 5:17 says "Therefore if any man be in Christ, he is a new creature: old things have passed away; behold, all things have become new." So the day you were baptized, that the falling glory was restored and when you continue in this glory to love Jesus by keeping His word, then the Father will love you and both will come to abide with you. John 14:23. If you have the Father, Jesus and the Holy Spirit making their home with you, you can imagine the magnitude of power that will be at your home, even your environment I mean the whole community, and also affecting your country. Prayer will yield instant answer, you touch someone and will receive instant healing. When God made His home with King Solomon, he never experienced war neither did he lack anything all the years of his reign, till he defiled God. 1Kings 4:20-30, 1Chron. 22:9. Because the Elohim made His home with him.

John 6:38 Jesus came down from heaven to do the will of God.

John 6:46 No one has seen God except Jesus. Exo. 33:20.

John 6:51 Christ is the living bread from heaven, the bread is the fresh of Christ, those who eat will live forever.

John 6:44 No one can come to Christ unless God draws him.

John 6:40 The will of God is that those who see Christ and believe may have everlasting life and will be raised the last day.

John 8:56-58 Abraham rejoice when he saw Jesus. The Jews were confused and said you are not yet fifty years and you have seen Abraham. Jesus said before Abraham I was.

John 12:26 Where I am there My servants will be, if any serves Me, him My Father will honor. Christ is ordained as the God of the world

Roman 5:8-10 God demonstrated His love towards us while we were sinners Christ died for us. God has the ability to save us through Christ.

1Cor. 6:19-20 Our bodies is the temple of the Holy Spirit. We are not our own. We are bought with a price

Hebr. 10:26 If we sin willfully now that we know the truth there remain no longer sacrifice for our sins.

Hebr. 10:14 By one sacrifice we are perfected for ever

Hebr. 9:28 Christ was offered once to bear the sins of many, those who wait will see Him, if they do not sin, for salvation.

1Pet. 2:24 He bore our sins in His body on the tree,by whose strips we are healed.

Gal. 3:13 Christ has redeemed us from the curse of the law haven become a curse for us for it is written CURSE IS EVERYONE WHO HANGS ON A TREE.

Eph. 2:14. Christ has broken the middle wall of separation.

So we have no excuse to reject Christ as our savior.

THE WORSHIP OF IDOLS:

After the advent of the sin of Adam and Eve, man was desperate for God and did not know where to begin and to end. Man knew there was God but cannot see God anymore. So man substituted God with objects and after time man's faith was diverted to those objects, which took man's faith in God. And this has been and till now, for some, idols has been their god. Psalm 106:35-40; Deut. 7:16; Lev. 17:7;

Gen. 11:31-32 "And Terah took Abram, his son and Lot the son of Haran, his son's son and Sarai his daughter-in-law, his son Abram's wife and they went forth with them from Ur of the Chaldees, to go into the land of Canaan; and they came unto Haran, and dwell there. And the days of Terah were two hundred and five years and Terah died in Haran."

Paraphrase:- In the time of Terah, syncretism was the best of godly worship and that was what Terah was practicing. And God accepted that because He saw Himself in only Terah mix with objects. The rest of the people in the face of the earth did not know God. That was what the

167

humans were practicing idol worship. Everybody had an idol as his god. So God intended to separate Terah and his family from the rest of the world. Terah, Abam's father made a figure of clay which was his object of worship because he cannot see God. Every morning, he will ask Abram to bring it out into the sun and in the evening he will bring it back to the room. There was a special room for this object. On day the weather changed all of a sudden. Terah told Abram to bring the object into the room, when it begins to rain for he was visiting a friend. As soon as he left, Abram went closer to the object and began to examine the object very carefully and he saw no life in it. He spoke to it, there was no answer. He asked the object to move, there was no movement. So Abram doubted his father's claim of that object to be god. So when it began to rain, he said to the object, my father said you are god, you created me. If you had created me and I can walk, then you being my creator must be able to fly. So it's raining, you must be able to walk to your room. The rain began to increase and there was heavy down pour and the object was destroyed, and Abram said this has no life. When Abram's father returned, he went to the room of the object but the object was not there, so he came outside and found it destroyed. He was angry with Abram, and Abram said, your claim of the object as god who created me, and it could not walk, does not make sense and I disagree with you and reject it to be creator, for god the creator is not made with hands. So after some days Abram's father died (god killed him so that the syncretism will not be brought to the promise land) and Abram was elected to separate to Canaan. From that day, God set His eyes on Abram and he became His friend and began to communicate with him, asked him to follow Him to complete the covenant of the promise land. Abram knew God to be Spirit and not an object. And Abram became a close friend of God and God loved him. So God said to Abram in: Gen. 12:1-3 "Now the Lord had said unto Abram, get thee out of thy country, and from thy kindred, and from thy father's house, unto a land that I will show you. And I will make of thee a great nation, and I will bless thee and make thy name great, and thou shall be a blessing: And I will bless them that bless thee, and curse him the curse thee: and in thee shall all families of the earth be blessed." And Abram did as God instructed him and was with him the rest of his days. Idolism is abomination to God, and God punishes that by death. We are given second chance because of the grace, through the death and resurrection of our Lord Jesus Christ. So if anyone is worshiping idols now is the final and second chance.

People who commit sin and repent are people who commit sin continually, and are people who are addicted with particular sin. If you sin and repent, you do not need repentance again. But those who sin and do not have the knowledge of repentance need to be saved through repentance. Those who are addicted to a particular habit need deliverance. Sin is habit, is not committed by a believer, a believer has no sin. Sin is habit that one accept to live with. Sin of fornication, sin of lie, sin of drinking, sin of worshiping idols, sin of stealing, sin of anger, etc. these are sins that is inside of people which they hold unto them. Sins are committed by people who repent, you do not repent if you have no sin. When sins are repented today, your Father in heaven forgives you and you say I don't want to do this again. Then tomorrow you are angry and ask for forgiveness, so the same sin that is inside you that was dealt with, those are the sins we say Father forgive our sins, and He forgave. But if there is a particular sin inside you, you do not need repentance, you need deliverance, it means your life is possessed by a demon of that particular sin, a demon of particular situation controlling your life. You may call it addiction, it is a sin. It does not make sense to see a believer doing the same sinful act and asking for forgiveness every time. The situation needs attention for deliverance.

So much of the situations we have, the first thing to deal with is the concept of sin. The biggest deliverance in life is to be delivered from the power that holds you captive into sin. We want to be delivered from a particular thing which is a problem but we don't want the sin to go. If you give the devil a small opportunity, it is as big as a complete world for him. It is time now either to follow Christ or to follow Satan. The bible said you either be hot or cold. If you are lukewarm I shall vomit you out of my mouth. The biggest problem to handle in life is not finances, it is sin. To sin means to miss the target. When you go to supermarket, no one brings the product to you. They are displayed and you have to chose from different locations. Even Satan does not force no one, but displays all kinds of sins and you chose the ones you love to commit from different locations. In the ancient world, even in our modern world. The bible says, if we sin we fall short of the glory of God, which should be yours, but because of sin, you miss the target and fall short. Any time you sin, you fall short, so sin will push you far from your glory. So the more you sin the more you fall short of God's glory. That's why when you pray nothing happens because sin had made you fall short of God's connection. "Answer to prayer is brought about by the glory of God." When you are in God's glory, when you speak a word, when you declare a word, when you decree, when you pray, it immediately takes place because you are connected in the glory. Now it does not happen because you have fall short of the glory of God, meaning you have dropped out. There is too much glory that you are supposed to experience but the bible says sin makes it impossible for manifestation. Many people come to church with sicknesses, even a disease is attached to sin. The bible says, he who forgives your sins and heals all your disease. Ps. 103:3; Is. 53:1-5; Ex. 15:26; Matt. 9:5; Jn. 5:8; Lk. 5:23;Mk. 2:9. Jesus is always interceding for us. The same air you breath for free, others have to pay to have it. You are born and alive, some were miscarriage, some were aborted, but God did everything to keep you alive which is the greatest miracle in your life. Is it for nothing? You are not alive because you want to be alive, but you are alive because God wants you to be alive for His own glory. God is keeping you for personal relationship with Him. John 14:23-24 "Jesus answered and said to him, If anyone loves Me, he will keep My word; and My Father will love him, and we will come to him and make our home with him," don't fornicate, don't be angry, don't covet, don't gossip. Those who know their God, don't care about what the world calls them for Jesus sake, Know that, this call is not by men, but only by Jesus Christ who makes it possible to live again, in Jesus Christ we move and exist and without Him, we are nothing and for us to die or live is Christ, for in our bodies we bear the mark of Christ Jesus. Phil. 1:21. I am fully persuaded that He who began good works in me, He shall also complete it. God's presence and manifestation is the definition of the word glory. Make our home means never fall short of God's glory. So if you keep His word, He shall come and abide with you, meaning God will move into your neighborhood, affecting other people, the peace of God will be in your neighborhood, you touch someone and he will be healed. If you have God in your neighborhood you cannot be broke, God is My Neighbor. When you sin you just miss God and Christ anointing and God cannot be your friend. Eph. 1:1-4 Blessed be the God and Father of our Lord Jesus Christ who had blessed us with every spiritual blessing in the heavenly places in Christ. 2Cor. 5:17 Therefore if anyone is in Christ he is a new creation, old things have passed away, behold all things have become new. I am nothing without Christ. Christianity is the anointing of the Anointed One, and Christianity is a love relationship with God and not religion. It is not something you were born with but a decision to change kingdom to have a love relationship with God, meaning to allow yourself to do away with human characters, to let go certain behaviors, ungodly behaviors and take over godly characters.

Exo. 32:1-10. God hates idolism and the main taboo in the house of God. Psalm 115:4-8 idols are motionless for they cannot talk. Psalm 14:1-2 The fool says in his heart, there is no God.[Psalm 53:1] Idol worship is the origin of all sin which has been the result in all mankind,inheriting a situation to sin and has led to many different kinds of sins. Gal. 4:8 "But then indeed when you did not know God you served those which by nature are not god's. Lev. 24:17 "Whoever kills any man shall surely be put to death." Because he has killed a nation. Lev. 19:31 "Give no regard to mediums and familiar spirits, do not seek after them, to be defile by them: I am the Lord your God". Lev. 20:6, 27 "And the person who turns to mediums and familiar spirits to prostitute himself with them, I will set My face against that person and cut him off from his people". [27] "A man or a woman who is a medium or who has familiar spirit, shall surely be put to death; they shall stone them with stones. Their blood shall be upon them". All these are abomination to God. Lies, cursing, hatred, backbiting, grudge in heart, homosexuality, fornication, adultery, murder, etc. Lev. 19:11-18. "Also if a man lies with a man as with a woman both of them have committed an abomination, they shall surely be put to death. Their blood shall be upon them". All these are the fruit of idol worship. Idol worship is one of the greatest offense against God the creator of the universe. God created man in His image therefore worshiping of idols means that man had belittled himself and made God a liar and as such God becomes angry for disrespecting and belittling God. God had in many ways warn us to refrain from idol worshiping. God warned the Israelites not to make images of any kind and not to bow down and serve them. After all the miracles and wonders God did, they easily forgot and turned from God to make a CALF and worshipped and sacrifice to, and made God wish to wipe them off the face of the earth. Idol worship is rebellion which is the root of witchcraft and is absolutely stubbornness which is sin. It leads to bloodshed and human sacrifices, fornication, adultery and many more.

QUESTION: How do we overcome SIN?

We can overcome SIN by the following with their supporting scriptures:

1. By the blood of Jesus Christ : John 5:6, Acts 20:28, Rom. 5:9, Rev. 12:11, Matt. 26:28, 1Pet. 1:18-19, Herb, 9:13-14, 20, 22, 28, Hebr. 10:12.
2. By the Flesh [body] of Jesus Christ : John 6: 27, 33, 48-51, 53
3. By the word of God, [read, believe and live with the word]: Hebr. 4:12, 1John 5:7, Eph. 6:16.
4. By the prayer of the righteous, [make solemn or reverent petition to God for help. It can be worship, praises, thanksgiving, confession, repentance, intercession request etc.] : Eph. 6:18, Matt. 26:41, Luke. 22:46, Matt. 6:5, Luke. 18:1, Jonah 2:1, Thess. 5:17, 1Tim. 2:8.
5. By fasting occasionally : Esther 4:16, Ezra 8:23, Daniel 9:3, Jonah 3:5.
6. By obedience to the voice of the Holy Spirit: Exo. 23: 20-22, Exo. 3:2, Acts 8:26, Acts 10:13, Acts 11:11, 12:7. Sin is very powerful and that is the only way to overcome it.

SALVATION

REASON FOR SALVATION: When man sinned and God separated from man, man began to search for a way to get back to God. Then man began to practice good works, it did not work out for him. Philosophy became a means of modest principle of character, it also could not bring man to God. Then philosophy led to religion which began the approach of drawing man to God, bringing out priest, prophets, men of God and the church began. Out of the church came women of God, then finally God interceded and brought His Son Our Lord Jesus Christ for the final completion of the reconciliation. Our Lord Jesus Christ was sent to the world **as a ransom to cleanse** the sins which separated God and Man, and Jesus Christ became the bridge through which man could get access of having contact with God. Man therefore turned from sin, cross through Jesus Christ to have connection with God. This shows that salvation does not depend upon man's good works, modest principle of life, or philosophy and the power of the mind, but depends upon the love and the mercy of God and the grace of Our Lord Jesus Christ who paid a ransom by the sacrifice of His life and the shedding of His precious blood on the cross. In the beginning the church comprise of a family with the father or the husband as the priest eg. Adam Gen.4:24; Jacob Gen. 28:13-15; Abraham Gen. 12:1-3; Noah Gen. 6:18. which had no evangelical base or purpose. But with the advent of Moses as he was called in the wilderness as God revealed Himself to him (Moses) for the salvation of the Church and the twelve assemblies. This was the twelve tribes of Israel which became an organization of a nation. under the leadership of Moses Exo. 19:6. A theocracy which involved the complete life of a nation, the political life, the social life and the religious life. To this we say God was the ruler, the commander- in- chief and even in this new testament era God is, because He is the King of Kings and the Lord of Lords. Then came Christ who was sent by the Father upon the Jews whom they rejected, and the rejection created a new advent for the world salvation, which raise the Pentecostal era, the emerging of Christianity, the Christ churches and their institutions of ministries. Know that ministry is an establishment within the church. Hence salvation is to set free or deliver from destruction, failure or harmful situation.

APOSTLE PAUL in the book of Philippians 2:12. said Therefore, my beloved, as you have always obeyed not as in my presence only, but now much more in my absence, work out your own SALVATION with fear and trembling.

SIDDHARTHA GAUTAMA (founder of Buddhism) said "Behold now brethren, decay is inherent in all things component, work out your SALVATION with diligence, be a light unto yourselves, for there is no other LIGHT than this."

Siddhartha Gautama, the founder of Buddhism, agreed with Apostle Paul that salvation is to be worked on with trembling, fear and diligence. Therefore salvation is to be worked on. Gautama did not propagate salvation, but re-incarnation which has nothing to do with the life after death. So Christianity is the relationship with God for the existence after death. Salvation is the thing of the spirit which is difficult for mankind to believe and for this, man seeks for the things of the flesh more that the things of the spirit.

There are three kinds of salvation to be worked on, once one accepts Christ.

1. THE SALVATION OF THE SPIRIT - swift or instant salvation known as PERFECTION.
2. THE SALVATION OF THE SOUL - persistent/ continuous salvation known as RIGHTEOUSNESS.
3. THE SALVATION OF THE BODY - ultimate or final salvation as HOLINESS.

THE SALVATION OF THE SPIRIT : Once you accept the Lord Jesus Christ as your Lord and savior, the Holy Spirit will continue to be touching you for the desire of baptism, because the spirit in you has been redeemed by the ransom sacrifice of the Lamb of God. Now comes a war and spiritual battle to protect the soul until baptism take place. The spirit components are of the intuition, the conscience, and the communion, which is the science of spiritual consciousness and relates to God, and it is the Godly awareness. The spirit in question is the biological spirit, which is beyond the scope of human understanding. It is the spirit that functions the body, without which the Holy Spirit cannot be received. It is the sacred force which communicates with the soul.

THE SALVATION OF THE SOUL : After accepting Christ and open up for baptism, as I said comes the spiritual warfare in the body against the soul. So once you are baptized, the spirit and the soul unite to work out for the salvation of the body, by your daily prayer, reading of the scripture and living by the scripture which is possible by fasting occasionally. The soul components are the mind, the emotions and the will, which is scientifically the psychological consciousness. The soul receives power from the Lord which in turn gives power to the body and renews this power every day. After the salvation of the soul, it is now connected to God the Father and has direct communication with the Father through Christ.

THE SALVATION OF THE BODY : The body receives salvation by the understanding of the word of God. Because the understanding of the scripture does the makeup of the body to resemble Christ which embodies you in Christ. It is the anatomic salvation where every organ of the body come to understand the anatomic science of salvation, and that person becomes righteous. In this case every part of the body understands its role in every activity of the body. eg, praying, fasting, studying the scripture, hearing from the Holy Spirit and daily personal errands. Always remember you cannot walk in someone's anointing. Anytime you walk in someone's anointing, you cannot move. The body now becomes waves and rays where the cosmic ray, the gamma ray, the ultra violet, the x-ray, the infrared, the micro waves, radio waves and radiant and nuclei are now active and receives the physiological consciousness. This is where the science of salvation is displayed. The presence of the person heals the sick, the dead is raised, the lame walks and blind receives his sight. God is full of science and without God there is no science. There are two sciences of bodily salvation: Physiology, and Psychology.

Physiology - the scientific study of normal mechanisms and their interactions which work within a living entity. It is the science that treats of the functions of the living organism and its parts, and the physical and the chemical factors and processes involved.

Psychology - It is the scientific study of the human electromagnetic celvic and its functions, especially those affecting behavior in a particular sense. In Greek it is the study of the phyche or soul.

The following names has the same meaning as salvation. Instead of saying salvation, one can choose to say redemption, or regeneration, or mystery or rescue or born again. They all mean the same thing.

Mystery : rescue beyond the knowledge of man; confessing the name of Jesus Christ and believing in his death, resurrection and ascension. Eph. 3:9 And to make plain to everyone the administration of this mystery which for ages pass was kept hiding in God which created all thing by Jesus Christ.

Redemption: To remove someone from captivity back to oneself. Or To take back. Eph. 1:7 In Him we have redemption, through His blood the forgiveness of sins in accordance with the riches of His grace that lavished on us with all wisdom and understanding.

Regeneration: Subject to spiritual renewal. Matt. 19:28 And Jesus said unto them, verily I say unto you, that ye which had followed Me in the regeneration [the renewal of all things] when the Son of man shall sit on His throne of His glory ye also shall sit upon twelve thrones judging the twelve tribes of Israel.

Rescue : To save or release one from custody under captivity. Acts 23:27 This man was seized by the Jews and they were about to kill him but I came with my troop and rescued him for I have learned that he is a Roman citizen.

Born Again : To be made again without sin. [rebirth or recycle]. John 3:3 Jesus answered and said unto him, verily, verily, I say unto you unless a man be born again, he cannot see the kingdom of God.

MEANING FOR SALVATION:- Salve is a medicinal substance applied to the skin to smoothing it to make the skin fresh and new, and God can use any substance [the word of God, water, olive oil, coconut water, water from the sea, water from the river ect. to make one new or give rebirth] 2Kings 5:14. This is physical medicine. But in the Christian sense Salvation is the saving of a person from sin or saving of a person from danger or difficulty, destruction or evil. It is a spiritual medicine. If you live in sin, you live in danger because you become vulnerable to the attacks of Satan. The bible says in Prov. 14:12. "There is a way that seem right to a man, but it's end is the way of death." And Proverbs 16:2. "All ways of a man are pure in his eyes, but the Lord weighs the spirit." There are so many people attending church who are not saved, and it's all the same good. Therefore, for someone to obtain salvation, that person must first have repentance, and his sins forgiven then be baptized and he or she is saved. Salvation is a free gift, which every human being must receive, no matter who you are or where you came from. Salvation leads to an everlasting life and redeems us from destruction, therefore we have been retrieved from the physical world to the spiritual world. This salvation is only found in Jesus Christ and nobody else. Acts 4:12. Salvation is beyond the knowledge of man which is a mystery. Eph. 3:9. "And to make all men see what is the fellowship of the mystery which from the beginning of the world hath hid in God, who created all things by Jesus Christ." The bible says it was hidden in God and was released to Christ. When the dominion was taken from man, all rights was taken from him and man lost the rightful ownership but God knew what would happen in future so He well protected it, the most precious ornament of life. If salvation had been lost, Jesus wouldn't have come to save us. Salvation is more powerful than dominion. Salvation was so precious to God that he did not leave it with anybody, but kept it in himself. It was the definite thing of God for the redemption of mankind, therefore it was kept in a highly secured environment, which was inside God. God knew the future and knows the deep thing of every human being, therefore He placed a very high security code on salvation. Salvation is a miracle by itself and supersedes all miracles and subdues all miracles. It supersedes healing and supersedes casting out of demons. When man sinned and died in spirit and realized his mistake and sought for a reconciliation, God also tried to find a way to regenerate man. Ezekiel 22:30. "And I sought for a man (the mediator of the new covenant) among them, that should make up the hedge, and stand in the gap before Me for the land, that I should not destroy it but I found none." The Father for his wonderful love for mankind sought for a propitiator. Do you remember Abraham pleading with God to consider the righteous among the people and God saying there is none among them, from fifty to one there was none except Abraham himself and God tried to use Isaac and Abraham pleaded for Isaac to live, God will bring a lamb. Gen. 22:1-8.

FUNCTION OF SALVATION:- Salvation is a gift from God to all humans without going to the mountains to spend forty days and forty nights without food or water, without taking shower and sleeping on the rock in the mountains or forty years of slavery for exchange. Our savior and Lord Jesus Christ, the God of salvation has taken it upon Himself and suffered that for us. Gal. 4:4-5. "But when the fullness of the time was come God sent forth his son made of a woman made under the law, to redeem them that were under the law that we might receive the adoption of son." Jesus reveal his purpose. Jesus came from million of miles, from heaven to the earth, left all his glory as a king, a ruler, as living God, perform miracles to confirm his majesty, to open the eyes of the blind, cast out demons, to let the dump talk and the lame walk, walk on the sea (only God can walk on the sea) because Gen. 1:1 says the spirit of God was at the creation moving on the waters. The bible says the people saw Jesus as he was walking on the sea as Ghost (spirit) and they were afraid. In John 3:1-6 Nicodemus a priest came to Jesus by night because he was protecting his position filled with power consciousness and completely in the flesh, he was so much attached to the worldly position and did not understand what Jesus said because his intention was to see more miracle but rather received salvation. To be born of water is repentance from deep within you and means to be baptized with water and that's what John the Baptist did. He baptized the people with water unto repentance and to be born of the spirit is the acceptance of the Holy Spirit and His tongues. And once you are born of the spirit your speech, your works, your character, everything that you do must display Christ and the Holy Spirit. You cannot have salvation without repentance. Once we receive salvation we are dead to sin and we become conscious of sin. 1Peter 1:23. "Being born again not of corruptible seed but of incorruptible by the word of God which liveth and abide forever."

1Peter 2:24 "Who His own self bear our sins in His own body on the tree, that we being dead to sin, should live unto righteousness. By who's strips ye are healed." King David said in Psalm 119:176. "I have gone astray like a lost sheep, seek thy servant, for I do not forget thy commandments." David was pleading with God to restore him spiritually but people of this modern era are much blessed with this free gift.

PURPOSE OF SALVATION:- Luke. 19:10. "For the son of man is come to seek and to save that which is lost." Here it was not man that got lost, but something spiritual, so precious got lost. Something which is higher than man which can be possessed by man, angel even Satan. The bible declares in: Gen. 1:26 HAVE DOMINION - LIGHT. So when the dominion was taken from man, the EARTH also was taken and man got lost and became a stranger and a captive on earth. Meaning the dominion was greater than man. Without the dominion man is spiritually dead in this world. What makes man precious is the dominion. The jealousy of Satan against man is because of the dominion. In Isaiah 14:12-14. Satan claiming to be above everything and, above God. But when Satan saw the dominion with man because the dominion is the power behind the word which cause Heaven and Earth to be in existence, which also gives path to man. He became aggressive and device devices against man. Rev. 12:7-11. Says the angels waged war against him and he was cast down and the saints conquered him by the blood of the Lamb and the word of their testimony. Job.9:24. The world is given into the hands of the wicked one. Because he has blinded the eyes of the legal owners and taken possession of it. And in. Gen. 3:2-6. Satan made a legal agreement with Eve for the exchange with fruit –man did not know the value of the dominion at that time and gave it out for food, Good for food – to make a woman beautiful; a tree to be desired to make one wise – something that carries intelligence and wisdom; Pleasant to the eyes – to be admired by men. Luke. 4:6. Satan made show of the power delivered onto him by Adam before Christ. And in: Matt. 28:18. Jesus also made show of the power given to him by the Father both on earth and in heaven (Eph.3:4-5). Satan saw that the power given to him was low so there he was conquered and caste out of the world again this time by Jesus.

(John. 12:31) Now is the judgment of the world, now shall the prince of the world be cast out. John 14:30. Here after I will not talk with you for the prince of this world cometh and hath nothing in me. Satan took the world as his own property, but blessed be to the Living God that He had retrieved it from the grip of Satan. And this was the terrible defeat on Satan by Christ. Colo. 2:13-15. Christ had quickened us together with him and forgiven us our trespasses. Blotting out our sins and took it out and nail it on the cross. Christ therefore spoiled the principalities and powers and made show of his victory openly triumphing over them in the satanic kingdom. Colo. 2:8. Jesus Christ now warns us to be careful that no man spoil us through philosophy and vain deceit after the logic and traditions of the world and not after Christ. Now the bible says; Colo: 2:9 We are complete in Christ, we now have all the weapons, the armor, the ammunitions to fight Satan and his kingdom. Confirmed in, Mark 16:16-18. Those of us who believe and are baptized, shall be saved: but those that believe not shall be damned. Salvation of man was a great war between Jesus Christ and Satan and Christ won the battle. He made show of it before the whole world and before mankind, and saw him rose from death of crucifixion, confusing the devil and scaring him and his host.

Salvation is a process through which the second birth from God the Father is given; It comes:-

1. By hearing the word of God.
2. By accepting and believing in Jesus Christ
   (a) confessing your sins.
   (b) confessing the name of Jesus Christ.
   (c) Accepting and availing yourself to be baptized.
   (d) By accepting to be delivered from the curses of the past.

You are now dressed in Christ military garment ready to enter the battle field. You are now David against Goliath. That is how heaven sees you now.

THE ADVANTAGE OF THE PHYSICAL BODY:-The only time for man to receive Christ is when one is human, having physical body, that is the only vessel Christ will need. 1Cor. 3:16-17 "Do you not know that you are the temple of God and that the Spirit of God dwells in you. If anyone defiles the temple of God, God will destroy him. For the temple of God is holy, which temple you are." 1cor. 6:19 "Do you not know that your body is the temple of the Holy Spirit who is in you, whom you have from God and you are not your own." Christ can only enter into the flesh and once a person dies Christ cannot enter into that person any longer because Christ does not enter into a spirit, He needs a full component of man to save the soul not spirit. Spirit can only possess physical body so having the physical body is an advantage to receive Christ and that is the purpose of being born with a physical body. Satan is jealous of you as human beings because you have the body, the soul and the spirit, you are like the God head bodily but Satan has only one component, the spirit, which does not satisfies him, because he needs to possess a physical body for his purpose, and until a physical body yields to him, he cannot achieve his purpose, that is the reason why human being have more spiritual attacks. If you die without Christ, you have missed your target which is the purpose in life. So once a person dies there is no salvation for such individual because the person has lost the physical body which is the vessel Christ needs to use to save the soul. Jesus cannot relate Himself with this person when the flesh is lost without Him. The bible says in Roman 3:23 "For all have sinned and fall short of the glory of God." We have already dropped out of the glory, so the more we sin, the far we are driven from the glory of God. Once Christ is rejected the target of the purpose in life is missed and the glory of God is also missed. There is enough glory for mankind to live in but sin has covered it and made it impossible for mankind. The advantage you have and live as human being today is extraordinary. Many did not have this advantage, they were miscarriaged, aborted, spent a day or two and died and even in the delivery process. This life is an advantage for you to receive Jesus Christ, do not miss this experience and precious life. When we turn to Christ who paid the price for our sins, the barrier between God and Man is removed, and God will hear us when we cry unto him.

PACKAGE:- And these signs shall follow them that believe: In my name 1. shall they cast out devils, 2. they shall speak with new tongues, 3. they shall take up serpent. 4. they shall drink deadly things like poison, attack with juju, voodoo, talismans, shrines and altars, they will have no effect on them, 5. they shall lay hands on the sick and they will recover. 6.We have received salvation and saved through Christ. 7. We can now come to the God the Father. 8. We are now children of God. 9. We can ask Him what we want and He will surely give us.10. That we also may go out to spread His word and win souls unto Him. 11. Satan is made a looser and God has won.

COMMITTING SUICIDE-:

People commit suicide because they do not have salvation and have no knowledge of the power of salvation. Mark 14:21 "The Son of Man indeed goes just as it is written of Him, but woe to that man by whom the Son of man is betrayed! It would have been good for that man if he had never been born." And Judas who betrayed Him committed suicide, Matt. 27:5. When one commits suicide his message is, he is not fit to continue to live in the world. He has given up on himself. If one commits suicide he had already passed judgment upon himself and condemned himself. Even in the world where there is grace, he could not spare himself, how can hell spare him after this life, meaning if you commit suicide there is no heaven for you. Judas committed suicide because he felt the punishment of what he did was condemnation by himself. Even hell does not want people who had committed suicide, meaning hell has rejected such a person. So do not commit suicide, there is no problem that has no solution. That which is impossible with man is possible with God. Christ is the solution to every problem. You think your problem is too great to handle but there is a second chance to live. You need to be born again to start a new life. Matt. 11:28 "Come to me, all you that labor and are heavy laden, and I will give you rest."

BENEFIT OF SALVATION:- In Psalm. 51:12. Restore unto me the joy of thy salvation. David searched for this package of the salvation and did not receive it, but Christ has delivered this package automatically unto Christians. 1Cor. 6:20. The Lord Jesus Christ paid an expensive price to retrieve us. Eph. 2:12. says, We had no hope with God in the world but Eph. 2:13. indicates, We are now brought near to God by the blood of Jesus Christ. verse 14. says The Lord Jesus Christ is our peace, our shepherd and had broken the middle wall of partition between God and man, and God is now visible and face to face with man.

BAPTISM.

What is baptism? Baptism means complete immersion or total immersion. It is a ceremony marking a person's admission into the Christian congregation by immersion in water at an age when a person is old enough to understand what this ceremony means, knowing and understanding good and evil. It is the new testament baptism. John 3:1-8. An infant can be presented for dedication to the Lord but not for baptism. Luke 2:21-22

Key Scripture:-1.1Cor. 12:13; 2. Hebr. 6:1-2; 3. Matt. 28:19; 4.Luke 11:13; 5. Matt. 3:11-12.

Institution of baptism: (Establishment) Matt. 28:19; Mark 16:15-16. It was a commandment from Jesus.

TYPES OF BAPTISM :-

There are four types of baptism that a person must receive to be declared a child of God. Each of these baptism is very important for one's admission as a Christian. These are:-

1. Baptism by one spirit into one body — Public confession (repentance acceptance, or baptism of repentance. Acts 2:38; Matt. 3:1-2; Matt. 3:11; It is the spirit of submission, humility).

2. Baptism in water — Position (where one declares his position in or give self to Christ, initiation into the body of Jesus Christ. Acts 8:29-39).

3. Baptism in the Holy Spirit. — Power (Acts 4:8-13. 2:2-4).

4. Baptism with Fire — Holiness (standing alone spirit. Acts 16:22-26 Acts 7:55-60). One does not look up to others to serve God. Acts 4:13.

1. Baptism into one body:- Rom. 10:9-10. Whenever a person without Christ surrenders to Christ, the Holy Spirit enters that person's life. Rom. 8:9 "But ye are not in the flesh but in the spirit, if indeed the spirit of God dwells in you. Now if anybody does not have the spirit of Christ, he is not his." As soon as one is drawn by the Holy Spirit into the body of Christ, he becomes a new born spiritual baby, the barrier to see God our Father is removed, and

through Our Lord Jesus Christ the believer can now see God. John 6:44,65Eph. 2:4-9, Eph.4:4-5, Eph.3:9, Rom. 10:9-10, Acts. 2:38-39. It is the symbol of the believer's identification with Lord Jesus Christ in his death, burial and resurrection. It is an open and public confession of the Lordship of Jesus Christ.

2. Baptism in water:- There are four kinds of this baptism in use, Sprinkling, pouring, effusion and immersion. But one thing we have to know is the term baptism means "TO DIP" that is total immersion. Since baptism is the identification of the death, burial and resurrection of our Lord Jesus Christ therefore Sprinkling, pouring and effusion cannot satisfy the purpose of Baptism of the new testament. John 3:23-27 Mark 1: 9-10, Acts 8:36-39. It is a change of mind, which makes one to put away the old things and walk in the works of Christ. Water baptism is the outward sign of repentance and forgiveness of sins through faith in Jesus Christ not through the performing of the baptism. It is the physical operation expressing our faith in God.

UNDER THIS BAPTISM ARE:-

1. The institution of water baptism. 2. The mode of water baptism. 3. The significance of water baptism. 4. Subjects of water baptism

THE INSTITUTION OF WATER BAPTISM:-

This is the time and command of establishing this kind of baptism. It marks when this baptism was established, how it was instituted, why it was established and what it is. Matt. 3:16, Matt. 28:-19, Acts 2:-38,41.

MODE OF WATER BAPTISM [KINDS] :-

SPRINKLING [CONSECRETION] :- This is done where water is very scarce eg. In the desert. It is an emergency baptism, that could be done to secure the member's faith in Christ as a Pentecostal believer or in the charismatic churches, that person must be re-baptized by immersion in water.

POURING [CONSECRETION] :- This kind of baptism is applied where the river has a high force of current or the water is under high pressure and could not be entered, or where there are no rivers, lakes or ponds. This is done with bucket from a well or where the river cannot be entered and poured upon the recipient and is acceptable water baptism.

EFFUSION [CONSECRETION] :- By means of gushing forth from tap of the pipe borne water, the recipient must be re-baptized in a river because it does not satisfy the new testament baptism.

IMMERSION :-[TO DIP] This is the Christ recommended new testament baptism symbolizing the Death, burial and resurrection of Jesus Christ. Matt. 3:16 :- Jesus when he was baptized went up straightaway out of the water and lo the heavens were opened unto him and he saw the spirit of God descending like a dove and lighting upon him. Mark 16:15-16. "And he said unto them, go ye unto all the world and preach the gospel to every creature. He that believes and baptized shall be saved but he that believes not shall be damned." So Jesus gave the bishops, apostles, pastors, evangelists, missionaries, the mandate or the power to baptize. Matt. 28:19. In the name of the father and of the son and of the Holy Ghost shall the converts of the new testament be Baptized. Matt. 3:13-17 Know that Jesus will not say something He does not do. Jesus Himself was baptized where there was enough water, in river Jordan at Aenon near the city of Salim. John 3:22-23 (It is most likely Jesus himself baptized the Disciples). John 4:1-2 When therefore the Lord knew how the Pharisees had heard that Jesus made and baptized more disciples than John, (though Jesus Himself baptized not, but His disciples. John 17:20; Luke 3:21-23.

Acts 2:38-41. "Peter said unto them repent and be baptized every one of you in the name of Jesus Christ for the remission of sins and ye shall receive the gift of the Holy Ghost." They believed, repented, confessed and were baptized. Have faith in Christ that he was crucified, Dead, buried and resurrected. It's just that. Sin prevents the Holy Spirit and once we are sin free, the Holy Spirit becomes our partner. because we do not choose the Holy Spirit but the Holy Spirit chooses us.

SIGNIFICANCE OF WATER BAPTISM:- The purpose of water baptism:- It is the symbol of the believer's identification with Jesus Christ in his death, burial and resurrection. It is an open and public confession of the lordship of the Lord Jesus Christ and acceptance of the Christian faith or the declaration of one's position in Christ as Christian. Rom. 6:3-4. "Know ye not that so many of us as were baptized into Jesus Christ were baptized into his death. Therefore we are buried with him by baptism unto death, like as Christ was raised up from the death by the glory of the Father even so we also should walk in newness of life.

Colossians 2:9-12. "For in him dwells all the fullness of the Godhead bodily. And ye are complete in him which is the head of all principalities and powers. In whom also ye are circumcised with the circumcision made without hands, in putting off the body of the sins of the flesh by the circumcision of Christ. Buried with Him in baptism, where in also ye are risen with Him through the faith, the operation of God who had raised Him from the dead."

SUBJECT OF WATER BAPTISM:-Baptism is saved for those who are prepared and believe that salvation is the only way to come back to God. This new testament baptism comprise of the following:-
1. Those who received the word Acts 2:41. (presently received the word).
2. Those who had received the spirit. Acts 10:47,44; 16:33-34; 18:8; 1Cor.1:16
3. Those who can hear the word. Acts 10:44. (might follow friends as an opportunity).
4. Those who hear and believe. Acts 16:30-34. (hear the word because it was available to them).

These are those qualified to be baptized. Baptism in water is a spiritual act or operation leading to the spiritual truth in Christ. In water baptism we are in effect sharing with Christ his death, burial and resurrection. Rom. 6:3-7, Gal. 2:20, Col. 2:12.

We must be baptized in water because :- 1. Jesus has commanded us to do so. Matt. 28:19. 2. It shows our conscience towards God. 1Pet. 3:21. 3. It's something Jesus himself did. Matt. 3:13-17. 4. The faith of the early churches was based on this. Acts 2:41, Acts 10:47-48. 5. It represent the cleansing of sins, by the blood and word of God Acts 22:16. 6. It create joy in heaven, and increase the capacity of God's kingdom. 7. We are transform from the world and removed from the kingdom of Satan. John 15:19

3. HOLY SPIRIT BAPTISM:- This baptism is the promise from our Lord Jesus Christ. The Holy Spirit is a gift and is not bought with money, it is a free gift to all who believe. Acts 1:8. We do not have to be confused with the Holy Ghost baptism and the anointing of the God. The anointing brings the casting out of demons, performing of healing and miracles. But the Holy Spirit baptism helps the believer to lead a righteous life and take responsibility in the work of God. This baptism brings forth the gift of the Holy Spirit- that's the anointing to glorify the Lord. 1Cor. 12:7-11. It gives boldness. Acts 2:14-15, 4:31;Rom.8:15-16. It also increases our love for the word of God and gives understanding. John 16:13; 1Cor.2:9-16. This baptism is received by faith (Gal.3:2-5) it is not struggle for, agonized, begged for, or bargained. It is a free gift of the Lord Jesus to his disciples to enable them walk as he did. Luke 11:11-13

4. BAPTISM WITH FIRE:- This baptism builds a magnetic field around the believer to repel the attacks (missiles). We become vessels more able to fulfill what God has planned for our lives. God has chosen to use our circumstances and the pressures of life to achieve this process of purifying our lives. Like the chaff (matt. 3:12) be burnt by unquenchable fire, we must be prepared to withstand. We must learn to take advantage of these pressures. Without these pressures we never be as God wants us to be to fulfill our full potential in Christ. Matt. 26:67. Matt. 27:27-31. We ask God to change us but when the pressures come we pray to God to remove it. 1Pet.1:7. (1Pet.4:12-19, 2Tim.2:3, Rev. 2:10).

CONFESSION:-I lift up my hands and accept Jesus Christ as my Lord and savior. I believe that Jesus Christ is the son of God who was sent by the father unto the world who shed his blood at Calvary and cleansed me and gave up his life that I may receive salvation. Lord I lift up my hands and confess my sins before you that you will forgive me. I will worship you with the rest of my life. In Jesus name. Amen.

THE LORD'S SUPPER.

Memory verses:- Matthew 26:26-30; John 6:53-58;
Luke 22:15-20; 1Cor. 11:24-30; Exo. 12:20-24

    <u>Introduction</u> :- The pass over is a type of deliverance from the slavery being symbolized with the consecration of blood of animals (the blood of the first born of the Egyptians: both humans and animals was used to sanctify the first born of the Israelites). That was the Passover of the night when the Lord passed through the land of Egypt but the new testament pass over is what we deserve for our sins to be washed with blood of Jesus Christ as has been applied to us by faith. The pass over would have been senseless and waste if the remnant was not consumed, likewise the blood of Jesus applied on the cross and His body consumed into the grave. So by the sacrifice of Our Lord and Savior Jesus Christ we are made to live by faith. The pass over was eaten with bitter herbs, as the bible says, eating the bitter herbs was not easy. What is bitter is bitter and it takes courage to eat in Exodus 12:12-14. Likewise the bitter herb represents public confession. For someone to abandon his old character is not easy. Jesus told the rich man, Go and sell your properties and share to the poor, abandon the old character or lifestyle and come to take this new character or lifestyle by following Me, and the man could not. Jesus said it is easy for the camel to pass through the eye of the needle than for a rich man to enter the kingdom of God. Matt. 19:24 That's what it takes for repentance by public confession, but that is the only means to seek for the kingdom of God. (Notice that none of the Israelites was consumed by the pass over) because they obeyed by eating the bitter herbs with the meat and applying the blood on their door frames. If we obey and come to Christ and repent and make public confession of our sins, we are saved and absolved into the kingdom of Christ. And finally participate in the Lord's super. The Passover and the Lord's Super are the same. The feast of unleavened bread came about when the Israelites were instructed to get ready to leave Egypt. They had no time to bake the normal bread but bread which did not stay overnight to gain volume and it became skim bread which is unleavened bread and it became part of the tradition of the Israelites to have the feast of the unleavened bread.

<u>Meaning</u>:- The Lords Super is the central act of the faith given to Christians by Jesus Christ Himself. It is an act to remind the Christian of his or her position in Jesus Christ, making personal examination before the participation. If we eat and drink this cup in a sinful manner we eat and drink judgment to ourselves, without thinking of the holiness of Jesus Christ. Therefore we will have no judgment if we first judge ourselves. He who judges himself is not judged. The Lord's Super symbolizes the remembrance of Jesus Christ's suffering, His death and the great love He had shown to the world Hence it will not just become Christian tradition but a Christian purpose to focus on and the sacrament to help us strengthen our faith. The PASSOVER is the same as 1. THE LORD'S SUPER, 2. THE LAST SUPPER, 3. COMMUNION, 4. EUCHARIST [thanking God for the work of Jesus Christ's sacrifice]. The elements of the Lord's supper are 1. the sacred bread and 2. grape juice. Christians believe the presence of the Lord Jesus Christ each time of the Lord's Supper spiritually.

Institution: It was instituted in the night when Jesus Christ and His disciples met together to eat the Passover and Dr. Luke explains, that which took effect on that Thursday night. This shows that as the Passover was instituted in the old testament in that night when the Lord passed through the land, Even so, in the new testament the Lord Super was instituted the night Jesus commanded the disciples to go and prepare a place for the Passover (which is the feast of unleavened bread), in Matt. 26:17-20" Now on the first day of the feast of unleavened bread the disciples came to Jesus saying to Him, where do you want us to prepare for you to eat the Passover? And He said go into the city to a certain man and say to him, The Teacher says, My time is at hand. I will keep the Passover at your house with My disciples. So the disciples did as Jesus has directed them and they prepared the Passover. When even had come He sat down with the twelve." The Passover and the Lord's Super are the same. Even though it was there by name as Passover at the time of Moses, it was being celebrated once a year, but The Lord came to fulfilled that anytime the Christian congregation met they should celebrate it as a remembrance of Him Luke 22:19, to keep in touch with Him till He comes.

<u>The Importance Of The Lord's Super To The Christian</u> :- The Lord's Super reminds us of the great sacrifice Our Lord Jesus Christ offered for our sake, His suffering before the Cross and that on the cross, which

originally pertain to us. By faith the Lord's Super becomes sacred meal possessing healing power. When we celebrate the Lord's Super, we are expressing our gratitude to God for His mercy and His acceptance of us for this new relationship as being part of the body of Our Lord Jesus Christ. The Lord's Super connects us to Jesus Christ as long as we keep celebrating it. It is a symbolic celebration which Our Lord Jesus established for His remembrance to acknowledge our participation in the benefit of His death and fellowship with Him till He comes. 1Cor. 11:26. "For whenever you eat this and drink this cup you proclaim the Lord's death until He comes." Jesus chose the unleaven bread of the pass over meal to represent His physical body which will be broken on the cross. As the bread was broken apart and distributed to the disciples during the meal, even so His body was broken on the CROSS. If the bread was not unleaven, it could not represent the body of Christ. He knew ahead of time that the unleaven bread will one day represents His body and must not gain volume because once it is allowed to gain volume that's swollen, His body also must gain volume or swell in the tomb, which means he could not rise, for any living thing that dies (sleeps) and gain volume by swollen is deteriorated and dead, and cannot rise again. That is the reason why He made it a law for the Israelites to have unleaven bread for the celebration of the pass over which represents His body. So any time the Jews eat the unleaven bread they eat the body of Christ but they do not believe in Jesus Christ as the SAVIOR but yet do His command for the remembrance of His death, resurrection and ascension. Exo. 12:8,34 and Luke 21:17-20. Jesus Christ instructed Christians to eat the Lord's Supper anytime they meet in remembrance of Him and the Jews do this almost every day or every Saturday unknowingly. Luke 22:19.

The Lord's Super Replaces The Passover :- The Passover was a feast which the Jewish people celebrate as a covenant with Jehovah for their deliverance from slavery out of Egypt. In this night a lamb was slaughtered and applied the blood on the door frames to separate the children of Israel from the Egyptians, which ended up killing every first born in the land of Egypt. It is assumed as a symbolic deliverance of God's people from slavery. It was the time of celebrating the Passover that Jesus replaced with the Lord's Super. Luke 22:7-20

The Lord's Super as a covenant :- The Lord's Super is in two parts, the bread which is the body of Jesus Christ and the wine which is His blood. Eating the bread which is the body of Jesus Christ gives us the opportunity to become part of the body of Christ, physically and spiritually and gives confidence in both realms. The wine which is the blood of Jesus is in some case called "the Cup" which had cleansed us of all our sins and totally forgiven and made us new creatures. 2Cor. 5:17. This is a new covenant, Luke 22:20 by which we are assured that Christ will never forsake us, as long as we continue to celebrate this for His remembrance. Luke 22:19; 1Cor. 11:25. This covenant is a legal agreement between Christ and us, and our relationship and future everlasting reward.

Who Should Participate in the Lord's Super :- The Lord's Super has no barrier of who should participate. The only qualification to participate is that the participant must be a Christian. You cannot participate in the Lord's Super and you do not know what you are doing. There are some warnings as to partake this celebration unworthy. It's for our benefit to heal us from our infirmities and intimate relationship with Jesus Christ and our connection with the Holy Spirit towards the second coming of Christ. If you operate a machine and you do not understand its functions neither the buttons, you can end up in terrible accident, being amputated and disabled. Likewise the Lord's Super, if you eat and drink it without understanding what you are doing, you may eat and drink it unworthy which can end up with a curse. A curse go so much far to generations upon generations. So let's understand what we are doing and have the blessing. 1Cor. 11:29 "For he who eats and drink in an unworthy manner, eats and drinks judgment to himself not discerning the Lord's body." Someone will like to ask, how many time do we have to celebrate the Lord's Super? As often as we meet depending on the financial capacity of the church and availability and willingness to participate. 1Cor. 11:25

Ministering the Lords supper :-

1. The minister must remember Ecclesiastes 3, there is time for every purpose, time for the Lord's Supper is not the time for prayer, preaching or partying.

191

2. Continually participating in the Lord's Supper helps the believer to maintain the spirit of Christ in him or her. He or she is always alert.

3. The pastor or the priest must supervise the preparation of the bread and the drink, which represents the body and the blood of our Lord Jesus Christ.

4. When everything(the table of the supper) is ready before the congregation, the pastor or the priest or the officiating minister will refer to what Jesus, Himself said of the Lord's supper in Luke 22:15-20 and also the quotation of apostle Paul recommendation in 1Cor. 11:24-30.

5. The officiating minister then blesses the table of the Lord's supper, and call the congregation starting with women first and then followed by the men, having the congregation sing one to three songs of the blood and salvation.

6. The officiating minister then prays over the ceremony to end it. Remember that when something is spiritually established, the physically aspect is already established.

The Blessing Of The Lord's Super :- We are sinners and were not qualified to celebrate the feast of the Lord's Super. It is just the grace of God that we also participate in this feast. As we participate we show our obedience and appreciation of Christ's sacrifice and God blesses us for our act of humility. With the celebration of the Lord's Super we are healed of our infirmities or sicknesses. So the blood of Jesus as we drink is a medicine without expiring date which has the potential to heal every sickness and every disease tormenting us as Christian. It is always a fresh and powerful medicine. This is a big guarantee and a breakthrough for the Christian.

TITHE

John 1:1 In the beginning was the word and the word was with God and the word was God. God worked with the word and the word is the bible. With HIM- the word, God speaks to us, God is our spiritual father, so if we neglect what the bible say, we become rebellious to God and our relationship with HIM, Lord Jesus.

MEMORY VERSE: Malachi. 3:8." Will a man rob God? Yet ye have rob me. But ye say, wherein have we robbed thee? In Tithe and offering."

Purpose: 1. Provide for the work of God. 2. Prove believer's faithfulness 3. Pay honor to God 4. To feed the widow and the fatherless. 5. Care for the priest(pastor, evangelist, prophets etc.).

MEANING:- Tithe is a covenant or agreement between God and his children. It is the tenth part of your earnings as children of God dedicated to the house of God. Therefore every child of God is oblige to pay tithe upon which the tithe payer will be blessed and protected. Tithe is a contribution God is more particular with. Tithe is for people with faith, you can't pay tithe if you have no faith in God. We are fortunate to be asked to pay tithe as Christians. Tithe identifies you as the child of God. God gave tithe to his children, as an identification, so that God can bless them. So as tithe participant you are special. The gift of the Holy Spirit depend upon your tithe and righteousness as tithe displays the faithfulness of the tithe payer. (Gen. 14:19-20, Heb. 7:1-6, Rom. 4:3,21-25).

REASON:- Gen. 1:1. The bible says, In the beginning God created the heaven and earth." He did not mix any chemicals to create the earth, he did not mix medicines or herbs together to create the earth but: "By the word He created the earth. Gen. 1:11. And God said, let the earth bring forth grass, the herb that yield seed and fruit-tree that yields fruit according to its kind, whose seed is in itself, on the earth, and it was so. We know that, this comprises also of the minerals like, gold, silver, iron ore, coal etc. Gen. 2:5-7. And every plant of the field and minerals before it was in the earth, because God has not rain upon the earth because there was not a man to work on the ground. But there went up a mist from the earth and watered the whole face of the ground. And the Lord God formed man of the dust of the ground and breathed into his nostrils the breath of life and man became a living soul. Now the rain had expose the gold, diamond, silver, bauxite, manganese, iron ore jasper, sapphire jacinth, amethyst, chrysoprasus, chrysolyte topaz and saduins. Gen. 1:21. God created every living creature that moveth, sheep, goats, cows, bulls, fouls and the great and small creatures of the sea and creatures of the air. Gen. 1:27-28. God created man and blessed man with wisdom and power to do wonderful things: planes, cars, ships, radio waves etc with materials God has put into the earth and the animals in the forest made accessible to man. The wisdom to make big factories to make money. And after making money we are entitled to pay tithe to God (that's to the church – for the work of God) but we forget about Him. So God spoke in. Malachi. 3:8. "Will a man rob God, Yet you have robbed Me. But you say, In what way have we robbed You? In tithes and offerings. Job 38:4. "Where were you, when I laid the foundation of the earth. Tell Me if you have understanding." God has made His earth and created us unto it and He is asking us to pay ten percent of whatever we make to him and some do not agree with Him. Isaiah 45:12. I have made the earth, and created man on it. Malachi 3:9-12. "You are cursed with a curse, for you have robbed Me, even this whole nation. Bring all the tithes into the storehouse, And try Me now in this, says the Lord of Host. If I will not open you the windows of heaven and pour out for you such blessing that there will not be room enough to receive it. And I will rebuke the devourer for your sake, so that he will not destroy the fruit of you ground, nor shall the vine fail to bear fruit for you in the field, says the Lord of Host; and all nations will call you blessed, For you will be a delightful land says the Lord of host."

The Lord is asking us to pay tithe (rent) on the earth we occupy, materials and all that we take. Some say when JESUS CAME He did not speak of tithe so tithe is not necessary but Jesus spoke in proverbs and even the disciples questioned Him why He always spoke in parables. This is what Our Lord Jesus Christ said about tithe: Quote Matt. 21:33-40. Hear another parable: "There was a certain landowner who planted a vineyard and set a hedge around it, dug a vine press in it and built a tower. And he leased it to vinedressers, and went into a far country. Now when winetage-time drew near, he sent his servants to the vinedresser that they might receive it's fruit. And the vinedressers took his servants beat one, killed one and stoned another. Again he sent other servants more than the first, and they did likewise to them. Then last of all, he sent his son to them, saying they will respect my son. But when the vinedressers saw the son, they said among themselves, this is the heir, come let us kill him and seize his inheritance. So they took him and cast him out of the vineyard and killed him. Therefore, when the owner of the vineyard comes, what will he do to the vinedressers? Verse 41 they answered, he will destroy those wicked men miserably, and lease his vineyard to other vinedressers who will render to him the fruits in their seasons". He also said in Matt. 23:23. "Woe to you Scribes and Pharisees, hypocrites! For you pay tithe of mint and anise and cumin and have neglected the weightier matters of the law: justice and mercy and faith. These you ought to have done, without leaving the others undone." Jesus said without leaving the commandment of tithe and all the laws of Moses, meaning He said, we have to pay tithe. Leviticus 25:23. says "The land shall not be sold for ever: "FOR THE LAND IS MINE" for ye are strangers and sojourners with Me." Tithe is a covenant we cannot break. Once we break, it becomes a curse on mankind. Even gifts we have to pay tithe on them, tax returns, compensations, and donations etc. And Numbers 18:29, says "Out of all your gifts ye shall offer every heave offering of the Lord, of all the best thereof, even the hallowed part thereof out of it." And again, all that Jesus is saying is that, The Father is asking mankind to pay tithe because that's the rent of the World we live in. God is saying I have given you the earth to live on and do every business you want even the things in and on the earth as material for your business but at the end of the month or the year you should bring me one-tenth of whatever you made as long as you live in the world. Jesus has confirmed the offering of tithe to the church, for the church is the house of God, the storehouse of God. At the end of the month we quickly have to pay our rent of our habitation, even if we do not have the means we do everything possible so that we are not thrown out. But that house is on the earth, as the landlord will throw the tenant out when he fails to pay his rent even so God will throw our houses out of the face of the earth with an earthquake, tornado, hurricane or volcano. We cherish to fear human being more than the creator. Even if our landlords throws us out, we are still living and do every business we like on the earth. But we honor the landlord more than our creator. When we fail to pay our tithe, we become enemies of God, what did David say: 1Samuel 25:21-22. "Now David had said, Surely in vain I have protected all that this fellow has in the wilderness, so that nothing was missed of all that belongs to him. And he has repaid me with evil for good. May God do so and more also to the enemies of David if I leave one male of all who belong to him by morning light." When we fail to pay our tithe, we become enemies to God, exactly like Nabal and his house became enemies to David.

FUNCTION:- In Malachi 3:1. Bring all the tithe into the storehouse and it's where the treasuries of the dedicated things and the treasuries of the house of God are brought, as said in 1Chron. 26:20. So it is sin not to pay tithe. And also incorrect payment of tithe is also sin and can lead to curse. The very day God placed you in your mother's womb that He made this covenant with you, so it's a violation as able human being not to pay tithe. Deut. 8:11-12 ;17-18. "Beware that you do not forget the Lord your God by not keeping His commandments, His judgments, and His statues which I command you today, lest when you have eaten and are full and have built beautiful houses and dwell in them". Verse 17-78 "then you say in your heart, my power and the might of my hand have gained me this wealth. But you shall remember the Lord your God for it is He who gives you power to get wealth that He may establish His covenant which He swore to your fathers as it is this day." It is God the father, the father of our Lord Jesus Christ who supplies you power, strength and knowledge to acquire the wealth you possess, therefore you need to honor him with your wealth to pay tithe of ten percent unto your God. **BENEFIT:-** Malachi. 3:8-10. God has talked to us cordially to bring the tithe on the things we take from Him, God is a living God and promise us abundant blessing. He has promised us protection and great popularity. He also promised us protection which is the HEDGE: Job 1:10. If you refuse to pay tithe, you loose the hedge (that's the fire of the Holy Spirit) God has set around you. So brothers and sisters try to pay your tithe to identify yourself as a child of God, the seed of Abraham and the heir of God. Proverbs. 3:9-10. "Honor the Lord with thy first fruit and your barns shall be filled with plenty."

EXTRACTS:- Hebr. 7:8-9 Exo. 16:36 Gen. 14:22-29; Gen. 28:20-22 1Cor. 16:1-2 Num. 18:21-28 Matt. 22:21;Matt. 23:23 Deut. 14:22-28 ; Deut. 8:18 Malachi. 1:7-8 Nehemiah 10:35-58

Deut. 26:12-15." When thou hast made an end of good tithing, all the tithes of thine increase of the third year which is the year of tithing, and hast given it unto the Levite, the stranger, the fatherless, and the widow, that they may eat within thy gates, and be filled. Thou shall say before the Lord thy God, I have brought away the hallowed things out of mine house, and also have given them unto the Levite, and unto the stranger, to the fatherless, and to the widow, according to all thy commandments which thou hast commanded me: I have not transgress thy commandments, neither have I forgotten them. I have not eaten any of it when in mourning, nor have I removed any of it for an unclean use, nor given any of it for the dead. I have obeyed the voice of the Lord my God, and have done according to all that You have commanded me. Look down from Your holy habitation, from heaven and bless Your people Israel and the land which You have given us, just as You swore to our fathers, a land flowing with milk and honey." This is a covenant and once you honor your part God is committed, He cannot get out of this covenant till He also honor His part. For it's His own words from His tongue through His lips. In Malachi. 3:10 -12, He has stated exactly what He will do in your life if you pay your tithe correctly and your offering.

Lev. 27:31-34 "And if a man will at all redeem ought of his tithes, he shall add thereto the fifth part thereof. All the tithe of the herd, or of the flock, even of whatsoever pass under the rod, the tenth shall be holy unto the Lord. He shall not search whether it be good or bad, neither shall he change it and if he change it at all, then both it and the change thereof shall be holy: it shall not be redeemed." Because tithe is a covenant, God has place strict measures on it and must be obeyed.

1Cor. 9:13-14 Do ye not know that they which minister about holy things live of the things of the temple? And they which wait at the altar are partakers of the altar? Even so hath the Lord ordained that they which preach the gospel should live of the gospel.

FORGIVENESS OF SIN

MEMORY VERSE: 2Corinthians 2:10-11. "Now whom you forgive anything I also forgive, for if indeed I have forgiven anything, I have forgiven that one for your sake in the presence of Christ. Lest Satan should take advantage of us for we are not ignorant of his devices." (the greatest device of Satan is unforgiveness).

2Corinthians 5:17. "Therefore if anyone be in Christ, he is a new creature, old things are passed away, behold, all things have become new."

MEANING: To completely forget someone's fault against us or to give up resentment (bitterness), Forgiveness is not by wisdom or power or knowledge of man, but of the mercy of God when we are broken in heart to walk with God.

THE LOVE OF GOD: God sacrificed the most expensive treasure in His custody, His Only Begotten Son Our Lord Jesus Christ to cleanse us of the grievous sin in the life of man, which brought condemnation to man. John 3:16-18. When we became His followers, we have been cleanse by faith, the old character and deeds is cancelled, we have started a new life, All sin is forgiven.

POWER OF CONFESSION: There has been no other way that man has received forgiveness of sin, other than repentance of sin and confession of sin. Roman 10:9-10, 2Corinthians 5:21.

TOTAL FORGIVENESS: We are totally forgiven when we have change of mind, repent and confess, and receive Jesus Christ as the Son of God and our Savior. 1John 1:9. This makes God to forget that we have ever sinned. Our godly memory is restored to us, condemnation is totally removed from us. Repentance and confession is the greatest weapon that draws God back to us and closes the gap between God and Man. It is the weapon which Satan hates and cannot withstand it.

TWO KINDS OF FORGIVENESS: (1). Godly forgiveness (2). Human forgiveness. God expect us to forgive so that He could also forgive us. Matt. 6:14 For if you forgive men their trespasses your heavenly Father will also forgive you. But if you do not forgive men their trespasses neither will your Father in heaven forgive your trespasses. (Matt. 6:12).

After we have forgiven the trespasses of others against us, then the heart and body has been prepared to receive forgiveness from God. It is obvious that our heavenly Father will forgive us our sins. Most of the sayings and activities of the gospel are spiritual and until you believe, you will not understand.

Peter was eager to serve the Lord with open heart and tried to know from Jesus where he will stand in forgiveness to others. Matt. 18:21-22 "Then Peter came to Him and said, Lord how often shall my brother sin against me and I forgive him? Up to seven times? Jesus said to him, I do not say to you up to seven times, but up to seventy times seven." Peter was convinced, Jesus said this, because the Jews hardly forgive, they usually like to revenge and it was the other of that time, that once you revenge, that person stops coming after you and this was according to the order of Moses. Exodus 21:24. eye for eye and tooth for tooth. But this resulted in a very serious and horrible violence and there was no peace among them, eg. Genesis 34:25-29. The sons of Jacob destroyed the city of Shechem when the son of Hamor raped Dinah the daughter of Leah and Jacob. They never forgive even when the king said his son will marry Dinah and was prepared to give all that they will request, and killed all the people in the city and took their properties and assets for the sake of Dinah. Hebrew 10:30-31, 26. As Christians we have to seek for settlement and not confusion and violence. Jesus is telling us to do the possible best we can to forgive and live in peace which will create a peaceful world environment and image. God does not live in violence environment and hate human violence. Matt. 18:15-17 "Moreover if your brother sin against you go and tell him his fault between you and him alone, if he hears you, you have gain your brother. But if he will not hear you take with you one or two more, that by the mouth of two or three witnesses every word may be established. And if he refuse to hear them, tell it to the church, but if he refuses even to hear the church, let him be to you a heathen and a tax collector." Tax collector have no mercy, no matter how much small one owes, they will levi your property to pay exactly the amount, meanwhile they are the worse cheats and embezzlers. Matt. 18:23-35 The parable of the unmerciful servant whom his Lord spared because he did not have the ability to pay his master what he owed him, but he was so wicked that his friend, a servant like him owed him very small amount which he demanded payment and his friend was not able and threw him in prison. When their Lord heard of his action, he called him back, threw him also and his family into an everlasting prison because there was no way for him to pay what he owed. When Jesus asked for forgiveness of sin for the world, Luke 23:34 "Then said Jesus, father forgive them: for they know not what they do." God began to pour all the sins of the world upon Jesus (extracted from the world). And because Jesus was holy in the flesh and in the spirit, the sins poured upon him became very heavy upon him and could not enter into his spirit, (when sin enter into the spirit it becomes a curse and make one die in the spirit and continue to torment the person till this curse is broken and the person is delivered and set free.). Mark 15:34 "And at the ninth hour Jesus cried with a loud voice, saying, Eloi, Eloi, lama sa-bachthani? Which is being interpreted, My God, My God why hast thou forsaken me." and John 19:28. "After this Jesus knowing that all things were now accomplished, that the scripture mighty be fulfilled, said, I thirst." His righteous spirit began to increase in strength and power and burnt off the sins poured upon him, John19:30. When Jesus therefore had received the vinegar, he said, It is finished: and he bow his head and gave up the ghost. After the sins were burnt Jesus then collected the sins and carry them and buried them in the grave and came back to life, Col.2:13-15." And having spoiled principalities and powers, he made a shew of them openly, triumphing over them in it." Jesus drove away the strongman and his army and chained the strongman under the sea and his ministers in the mountains, Jude 6. "And the angels which kept not their first estate, but left their own habitation, he had reserved in everlasting chains under darkness unto the judgment of the great day." So when we ask for forgiveness of sin, God by forgiving us our sins, extract the sins from the spirit to leave the spirit clean and righteous, he then pours the sins upon the flesh, which means we also have our part to play for the forgiveness of our sins, there is no easy attitude in the things of God. The fire of the righteous spirit given by Christ battles to burn the sins. The moment we sin again the fire of the righteous spirit of Christ is quenched and the sins enter back into the spirit and demons and evil spirits take advantage and we are conquered. John 8:11; She said, no man, Lord. And Jesus said unto her, Neither do I condemn thee: go, and sin no more. Matt.12:43-48. "When the unclean spirit is gone out of a man, he walks through dry places, seeking rest and finding none. Then he said, I will return into my house (if someone dwells at a place for a long time he dominates the place spiritually and physically) from hence I came out: and when he is come, he findeth it empty, swept, and garnished. Then goes he and takes with himself seven other spirits more wicked than himself, and they enter in and dwell there: and the last state of that man is worse than the first. Even so shall it be also unto this wicked generation." A paralyzed man was carried by friends through the roof in front of Jesus who received his healing instantly when his sins were forgiven him by Jesus. Mark 2:5. We also need to repent and confess our sins to receive forgiveness. 1John 1:9 If we confess our sins, he is faithful and just to forgive us our sins and to cleanse us from all unrighteousness. Confessing our sins and being obedient attracts God's favor. One thing we have to understand is that favor is a behavior which gives a person an advantage even if it is unfair. Once you have been forgiven your sins, you can attract favor and it comes by meekness.

CONCLUSION: Forgiveness is so important to God that every book of the bible talks about it. Once you are saved by the sacrifice and the blood of Jesus, God desires you to be His home made image and not a mass product image. So God has said, even when we are casting in our offering and there we remember that we have something against another person or brother in faith we first have to go and make peace with him then we can come and cast our offering in the offering bowl else the offering is not acceptable Matt. 5:23-26. Matt. 5:9 "Blessed are the peace makers for they shall be called the Sons of God." (your adversary will complain bitterly against you and cause your down fall and make sure that you be like him and both of you will fall into hell). Deuteronomy 32:35. "Vengeance is mine and recompense, their foot shall slip in due time, for the day of their calamity is at hand, and the things to come hasten upon them." So it is not for us to judge people who offend or sin against us. It is the Lord who has the power to judge the person. Luke 15:20-24 We also have to remember the prodigal son, his father did not rejected him but accepted him back in the family. The father forgave him like you and I, Jesus Christ has forgiven us all our sins, why do we not also forgive others. Even though the prodigal son was totally forgiven, his guilty conscience limited him of his liberty in the family and his control over the family properties and was afraid to certain measures in the house. Once we forgive others, their guilty conscience will limit their relationship. It's natural.

THE FRUIT OF LIFE

MEMORY VERSE:- Romans 10:14-15

TOPICE: WALKING IN THE SPIRIT, AND BEARING FRUIT (Gal. 5:16-26.) Vs.16-This I say that walk in the spirit, and ye shall not fulfill the lust of the flesh. Vs. 19-now the work of the flesh are manifest which are these.

THE FRUIT OF THE FLESH

The fruit of the flesh is the things that we do that does not glorify God. Things which lead us into sin. Once we are in the flesh we do not talk about things of God, but things that glorify us and exalt the devil. One may ask after all, what are the things of the flesh. Some of the things of the flesh are explain below.

Adultery : voluntary sexual intercourse between a married person and unmarried person or between different married couples. 1cor.3:16-17; Prov. 6:32-33; Lev.20:10; Mark 10:11-12; 1Cor.6:16; Prov. 30:20

Fornication- : sexual activity between unmarried persons. Deut.22:23-24,28-29;Heb.13:4; 1Cor. 6:16;Cor.7:1-2; Prov. 31:3.

Lasciviousness: action or feeling expressing and influencing sexual desire, that's lust. Prov.23:33; Col. 4:6;2Tim2:16.

Idolatry : the worship of idol, too much devotion or admiration to idols, materialism and paganism. Eze. 8:9-16; Exo. 32:2-4.

Variance : having difference of opinion or disagree. (in conflict). Deviate.

Sedition : word or action intended to make people rebel against the authority of the state (Brain wash or undermining) of the leadership of a religious body. Acts 13:6-12

Hatred : very strong dislike, animosity, prejudice or hostility.

Witchcraft : The use of evil powers. Lev. 19:31; Lev. 20:6,27;Exo. 22:18;2 Sam.21:6 2King 6:28-29; Acts 19:13-17.

Uncleanness : Spiritually impure, lack of spiritual purity. Being talkative is a sin, talking against a brother, against your pastor, staying on the phone for hours with vain talk, inquisitiveness, insinuations and talking bitterly behind brother, all these are uncleanness, evil and sinful. Prov. 16:25; Lev.21:12; Lev. 19:12; Eph. 4:31; Prov. 13:31;

Wrath : extreme anger. Prov. 16:14.

Strife : violence disagreement, state of conflict. 1Sam. 19:1.Eze. 8:17-18; Hosea 4:4. **Heresies :** Opinion that is contrary to what is generally accepted. eg. religion. 1 John 4:1-3; Mark 9:38-40; 1 Cor. 10:27-28; Matt. 7:15-23.

Envy : Feeling of discontent and bitterness 1Sam.18:28-29: Mark 15:10.

Murder : Unlawful killing of human being intentionally. Matt. 5:21; Exo.20:13;2Sam.12:9. **Reveling. :** Making merry, noisy celebration, Being much interested in ungodly things; reveling until dawn. Prov. 21:17a.

Emulation : competitive action - trying to be better than the others or effort to excel over others or prideful look, eg if I am not there nobody can do it. Prov. 6:17; 16:18.

Drunkenness : the habit of excessive use of alcohol. Gen.9:20-24; Gen.19:30-38; Prov.23:3132,21, Prov. 31:3-6; Prov. 20:1; Prov.5:11-12,22; Joel 1:5;Hab. 2:15; Prov.21:17b; Dan.1:8; Rom. 13:13; Eph. 5:18.

And Such Like : Smoking, Pride, 1Cor. 3:16-17; Lev. 19:11,13; Prov. 16:1-Prov. 16:18; Job 41:20; Laziness: Prov. 19:15,24; 20:4,13; 6:9-11; 22:13; 18:9; 6:4-12; 21:25;12:27; Defrauding: Prov. 22:22; 28:3; 29:13, Stealing: Exo. 20:5, Lev. 19:11, Josh.7:19-25, Eph. 4:28

THE FRUIT OF THE SPIRIT

Goodness : The quality of being kind, quality that nourishes growth, favorable character, praise worthy character, fertile, Acts 10:38; Matt. 14:14; Col. 3:14; Gal. 6:9-10, Heb. 13:16; Eph. 6:8-9; Prov. 28:27; Prov. 19:17; Deut. 15:7-8.

Temperance : Calmness of the mind, composure, self restrain in one's behavior, moderation (control in behavior, self control). 1Pet. 1:6, Gal. 5:23, Acts 24:25.

Faith : Trusting in the invisible to be visible, strong believe, believe and trust in God and loyalty to God. Firm believe in something for which there is no Proof (trust is the main icon of faith), Questionable confidence. Heb. 11:1-6; Rom. 1:17; Rom. 10:17.

Love : Helping others, Putting one's life at stake for others, Helping to make the church what it is supposed to be, and to put new life into people. 1Cor. 13:4-8; 1John 3:16; Rom. 5:8; 1John 4:10; Matt. 22:36-40 (Deut. 6:4-7; Prov. 17:17; Heb. 13:1,3; Deut. 7:9 (Exo. 20:6); Matt. 5:8.

Joy : Feeling of great happiness, the emotion expressed by well - being, success, good fortune, the prospect of possessing what one desire. The joy of a Christian is to do the will of God and be blessed, and when we refuse to do the will of God we loose the joy in Christ. James 4:6; John 15:11; Acts 20:24; Matt. 25:21.

Peace : The state of violence free from within and outside, absolute security and externally from oppressive thoughts, emotions and actions. John 14:27; Col 3:5.

Meekness : Humbleness, Obedience, gentleness, submission, having no resentment (ill-feeling). Mark 7:25-30; Matt. 5:5; 11:29.

Forgiveness : Allowing room to completely forget an error. 2Cor. 2:10-11; Matt. 6:14-15; Matt.18:15-17; 2Cor. 6:15-18; Matt. 18:21-35; Rom. 16:20; Matt.5:9; Lev. 19:18; Gal.6:1-10; 2Cor. 2:10-11; Gal. 5:25-26; 2Cor. 5:14-19;Luk.15:20; Matt.18:23-35; Matt. 5:39-48. With these we know what to do and what not to do. Which things may lead us to be sinners and which good lifestyle we must lead as Christians.

THE TRINITY (THE FATHER, THE SON AND THE HOLY GHOST).

<u>Gen. 1:26.</u> Then God said, Let us make a man in our image, according to our likeness, and let them have dominion over the fishes of the sea and over the birds of the air, over the cattle, over all the earth, and over all creeping things that creep on the earth.

The word <u>OUR</u> in the above verse signifies that God is not alone but more than single entity. This confirms the Trinity. God is saying here that He is three entities in one and He and the other two entities are in agreement to make man in their likeness as stated in Gen. 1:26, 1John 5:7, and him.

Hence God consist of:

THE FATHER — the soul — The mighty invisible God which dwells in unapproachable light, the Omnipotent, the Omnipresent, the Omniscient. Exo. 33:20; 1Tim. 6:16; Rev. 16:18.

THE SON — the body — The physical aspect of God, the image of the invisible God, the expression of the Father manifested, the vocal and the power. Col. 1:16-17. The Alpha and Omega, the Beginning and the End, The First and the Last. Rev. 1:8

THE HOLY GHOST — the spirit — The unseen having all power and a great Light, the might fire, the producer and operator of God. Acts 2:4

Hebr. 1:8. But unto the son he said Thy throne, Oh God forever and Ever. Amen. So Christ is God. Man is the representation of the trinity. The father is in the Holy Spirit, and the Holy Spirit in Jesus Christ. Christ is the physical aspect of God the father. God the father is the power, the soul of the unique God,and the three are one as:

<u>THE TRINITY</u>. <u>1 John 5:7</u> "For there are three that bear record in Heaven, *the father, the Word*, and *the Holy Ghost*: and these *three* are *One.*"

Gen. 1:27. "So God created man in his own image, in the image of God he created him, male and female he created them." God now becomes single in this verse. So God is three in one. The TRINITY. The word <u>HIS</u>, simply proves that the three are one, because the word <u>our</u> was no more used so God is three in one. Exo. 3:14. God said to Moses, I AM WHO I AM. This is what you are to say to the Israelites: I AM, has sent me to you. John 8:58. I tell you the truth, Jesus answered, before Abraham I AM.

Hence the three are I AM. Therefore the man being the image of God, being created with all the qualities of God:

1. The Body as Christ - [the body loves the world, and between God and Satan which is exposed to all the worldly influences-Pleasures, wealth, worldly joy, hardships and oscillation actions of life, reveals the father to the world, the grace unto mankind].

2. The Soul as the Father - [the soul communicates with the father, purified from sin, the only sin that enters the soul is fornication and murder, only the originator commands and instruct the soul. The soul is not visible and not touchable. When the spirit is killed the soul has no strength but just support the body and has short life span].

3. The Spirit as the Holy Ghost - [the action maker who uses the body for all instructions from the soul. Sin kills the spirit.] So the theory of man being the image of the three, God the Father, the creator is perfectly proven. The spirit is not visible but could feel and see His actions.

THE SOUL COMPONENTS:

1. The mind - the intellect [memory, reasoning, creativity.]
2. The emotion- feeling [desire, concern.]
3. The Will - the ability [responsibility.]

The soul is the spiritual principle embodied in human being, the real man which is immaterial. The soul is the storage house of the body. Whatever you do, either good or evil is recorded in. The soul makes you reason, because it has the mental body, the intellect. It makes you think and be creative. It is the soul that makes you feel pain, when hurt and burn. It gives you desire, a taste for earthly things as well as spiritual things and the will of control. You become concern about something by the soul's emotional body. The soul supplies the ability to do something. If the soul refuses to respond, your ability to create, to invent, to study and to memorize will be impaired. But the soul itself does not act even though he has all these qualities. The soul is always spiritual. He is always in contact with God. His contact with God will come to reality only when we convert the vocal to the body from the spirit which is the Will, then we become magnificent to give glory to the Father in all our deeds because the Father created us for his glory. If one of the entities is lost eg. the spirit, the soul will still be performing his normal functions but without the spirit, the body becomes paralyzed or lost of senses [palsy or Alzheimer]. It's the result of lack of the word of God. Isaiah 43: 7. Everyone who is called by my name I have created him for my glory, whom I formed and make.

THE SPIRIT COMPONENTS:

The heart - house of the spirit and the thinking instrument : transmits to the brain and ensure the brain function. When the heart breaks down the spirit also collapses.

The senses - the transmitting agents : nose-smell, eyes-sight, ears-hearing, skin-feeling, tongue-taste and hand-touch. This is well experienced during deliverance meeting by the Holy Spirit.

The spirit in question is the biological spirit. The spirit is beyond the scope of human understanding, He is the possessor of the being. The spirit is the fusibility giving force, without which you cannot receive the Holy Spirit, the sacred force which communicates with the soul. The spirit enable the human to think, walk, act, memorize, to see, in short to have the qualities of humanity. The spirit allows the man to live consciously when is properly cared for. He is left in an unconscious state when is not properly care for, where the person cannot differentiate evil and good. Evil becomes as good. Godly understanding is lost. In theological sense the spirit is called light so the light is quenched. This light is light from God. So Jesus said when I go I will send this light to you, he will help you and remember you of whatever I have told you. John 1:4-5. "In him was life and the life was the light of men and the light shines in darkness and the darkness comprehend it not." It is the spirit which takes action. Without the spirit nothing will be achieved. This spirit is not the Holy Spirit but our intimacy with God by confessing Jesus Christ, God sends His Holy Spirit which cleanses and purifies and brings about the fusibility with biological spirit. This Godly spirit is given by the Lord Jesus Christ to those who believe in him and love him and live with His word. John 14:21,26,15. The spirit body is the body of Grace. It is the body by which we shall resurrect with. The spirit translates the command of the soul [the father] to the body [the son].

THE BODY: is the temple of the SOUL and the SPIRIT in which both dwell and function. Without the body these two cannot function and made active. It comprises of the tissues and organs (flesh, heart, lungs, intestines, brain, lever, kidneys, etc.), and the water (two part hydrogen and one part of oxygen - and make about sixty percent of the human body), and the blood (platelet-which prevent hemorrhage; the plasma-mixture of water, protein, mineral; white cell - for the body defense; red cell - the oxygen transporter and the blood vessel - which contains the blood networking). The body is an essential part of the human and represents Jesus Christ.

The whole human system functions like a car:

1.) The human physical body — The car body
2. The soul body — The engine
3.) The spirit Body — The operator

The car body contains the engine and the operator. The engine does not operate the car. Someone must be at the control panel to control the vehicle. The spirit puts the power supply into work.

Most people usually do not see the value of their gift in them until it's presence is lost. The Lord Jesus said, you will not see the value of this light in your mist but if I go away then I will come in the form of the spirit to you and this is the one who does the fireworks, He knows all things and capable of all works. The physical body is destroying the spirit, we feed the physical body and neglect the spirit body so the spirit body becomes powerless. We care more for the body than the spirit. Neglecting things like fasting, prayer and meditation means neglecting the spirit which is the operator of the being, therefore we only grow in the physical body and the spirit made retarded. Eating too much and physical desires are abuse to the spirit so you cleave to lust of the eye, the lust of the flesh and pride of life (1John 2:16). Feed the spirit and you will have good body. Negativity, evil thoughts, depression etc. make you spiritually impaired. When you are intuitively off balance, it means you are too physical. Know that your physical being is not the real you. The real you is the soul which will account for all the activities man lived.

People argue that God can't be three in One but there are so many examples that show that it is possible, that, what we hear is true. For instance the egg of a chicken, comprise of three elements, the shell, the yoke and white jelly. Each of the three is egg and the composition of the three together is also egg. So are The Father, The Son and The Holy Spirit constitute Almighty God as the egg.

The appearance we see as a man, is created with the composition of:
1. The Body which represents Jesus Christ
2. The Soul which represents the Father
3. The Spirit which represents the Holy Ghost
4. So the man being the image of God is clearly proven.

So man is a child of God, and is God the Child, as our Lord Jesus said in:

John 10:34. "Jesus answered, Is it not written in your Law I have said, You Are Gods, to whom the word of God came, and the scripture cannot be broken." and David also said: Psalm 82:6 "I said, You are "gods"; you are all sons of the Most High." But man has belittled himself and abused himself with sinful acts which had made him lost the godly quality in him, filled with earthly desires. A person learns to become supreme through positive prayers, positive meditation, positive fasting, proper exercise, healthy dieting, being self encouraged, not egoistic, charitable, being waiting always upon the Lord, and remembering to submit to the Lord your maker, Matthew 22:37 Love the Lord your God with all your heart and with all your soul and with all your mind. When we give our love to God in Christ we shall receive back our lost spirit in Christ Jesus. Let us leave the physical body and cleave on the spirit. Because the scripture says we shall rise with a new body which is not this physical body so we must begin to practice to leave this physical body. All the power is stored in Christ and Christ has made provision for us to tap but it is up to us to make the effort to tap this power. Luke. 10:17-19 "The seventy returned with joy and said, Lord even the demons submit to us in your name. He replied I saw Satan fell like lighting from Heaven. I have given you authority to trample on snakes and scorpions and to overcome all the power of the enemy; nothing will harm you. THE FATHER : is the soul, the mighty, who dwells in unapproachable light. THE SON : is the body, the physical aspect of God, the seen God, expression of the father manifested, the producer, the vocal and the power. THE HOLY GHOST: the spirit, the unseen, having all power and a great light, the mighty fire, the operator of God. We are the image of the three in- one God. In conclusion man being the image of God, soul, spirit and body has the qualities of God in him and for those qualities to function must draw near to God.

THE POWER IN THE BLOOD OF JESUS CHRIST.

All in the history of Israel, forgiveness of sin requires blood sacrifice. Blood sacrifice is considered as a way of deliverance for mankind and also for a nation. Nothing was considered purified without the mark of shed blood of animal. Even until now, in certain parts of the world where voodoo is practiced, annual blood sacrifice is still being used as sin offering to consecrate humans and properties and nations.

Leviticus 17:11. For the life of the flesh is in the blood, and I have given it to you upon the altar to make atonement for your souls: for it is the blood that makes atonement for the soul.

The blood represents the life force of the living soul. The eating of blood was strictly prohibited in the kingdom of children of God, and the following bible verses confirm it:

Gen. 9:4-6. "But you shall not eat the flesh with its life, that is, its blood. Surely for your lifeblood I will demand a reckoning; from the hand of every beast I will require it, and from the hand of man. From the hand of every man's brother I will require the life of man. Whoever sheds man's blood, By man his blood shall be shed; For in the image of God He made man."

Leviticus 17:13-14." Whatever man of the children of Israel, or of the stranger who dwell among you. who hunts and catches any animal or bird that may be eaten, he shall pour out its blood and cover it with dust; for it is the life of all flesh. Its blood sustains its life. Therefore I said to the children of Israel. You shall not eat the blood of any flesh, for the life of all flesh is its blood. Whoever eats it shall be cut off."

In pagan worship the drinking of blood was incorporated into ritual practice where the participant was believed to have captured the life force of the creature by eating it's blood.

Hebr. 9:22 "And according to the law almost all things are purified with blood and without shedding of blood there is no remission."

Because when Moses had spoken and laid down the principle intentions of the agreement to all the people according to the law, he took the blood of calves and goats with water, scarlet wool and hyssop and sprinkled both the people, the books, the alter, almost everything pertaining to divinity in the tabernacle and the tabernacle for a complete atonement and all was considered to be sanctified and holy. Also the bible says in Exodus 16:16 "So he shall make atonement for the Holy Place, because of the uncleanness of the children of Israel, and because of their transgressions, for their sins; and so he shall do for the tabernacle of meeting which remains among them in the mist of their uncleanness." The atonement was casual intersession of deliverance which never took away ones transgressions completely. It was a way which was provided out of His love for the sake of the people. With all the rebellion God did not abandoned man, He continued to seek for our welfare to communicate with Him. But in this new testament era the animal blood sacrifice for the sin of mankind has no value and does not valid, because the bible says in Romans 3:23 "All have sinned and come short of the glory of God. Therefore it is not this our modest sins that make us come short of God's glory but the sin by which we are born." Romans 5:12." Therefore just as through one man sin entered the world and death through sin and thus death spread to all men because all sinned". And again Romans 5:18. "Therefore, as through one man's offense judgment came to all men, resulting in condemnation, even so through One man's righteous act the free gift came to all men, resulting in justification of life." So we see that we are justify by the shedding of the blood of Jesus Christ being the eternal purpose of God and the blood of Jesus is still in progress in our lives perfecting our salvation. The bible says in Luke 22:43-44 "An angel came from heaven and strengthened Him whilst He was in agony and prayed earnestly and His sweat became like great drops of blood falling down to the ground." This shows us to know that Jesus began shedding His blood for the redemption of the world at the time of prayer before they arrested Him. The crucifixion started from the time of prayer before He made the final completion of settlement on the cross. This mean, it was not human beings who shed His blood for the great mission on the cross but He gave it up at His own will on the cross. The sacrifice of Christ was not the plan of man, and for this, Pilate sought for a way to release Jesus. He even sent Jesus to Herod so he can take advantage of Herod's judgment but that did not work for him. The people intensified their cry that crucify Him! crucify Him! "Let His blood be on us and our children" Matt. 27:25, this is just another way of saying, how can we have salvation if you let this man go. And that made Pilate to give Him up to be crucified so that the scripture might be fulfilled. If what the scripture has said did not come to pass, there wouldn't have been any salvation, but this is the doings of the Lord. Therefore Hebr. 9:12-14 says "Neither by the blood of goats and calves but by His own blood He entered in the holy place having obtained eternal redemption for us. For if the blood of bulls and of goats and ashes of heifer sprinkling the uncleaned, sanctifies to the purifying of the flesh. How much more shall the blood of Christ who through the eternal spirit offered Himself without spot to God purge your conscience from dead works to serve the Living God." Jesus Christ has given us the opportunity to come back to serve the Only True Living God.

1Peter 1:3,18,19 "Bless be the God and Father of our Lord Jesus Christ which according to His abundant mercy hath gotten us again into a lively hope by the resurrection of Jesus Christ from the dead." Knowing that you were not redeemed with corruptible things like silver or gold from your aimless conduct received by tradition(tradition follow laws but Christianity follow grace) from your fathers. But with the precious blood of Christ as of a lamb without blemish and without spot.

1John 1:7 "But if we walk in the light, as He is in the light, we have fellowship with one another, and the blood of Jesus Christ His son cleanses us from all sin."

Gala. 3:10 "For as many as are of the works of the law are under the curse for it is written, curse is everyone who does not continue in all things which are written in the book of the law to do it." Because we do not do all that is written in the book of the Law, our judgment was the curse of the cross but for God so loved us He gave His only begotten Son that as we believe in Him we will not perish but have an everlasting life and Jesus was sent to the cross in our stead. Since Jesus went to the cross, It has not been heard or read, anybody has been executed by the cross. Those two criminal with Jesus were sentenced ahead of Jesus. Our fathers follow tradition and culture and we all came under curse but by the blood of Jesus Christ we are saved. The blood of Jesus Christ is a powerful redeemer.

Eph 1:7 "In whom we have redemption through His blood, the forgiveness of sins according to the riches of His grace." He has brought us out of captivity, as the Israelites were brought out of Egypt. We were in the kingdom of Satan practicing all kinds of moralities and having nothing to do with what was written in the book of the law and for this we were under curse but now we are redeemed.

CHANGE. Change is an important ornament either in humans or in nations. Without change the statistic improvement of a person or nation will be buried. Roman 12:1-2 "I beseech you therefore brethren by the mercies of God that you present your bodies a living sacrifice, holy, and acceptable to God which is your reasonable service. And do not be conformed to the world but be transformed by the renewing of your minds that you may prove what is that good and acceptable and perfect will of God." When we present our bodies as living sacrifice, holy and acceptable to God and that is best service we can give to God. When we do not conform to this world governing system, then we are transformed and our minds are renewed. Renewal of our minds is transformation. Transformation is a change which brings about growth. In otherwise when someone grows, he must develop and that development must bring about prosperity. Prosperity from God has no impediments and sorrow Prov. 10:22. "The blessing of the Lord makes one rich and He add no sorrow with it." It will automatically stay to glorify God. Anything which has no change does not grow and anything that does not grow cannot develop. Someone who is not prepared to change is not prepared to grow and will not develop. Development brings about prosperity and that person or nation which does not want to change and cannot grow to develop is an outcast to prosperity. One funny thing is people want to prosper without developing, but know that you cannot reach the top of the mountain without climbing, you have to do some climbing to reach the top. Pastors preach about prosperity which is good, without preaching change, growth and development. Yes manna can happen but how often and how many people are blessed enough to receive such manna in this our time. We need to develop to prosper. How can we prosper without growth and developing. Nations remain poor because they do not want to change and because they do not want change, they cannot develop therefore they remain poor and join the EPIC (ending poverty in community) and they have no respect in the world's economic system among nations. So if one want to prosper then he must be prepared for a change.

To have a change, one has to encounter with God. It is God who will give the person heart for that change. He is the one who help us in all that we do, on our jobs and every day activities. In Moses era God sent manna but in this time of grace, we are in era of action. God will help us only when we take action. It is the desire of God to give us a future, hope and peace and not affliction, oppression and evil. Jeremiah 29:11. In Isaiah 41:10 says "Fear not, for I am with you. Be not dismay, for I am your God, I will strengthen you Yes I will help you, I will uphold you with My righteous right hand." So this time of grace do not expect manna from heaven but He is your God, your help, your strength and your health. God is ready to help everyone for change to grow unto development and make you prosper and be prosperous and proper. Development brings about invention and creation which leads one to prosperity. Change is development and it leads to growth which is a valuable component that brings quantity from quality. When we have quality we can produce in quantity. When you walk with God, no matter what you are or who you are, your name will change. Abram walked with God and his name was changed to Abraham. Likewise Sarai walked with God and her name was changed to Sarah and Jacob when he walked with God, his name was changed to Israel. These people encountered with God and their names were changed. Encountering with God cause a change in one's life. Genesis 17:15-16; Genesis 32:26; Genesis35:10-11; Genesis 17: 5-6. As a Christian you have also encountered with Christ so you must also have a change and develop, Eph. 4:23 : "And be renewed in the spirit of your mind": This will enable you to have a change of mind, and when you have change of mind, you will :

1. discover your purpose in the world,
2. recover your purpose in the world,
3. fulfill your purpose in the world and,
4. subdue your purpose and have dominion of your purpose in the world.

Moses discovered his purpose and encountered with God, who helped him to change, cause growth in his life, developed and prospered and was able to fulfilled his purpose. He had a royal lifestyle but obtained a godly lifestyle by the hand of God.

Matt. 9:17 says "Nor do they put new wine into old wineskins or else the wineskin breaks, the wine is spilled and the wineskin are wasted. But they put new wine into new wineskins and then both are preserved." It is just saying that when the new wine is put into a bottle, fermentation occurs and pressure is built up so change has occurred. If it is an old bottle, it will not be able to withstand the pressure and will explode, but if it is a new bottle it will be able to withstand the pressure and both the bottle and the wine will be preserved. Likewise when we accept Christ and His word be in our new bodies there will be a change in our lives and will result in our growth and development, and prosperity will begins to show up. God is ready waiting for us to avail ourselves to pour fresh oil in us but that fresh oil cannot be poured into the old man, it is our duty to present a new man so God can fill the new body with the fresh oil, which brings about creations and inventions and give us the heart to produce it. Gen. 1:28 says, "Then God blessed them, and God said to them, Be fruitful and multiply; fill the earth and subdue it, have dominion over the fish of the sea, the birds of the air, and over every living thing that moves on earth." God wants every human being to be successful, therefore He wants us to live in His glory, successful in His abundance not poverty in His abundance. He wants us to invent and produce and fill the earth with our invention and be known all over the world, and become spiritually, physically and financially successful, then God will be glorified because He has created us for His glory so that the prophecy of being fruitful and multiply, and fill the earth and subdue to have dominion, shall come to pass. Then God becomes a true and faithful God who honors His word.

It is the change, the growth, the development and the prosperity in our lives that proves the existence of God and His faithfulness in our lives. God sees no failure in us but because we do not love God that's why we see failure in our lives. He sees us as His kind. In God there is no failure, so be in God and see no failure of sickness, disappointment, affliction, oppression, infirmity, poverty, mental and physical illness and so on. Man is created the image of God as in Gen. 1:26-27." And God said, Let us make man in our image according to our likeness; let them have dominion over the fish of the sea, over the birds of the air, and over cattle, over all the earth and over every creeping thing that creeps on the earth." So God created man in His own image; in the image of God He created him; male and female He created them." He created us with the dignity to invent and to transcend above all creation. Roman 6:1-18 says "What shall we say then? Shall we continue in sin that grace may abound. And having being set free from sin you may become slaves of righteousness." therefore we sin, if we do not implement the gift God has given to us through the change, as we have been set free from sin, now we become the truth of His blessing, which will give Him all the praise and adoration. No human being is created poor because every being is precious in the sight of God, and is full of talents and riches. Hence if we seek for change, there will be growth which will bring about development and finally prosperity will be the end result. unto Himself, by Him I say whether they be things in the air or in heaven." By one man, Jesus Christ, the whole world has been redeemed, and those sins will not be imputed against us. Once anyone accept Jesus Christ as his savior and Lord he is made free, the past is over. Our fathers followed worldly tradition and culture and we are all under curse saved by the blood of the lamb. The blood of Jesus Christ is a powerful redeemer.

1John 2:2 "And He Himself is the propitiation for our sins, and not for ours only but also for the whole world." So this is the greatest miracle in the history of the world that one man's blood has saved the whole world given the chance to receive salvation by confessing the name of Jesus Christ. This is the blood that heals your diseases, the blood which is the medicine without expiring date which has the miraculous potential to heal every disease by faith. There are two weapons given to the Christian for his welfare, [1] the blood of Jesus Christ which heals all our diseases and [2] the name of Jesus which make every prayer possible.

THE PROMISE LAND.

The Old Testament Promise land

In the old testament, the promise land was known as CANAAN. Abraham's father was mandated to go to Canaan but unfortunately died in the process of his journey to Canaan in HARAN. Genesis 11:31-32. Abraham's father Terah believed in God but represented God with objects, and did not know he was practicing idolatry. He did not give his heart completely to God unknowingly, but was religious and godly than the rest of the people. His improvised and partial friendly with God became the true worship of God at that time and paved way for the promised land. Why the promise land? Because God wanted to separate Terah and his descendants from the rest of the sinful world at that time so they can commit themselves as a nation to God. Ur was the place of conception of the mission of Canaan to Terah in the city of Chaldeans, meaning Ur was where Abraham's father lived before the revelation of Canaan was revealed and assigned to him. Chaldea was known as Mesopotamia, it joins Armenia and Euphrates. It was a land where more wheat was produced. This was the ancient name of Persia being southern part of Babylonia. Canaan was known as low land situated at the west of the Jordan and the Red Sea and between these waters and Mediterranean was given by God to Abraham and his descendants, the children of Israel. After the death of Abraham's father, Abram was frustrated. But his relationship with God was very strong, He believed in God, trusted God and sought His presence always, Abraham saw the mistake of his father and corrected that mistake by serving God without objects and this was the result of the continuation of the mission resulting in Gen. 12:4-5. Now the Lord had said to Abraham "Get out of your country, from your family and from your father's house to a land that I will show you. I will make you a great nation; I will bless you And make your name great; And you shall be a blessing. I will bless those who bless you And I will curse him who curse you. And in you, all the families of the earth shall be blessed." The bible says, Abraham departed as the Lord had commanded him to take everything and follow Him to the promise land which was mandated to his father, Terah. And Abraham was seventy-five years old when he departed from Haran Then

217

Abraham took Sarah his wife and Lot his brother's son, and all their possessions that they had gathered and the people whom they had acquired in Haran and they departed to go to the land of Canaan. So they came to the land of Canaan." Abraham obeyed God and believed whatever God told him to be true and acted, left his country and departed as God said. God blessed Abraham as He promised. The bible says Abraham was very rich in Cattle, in Silver and in Gold. Abraham never stopped remembering God, wherever he went, he called on His name. Gen. 13:1-4. After the conflict with Lot he finally came to the land of Canaan. Isaac was born in the land of Canaan, Sarah, Isaac's mother and Abraham's wife died in Canaan Gen. 23:2. Sarah was buried at Canaan Gen 23:19. Abraham lived and died in Canaan and was buried at Canaan near his wife Sarah Gen 25:10. This means God fulfilled His promise by bringing Abraham to the promise land. So Abraham brought the Hebrews to the promise land as God's people. Hebrew was the ancient name of Israel. But the twelve tribe rebelled against God by rejecting the revelation God gave to Joseph and plotted to kill him. Even the father whose name is Jacob rejected the revelation. And God has to glorify Himself somewhere else. For them to know that Joseph's anointing on him was from God, and that revelation has to come to pass, so God was glorify in Egypt instead of Canaan - Israel. God said, the whole Israel, the twelve tribes and Jacob himself will bow before Joseph as the dream said so for rebellion they were damned to slavery and remained in Egypt. And as time went by they became and remained slaves which made them begin to cry unto God. And God who abide by His promise has to intervene by the hand of Moses back to the promised land. The creator did not stop creating human beings either bond or free for His glory, therefore He desired to save all and that led to the advent of Jesus Christ, His prophecy, His birth, His life and works on earth, His crucifixion, His resurrection back with the disciples, His ascension and His deity, resulting in the final completion of salvation not to Jews only but the world as whole.

New Testament Promise Land :-

Christ has appointed unto us a kingdom, where all the Christians will be led by Christ to the promise land of Heaven and this is the new testament Promise Land. The new testament promise land is different from the old testament promise land, in that about the old testament promise land, the people knew where they were going but did not know how to get there, but the Christ promised land is more complex and difficult for one to believe and explain, which means the Christian faith is more stronger than the Hebrews faith to the promise land for (1) the Christians do not know where that promise land is located but (2) know how to get there and how it's going to come. If our hope, the Lord and our savior Christ Jesus fails to come back then all the Christians have failed and misled and are in terrible trouble. But we trust in Him because He is God the Son. And God does not lie. As Christians we strongly have that faith and cannot be disputed. Some people had gone there and are still there, Enoch, Elijah and Jesus Himself and Jesus took the disciples to the mountain and transfigured and show them those people with Him, Enoch as Moses and Elijah. As Enoch and Elijah continue with Him so Jesus urges Christians to continue with Him. Luke 22:28-30. "But you are those who have continued with Me in my trials. And I appoint upon you a kingdom as My Father had appointed unto Me. That you may eat and drink at My table in My kingdom and sit on thrones judging the twelve tribes of Israel." Even when we do not have His physical presence, we continue with Him till He comes back. We have the faith that He will come back, which Christians are having super faith beyond the faith of Abraham, believing to receive what does not exist, a destination very difficult to describe and not easy for any ordinary Christian or person to believe. A believe, some may call it craziness. Abraham knew where he was going, he knew Canaan existed and where it was situated but heaven who can tell where it could be found but we believe and trust God to be there for us, a destination we are yet to reach. Jesus is the Lamb and the church is the bride and so Jesus says those who will continue in this call will share with Him the marriage supper celebration, Quote "Rev. 19:9. Blessed are they which are called into the marriage supper of the Lamb."

Jesus has promised Christians that He is going to prepare the promised Land and come back to take those who will wait John 14:1-3. "Let not your heart be troubled; you believe in God, believe also in Me. In My Father's house are many mansions; if it were not so I would have told you. I go to prepare a place for you. And if I go and prepare a place for you, I will come again and receive you unto Myself; that where I am, there you may be also." He had even promised us that whatever Christians had left behind and followed Him will not be wasted but they will receive hundred fold in this period of salvation on earth and in heaven. Matt. 19:28-30. In 2Peter 3:13. "Nevertheless we according to His promise look for new Heaven and a new Earth where in dwells righteousness." So the place Our Lord and Savior Jesus Christ is preparing, is the new heaven and the new earth meant for those who will patiently wait for His second coming.

Jesus said in John 3:11-12 "Most assuredly, I say to you We speak what We know and testify what We have seen and you do not receive Our witness. If I told you earthly things and you do not believe, how will you believe if I tell you heavenly things."

We have to consider that things of the old testament are physical and that of the new testament are more of the spiritual realm. Eg. The old testament baptism was the circumcision of the foreskin but the new testament circumcision has nothing to do with the foreskin but the receiving of the Holy Spirit or Holy Ghost baptism. If right now you will repented and accepted the Lord Jesus as your Lord and Savior, you will be saved and will be part of the mission to heaven. Because by grace we are saved through faith in Jesus Christ which is gift of God and not ourselves.

WHY SMOKING CIGARETTE.

Smoking is sin in the house of God (the Lord). Because the bible says the body is the temple of God, and the temple of God is where the angels of God and the Spirit of God dwell. So when you smoke, you drive the spirit of God and the angels of God away or suffocate them to evacuate them out of the temple. The man who smokes, he brings toxic chemical into the temple of God, that's the body, to kill the angels of God and the Holy Spirit. So the smoker is a killer and a criminal because smoking is a crime. Every criminal is liable for judgment and liable for punishment.

CHEMISTRY OF CIGARETTE SMOKE:-

Scientist have found that Cigarette Smoke contain nicotine, carbon monoxide, carbon dioxide, nitrate methane, nitrogen dioxide, hydrogen sulphide, carcinogenic (tars), methyl alcohol, glycerine, glyco (alcohol and esters), acetaldehyde, acroliein, acetone, prussic acid, carboxyle derivatives (acids), chrysene, nicotrosamines (alkaloids), cresols (phenols), radioactive compounds (nickel, polonium, plutonium), hydrocarbon (benzopyrene, benzene, isoprene, toluene, arsenic, cadmium, naphthylamines. This is the chemistry of cigarette smoke which are dangerous chemicals. They are all dangerous toxics. It has been found by scientist and medical doctors that the tars(carcinogenic) in the cigarette smoke create a film deposit on the walls of the respiratory tract and the lungs and cause them change color to become black and is the cause of many lung cancer diseases. If a smoker smokes a pack of cigarette per day, it's equivalent to a small beer glass of tar per year, into the lungs which may also sum up to 225 gr. on average. Carbon monoxide (Co) is an asphyxiating gas which is normally produced by car exhaust fumes which is 1.5% of the composition of the fume. That of cigarette is said to be higher than that of the car which is 3.2% of carbon monoxide and slowly asphyxiates the blood and needs twelve to twenty-four hours to dissipate, which could result in blocking of the arteries. Nicotine is a powerful insecticide and poisonous for the nervous system which also cause addiction, a demonic chemical. According to scientists, four sticks of cigarette contain fifty milligrams of nicotine which is enough to kill a man if used as an injection into the blood stream. The nicotine is diluted in the smoke which take a short time to reach the brain, stimulates the brain cells and block the nervous impulse and cause addiction. Nicotine speeds up heart rate and cause contracting and hardening of the arteries, the heart then pumps more and receives little blood putting the heart in a terrible labor or over work and can cause heart failure, and lead to death.

POLITICS OF CIGARETTE:-

No Government will allow his citizens to smoke but for the sake to maintain the factory and the workers and the taxes, governments encourage the existence of the cigarette factory. For this Jesus has cause governments to provide a law against smoking. On every pack of cigarette it is written : DANGEROUS TO YOUR HEALTH; WHICH MEANS YOU DON'T HAVE TO SMOKE AND THE SMOKER IS LIABLE FOR PUNISHMENT, WHICH COULD BE SPIRITUAL, and we see smokers getting terrible illness. Smoking is committing a slow suicide, and committing suicide is a crime. Cigarette smoking is not good for our health. Someone may say Why? and this alone is not enough. Cigarette is obtain from tobacco with little amount of nicotine added to it which can lead the smoker to a very serious illness as stated above. So we say cigarette is a refined tobacco with insecticide(nicotine) and toxic sheet of paper and a filter, which are all chemically processed. Now when we smoke cigarette, this tobacco turns to carbon dioxide and carbon monoxide, and such as tars(carcinogenic). When carbon dioxide and carbon monoxide are combined, they produce FREE RADICALS(free electrons) as proven by scientist. Free radicals are electrons without atoms (very harassing and aggressive electrons). An electron and an atom when combined or put together produce ENERGY. The human body has already its atoms and its equivalent electrons which give us energy. Each puff of cigarette contains thirty-two (30-32) electrons (as proven by scientists) multiply by the number of puffs per stick of cigarette multiply by the number of sticks of cigarette we smoke per day. The electrons from the smoke admitted into the body struggle with the electrons already in the body and eat up the body atoms produced, meant for the citizen electrons, why? because they are fresh and they are strong. These foreign electrons(free radicals) do not last for long, they last for twenty-four hours and within this period they cause terrible harm to the body. They are like Boko Haram(free radicals), this organization will die out in couple of years but it will cause terrible and horrible tragedy, if not stopped. So stop free radicals (the boko haram in your body) by stopping smoking. The remaining electrons which have no atoms must also live, so they slowly attack the body cells. And any sickness can be a major illness after many years.

THE DEVIL OF CIGARETTE SMOKE

Illness mostly known are : 1. STROKE; 2. CANCER' 3. TUMOUR; 4. ULCER and so on. Carbon is an element which, when taken in excess make one feels tired always, leading to serious sickness. So we say carbon produce fatigue. So when free electrons are in excess they invade the heart to influence the brain and cause the following:

1. SELFISHNESS 2. GREEDINESS 3. JEALOUSY 4. CORRUPTION 5. HATRED. These are great enemies of the world. They are enemies fighting mankind to destroy them. We now know them so let us be cautious, and avoid them.

NITROGEN = 14 atoms + 28 electrons or molecules (as published in news letter yrs ago). CO_2 = 44 electrons + No atom (published in news letter yrs ago).

By these mathematics we can now be very careful with cigarette smoking. This smoke kills hundreds of people a day. It is as dangerous as the gun even terrible than the gun. The gun kills one at a time but the smoke kills hundreds at a time and the worse of it, some of the victims suffer illness for many years before they are killed. If we can stop cigarette smoking, our cities will be wonderful cities to live. It's stressful and uncomfortable if non smoker has smokers around him smoking. Truth is only one and that's the truth, smokers are selfish and do not consider how other people feel when they are smoking around them, even when others are dying they only think of their satisfaction at that particular moment. The bible says in; 1Corinthians 3:16-17 "Do you not know that you are the temple of God and that the Spirit of God dwells in you? If anyone defiles the temple of God, God will destroy him. For the temple of God is holy, which temple you are." Again 1Corinthians 6:19 also says "Do you not know that your body is the temple of the Holy Spirit who is in you, whom you have from God, and you are not your own? For you are bought at a price; therefore glorify God in your body and in your spirit, which are God's." This is a plain sayings and you do not need explanation therefore why do people smoke. They are killing themselves and killing innocent people. The smoker and the sniper are no difference.

IDLE WORDS.

The bible advices us that the words that proceed out of the mouth of a person forms the boarders[coast] of your life. Word is powerful, swift, and dangerous, and anything can happen to where it's landed. Therefore whatever you say with your mouth will surely come into reality in your life. Words are spirit therefore once a word is spoke unto a person it mixes with the spiritual pattern of the person and gradually draws the pattern of the object, which becomes the ghost of that object and completely create that object to be the boarders of that person's life. When an architect wants to put up a building, he first imagines it and then put it on paper that forms the ghost, the blue print and with the ghost he will determine the cost of the project, then it is put into physical realm and we see with our eyes a mighty building. Curse, blessings, and prophecy is like that. So once we say something unto a person it is spiritually inscribed in his life which begins to rule his life afterwards. In John 3:11-13. says, "Verily, verily, I say unto thee, we speak that we do know, and testify that we have seen; and ye received not our witness. If I have told you earthly things, and ye believe not, how shall ye believe, if I tell you of heavenly things? And no man hath ascended up to heaven, but he that came down from heaven, even the Son of man which is in heaven." There are things which are very difficult to believe because they are spiritual, it is descend. Only by the spirit of discernment those things could be comprehended.

In Mark 7:15. "There is nothing from without a man, that entering into him can defile him; but the things which come out of him, those are they that defile the man." Jesus continue to explain in Mark 15:18-23. "Do ye not perceive, that whatsoever thing from without entereth into the man, it cannot defile him. Because it entereth not into his heart, but into the belly, and goeth out into the draught, purging all meat? And said, that which cometh out of the man that defile the man. For from within, out of the heart of men, proceed evil thoughts, adulteries, fornication, murders, thefts, covetousness wickedness, deceit, lasciviousness, an evil eye, blasphemy, pride, foolishness: All these evil things come from within, and defile the man." So man by the above acts produce evil spirits into the world. So in Matt. 5:21-22 "Ye have heard that it was said by them of old time, Thou shall not kill: and whosoever shall kill shall be in danger of the judgment. But I say unto you that whosoever is angry with his brother without a cause shall be in danger of the judgment: and whosoever shall say to his brother 'RACA' shall be in danger of the council: but whosoever shall say, 'THOU FOOL' shall be in danger of hell fire." Jesus came to eliminate evil spirits because they are dangerous in the life of man, so He was casting them out and make sure they do not live, and if mankind should use violence evil word to cause the production of demons such person will face the council and the hell fire (meaning you will face God the father, God the son and God the Holy ghost) as the council and be delivered to Satan as the hell fire. That is the punishment and the consequences of bleeding unclean spirits into the world. It is very sad to hear a mother tells her own child 'stupid,' injecting the spirit of stupidity into a child, conceived nine months, to torment the child, forgetting the pain she went through for the nine months. It's just sad. People insult God, they insult Christ and insult the Holy ghost but the bible warns that they should be careful for what comes out of their mouth, because it will

definitely bring curse upon them.

Matt. 12 31-32. "Wherefore I say unto you, All manner of sin and blasphemy shall be forgiven unto men: the blasphemy against the holy Spirit shall not be forgiven unto men. And whosoever speaketh a word against the son of man, it shall be forgiven him: but whosoever speaketh against the Holy Ghost, it shall not be forgiven him, neither in this world, and neither in the world to come." The new testament again says: in vs. 36-37 that every idle word that men shall speak, they shall give account thereof in the day of judgment. For by thy word thou shall be justified, and by thy word thou shall be condemned. Lev.24:15-16. "And thou shall speak unto the children of Israel, saying whosoever curseth his God shall bear his sin. And he that blasphemeth the name of the Lord, he shall surely be put to death, and all the congregation shall certainly stone him: as well the stranger, as he that is born in the land, who blasphemeth the name of the Lord, shall be put to death." Blasphemy against the Holy ghost is very serious offence and God warns mankind to refrain from that, because of it's bleeding of unclean spirits and the curse it brings unto mankind. For that Christ destroyed evil spirit and gave us power to continue to destroy them and their works. In Luke 9:1. "Then He called his disciples together, and gave them power and authority over all devils and to cure diseases."

And Luke 10:8-9. "And into whatsoever city ye enter, and they receive you, eat such thing as are set before thee, and heal the sick that are therein, and say unto them, the kingdom of God is come nigh unto you." Christ has given us power over serpents, and scorpions and over all the power of the enemy but we have to use this power carefully. These evil spirits or unclean spirits don't cease trying, if one plan fails they try another plan, they go to churches, to the markets, grave yards, in the sea, holes, in the air, jungles etc. but the bible says we are complete in Him which is the head of all principalities and powers. Jesus told us exactly where to instruct the demon to go, revealing the power of the word of God and encourage us to be specific in our prayer with authority given to us over demons. When we tell the mountains to move, we should tell it where to go. Matt. 21:21-22. Else it will be loitering and possess an innocent person or will not move at all, because it does not know where to go, Matt. 12:43-45. We do not have to play with the enemy.

Idle words fuses with ones ability of determination and encourages various difficulties. People talk their difficulties because there is no sufficient space in the mind for that knowledge of difficulties. It is unwise to tell ones secret to one who is not necessary to be told. Ones progress is a secret affair so if you want to progress keep your mouth shut and keep your eyes and ears opened and do what you have to do. What comes out of your mouth forms the boarders of your life so be careful of the words that issues out of your mouth.

Idle Words brings the denial of God's help in time of need and judgment. Words have power, every word carries power and once the word is spoken power will be released.

2Timothy 2:16. "But shun profane and idle babblings for they will increase to more ungodly."

Words can cause terrible damage or cause wonderful good things or healing. Good words that come out of the heart cause manifestation outside likewise bad words.

Jesus said in John 6:63. "It is the Spirit which gives life, the flesh profit nothing. The words that I speak to you are Spirit and they are life." Because Jesus was speaking good words, they are spirit that carry life and give salvation.

Proverbs 4:23 Keep your heart with all diligence, For out of it springs the issues of life.

People with heart troubles are always confused because the heart is the instrument for understanding and is disorganized. Bitterness escalates heart troubles and results in hatred.

Matt. 12:36-37. "But I say to you that for every idle word men may speak, they will give account of it in the day of judgment. For by your word you will be justified, and by your word you will be condemned." So each and everyone shall account for the words that we spoke as idle as they are.

Roman 6:16. "Do you not know that to whom you present yourself slaves to obey, you are that ones slaves whom you obey whether of sin leading to death or of obedience leading to righteousness."

What is secret is that which consists of your Christian faith. Words could be deadly or could be fruitful, a life giver. As new Christian or a baby in Christ, you expect God to honor your desires and God understands that because that's the order of babies, but for a matured Christian your expectation is to obey and do the will of God and that's what makes you a Christian.

Ephesians 4:29-31. "Let no corrupt word proceed out of your mouth but what is good for necessary edification, that may impact grace to the hearer. And do not grieve the Holy Spirit of God, by whom you were sealed for the day of redemption. Let all bitterness, wrath, anger, clamor and evil speaking be put away from you with all malice."

Lev. 24:14. "Take outside the camp him who has cursed then let all who heard him lay their hands on his heard, and let all congregation stone him."

In the time of Moses those who curse or speak idle words are eliminated from the face of the earth. But for the grace of Jesus Christ, we live. So stop cursing.

Colossians 3:8-9. "But now you yourselves are to put off all these, anger, wrath, malice, blasphemies, filthy language out of your mouth. Do not lie to one another since you have put of the old man with his deeds."

CHAPTER FOUR

THE HOLY BIBLE

The word BIBLE means – Basic Instruction Before Leaving Earth.
The word HOLY means — He Only Loves You.

Therefore because He, Jesus loves you, you must be able to acquire his basic instruction and apply them before leaving this material earth, to enable you to have a better accountability. Judgment is the final application to come upon man before the final destination. In otherwise Holy Bible means He Only Loves You of The Basic Instruction Before Leaving Earth, meaning all are required to know the bible. The bible is the name given to a revelation in a study containing different books compiled and bind into a single book. The bible means book. A word derived from a Greek word "LA BIBLA." This bible is the one we call the "THE HOLY BIBLE." The bible is a complete library and contains all the revelations and books of the spirit and the living. It is the word of God, full of grace and full of truth, the bread of life,sent from above for a sacrifice unto salvation. The holy bible is the proof of the "SCIENCE in GOD." It is the DIVINE FORMULA which is applied to solve the problems of life. In some case the bible is referred to as:-

1. The scripture - the recorded spoken word of God.
2. The Oracle - the spoken word of God.
3. The word - the voice of God.
4. The Testament - testimonies and revelation.
5. Covenant - agreement for salvation between God and man.
6. The Law - the spoken order or command from God.
7. The Canonical - the sacred books

The bible is made of two parts namely:-

1. the old testament - the mosaic and prophetic covenant and the writings
2. the new testament - the new covenant: works and revelations of Jesus Christ.

The bible contains 66 books :-

a. 39 books of the old testament.
b. 27 books of the new testament.

The old testament is divided into four parts:-

1. **Genesis to Deuteronomy** - the Torah, being the Law known as the Pentateuch, which is the five books of Moses. [The Pentateuch is the instruction according to the time - communiqué.] There is confusion about the books that Moses wrote. We have been hearing of six and seven book of Moses and eight, nine, and ten books of Moses, there is nothing like that. Moses wrote only five books, the rest are occult made books by secret societies, imagined, formulated and written to suit their own occult purposes. These societies invented them. As a Christian if you read those books you can be possessed and your salvation will be useless and meaningless. The old testament is known as TANAKH, which is the Jewish bible, made of the Torah - the Jewish laws, the Neviim - the prophets, and the Ketuvim - the writings or poets. The Tanakh is the canonical collection of the Jewish text compiled and preserved as the sacred book of the Jewish people. The Talmud is the center piece of the rabbinic Judaism being the Jewish cultural life, the Jewish ethics, the Jewish civil and ceremonial laws, and has two components, (1). the Gemara - the component of the Talmud which is the written rabbinical analytic theology and (2). Mishnah which is the oral rabbinic theological literature. So the combination of the Gamara and the mishnah constituted the Talmud. There are the Babylonian talmud and Jerusalem talmud. More attention is given to the Midrash that is the exegesis which is

the explanation and interpretation by the ancient judaic authorities of the Tanakh.

2. **Joshua to Esther** - History. the Gemara **3. Job to Song of songs** - Poetry [poems]; the Ketuvim **4. Isaiah to Malachi** - Prophets [prophecies] the Neviim

The new testament is from Matthew to Revelations.

They are also divided into four parts namely:-

1. Matthew to John - Gospel [biography of Jesus Christ - God Himself came down for the salvation of the world].
2. Acts - History [the acts of the apostles].
3. Romans to Jude - Epistle [correspondence – Laws - the communiqué].
4. Revelation - Apocalypse [the prophecies].

So the old and the new testaments are identical. They have four identical features:

1. the Law; 2. History; 3. Poetry (correspondence); 4. Prophecies.

THE BOOKS OF THE BIBLE AND THE AUTHORS

THE OLD TESTAMENT

1 Genesis - Moses; 2. Exodus - Moses; 3. Leviticus - Moses; 4. Numbers - Moses ; 5. Deuteronomy – Moses; 6. Joshua – Joshua ; 7. Judges – Samuel ; 8. Ruth – Samuel; 9. 1Samuel – Samuel; 10. 2Samuel – Nathan(1Chro. 29:29); 11.1Kings –Jeremiah; 12. 2Kings – Jeremiah; 13. 1Chronicles – Ezra; 14. 2Chronicles – Ezra; 15. Ezra – Ezra; 16. Nehemiah – Nehemiah; 17. Esther – Unknown(but some say Ezra); 18. Job – Job; 19. Psalms – David; 20. Proverbs – Solomon; 21. Ecclesiastes – Solomon; 22. Songs of Songs – Solomon; 23. Isaiah – Isaiah; 24. Jeremiah – Jeremiah; 25. Lamentations – Jeremiah; 26. Ezekiel – Ezekiel; 27. Daniel – Daniel; 28. Hosea –Hosea; 29. Joel - Joel; 30 Amos - Amos; 31 Obadiah - Obadiah; 32.Jonah - Jonah; 33. Micah - Micah; 34.Nahum - Nahum; 35. Habakkuk - Habakkuk; 36.

Zephaniah - Zephaniah; 37. Haggai - Haggai; 38 Zechariah - Zechariah; 39. Malachi - Malachi Moses wrote 5 books; Jeremiah wrote 4 books; Samuel wrote 3 books; Ezra wrote 3 books and Esther.

THE NEW TESTAMENT

1. Matthew - Matthew; 2. Mark - Mark; 3. Luke - Luke; 4. John –John; 5. Acts – Luke; 6..Romans - Paul; 7.1Corinthians – Paul; 8. 2Corinthians – Paul; 9. Galatians - Paul; 10. Ephesians – Paul; 11. Philippians- Paul; 12. Colossians- Paul; 13. 1Thesselonians - Paul; 14. 2Thesselonians - Paul; 15.1Timothy – Paul; 16. 2 Timothy – Paul; 17. Titus - Paul; 18. Philemo - Paul; 19.Hebrews - Paul; 20. James - James; 21. 1Peter – Peter; 22. 2Peter – Peter; 23. 1John – John; 24. 2John – John; 25. 3John – John; 26. Jude – Jude; 27. Revelation - John.

Paul wrote 14 books; John wrote 5 books; Luke 2books; Peter 2 books.

Jesus said in Matthew 5:17 :- "Think not that I am come to destroy the law or the prophets: I am not come to destroy but to Fulfilled." The new testament did not come to condemn the old testament but rather the new testament is the update of the old testament which is to put Satan in pain and put him out of business, if mankind stay out of sin, Satan is out of business. So we see that the new testament and the old testament are identical: both have history, prophecy, Laws, and poetry. The new testament did not condemn the old testament but rather made it Complete. So the bible say you cannot add nothing and you cannot take out anything from the scripture. The holy bible is a divine formula which is used to obtain divine answers. There is no problem in life without formula, every verse of the bible is a solution to someone's problem. Applying the principles of the bible in your life in the name of Jesus is that divine formula, ordained to work miracles.

eg. love + charity + hope + peace = prosperity and love + faith + hope + peace = salvation.

The bible is filled with all the subjects of the world. Eg.

1. **Medicine -** King Hezekiah was sick unto death and he was given medicine to heal. 2Kings20:7, King Asa disconnected from God and connected with physicians 2Chro.16:12

2. **Engineering -** King Uzziah built war machines; 2Chro. 26:14-15 - Bezaleel molding of gold and silver cutting of stones and calving of timber; Exo. 31:1-5 Noah built the first ship Gen. 6:14

3. **Politics -** Jethro the father-in-law of Moses advises Moses to appoint ministers Exo. 18:13-27

4. **Management -** Planning - Luke 14:28-30

5. **Science -**the revelation of advancing and reversal of the day as a sign to Hezekiah by prophet Isaiah -2Kings 20:9 -11, scientific accuracy about marriage(the chemistry of love) -Matt. 19:4-6, 2Kings 4:34 Elisha stretches himself to keep the body of the dead boy warm to bring him back to life(transfer of body heat) the tender branches of the trees indicates that summer is near. Matt. 24:32, (agriculture).

6. **Accounting -** Jacob's counting and recording of the flock -Gen. 30:31-32 Taking inventory & reporting.

7. **Marketing -** Joseph sold to all nations -Gen.41:56-57

8. **Economics -** Joseph takes over Egyptian economy - Gen 41:39:40,48-49, made nation of Egypt rich. The prophet Elisha Predicting the STOCK EXCHANGE of the next day in 2Kings 7:1 "Then Elisha said, hear the word of the Lord. Thus says the Lord: Tomorrow about this time a seah (2 gallons approx.) of fine flour shall be sold for a shekel, at the gate of Samaria." Which came to pass. In the time of Elijah, the stock exchange was dependent on the word of the prophets, since there were no computers, and people traded according to the prophesies (predictions) of the prophets. So if you want to have a great business or education, consult the bible. Every verse of the holy bible has healing power, miraculous power and blessing for mankind. All these will manifest through the heart. It's very important to take care of your heart because it's the communication center of the word to the spirit. And you can take care of it by avoiding the holding onto offences such as bitterness, anger, hatred, pain of the past, envy, jealousy, violence and all forms of wickedness. Christianity depends on the heart. With our heart we know Christ and we know that Jesus has the power to heal, bless, deliver and saves, and we are committed to Him. With the offences in the heart, the bible becomes history

book. The holy bible is a mirror through which one reads and look at himself in God's word. So with those offences in the heart, it darkens the sensors of the word, making the transmitters incapable to communicate and cannot enable the reader to see himself in the word of God. Sometimes we pray that our enemies die so we can be blessed, but God has said in Psalm 23, I will prepare a table before you in the presence of your enemies, God is an intelligent God, if your enemies are not alive, that table is useless. Your enemies must live to see the blessing of God in your life to let them know the greatness of God in your life. This shows that it is waste of time to be hampering over your enemies. Jesus said pray for them. Train your heart to ignore the offences, be cleansed

and be perfect.

THE BIBLE SLOGAN

This is my bible. It is the word of God. - John 1:1-5
Full of truth and full of grace - John 1:14
It is the bread of life - John 6:48
Sent from Heaven - John 6:29, 33, 38, 42
For a sacrifice unto salvation - John 19:15,18.
I believe every word, written in it.
Father help me to walk before you and be perfect through Your word.
In the mighty name of Jesus Christ.

The bible is a book,written out of inspiration for every human being to study. It is the map and the global positioning system of life. Life based upon the bible will never go into a ditch because the word BIBLE signifies BASIC, INSTRUCTION, BEFORE, LIFE, ENDS, It is the basic instruction for every being to abide by before he dies.

UNDERSTANDING GOD

The bible say God is omnipotent, omniscient and omnipresent; by which the Greek explain as:

Omni - meaning All

Potenza - power and authority

Praesent - in everywhere; form of space, nothing is hidden from.

Scienta - Knowledge, full of science; science is knowledge: it is the proof of the existence of God, full of wisdom. Science is knowing almost everything.

Omnipotenza - Omnipotent - EL-Sabaoth, All powerful Rev. 19:6, Colo. 2:9-10, Matt. 28:18.

Omnipraesenta - Omnipresent - El-Shammah, All seeing and in everywhere, Matt. 18:20.

Omniscienta - Omniscient - El-Roi, All knowing, having solution to every situation. John 1:47-49.

There are certain scientific situations, only God can explain or prove them. Raising the dead, healing the sick and prophesies, through whoever avails himself and ordained by God for such works.

Melchizedek, the king of Salem(Canaan) shared sacrament with Abraham in the name of El-Elyon (Most High God) Gen. 14:18. When God asked Abraham to leave his country Ur (Syria) and head to Canaan, God was already there in the person of Melchizedek, Gen. 12:1-4.

Eloah - Singular

Elohim - Plural

El - God represents both singular and the plural

El-Shaddai - God of sufficiency, God who is enough, Almighty God.

Jesus is the physical part of God, which communicates with world (humanity): the terrestrial bodies.

The Holy Ghost is the part of God which communicates with the angelic world: the celestial bodies. The speed of the Holy Ghost is unimeasurable, even so is the Godhead bodily, that's The Father and the Lord Jesus Christ.

God is a great Light and communicates with the two: Jesus Christ and the Holy Ghost. The three has the power to come together or to compress into One Entity - the TRI-NITY.

El-Micha - Likeness of God, Image of the invisible God. He who is like God.

El-Gabri - The Mouth of God. Messenger of God. information and communication.

El-Rapha - The healing power and Deliverance God and justice Gen. 15:22-26.

El-Isra - One who struggled with God.

El-Rahee - God who see. Gen.16:13.

El-Hakavod - The God of glory Psalm 29:3.

El-Sali - The God of my rock Psalm 42:10.

El-Emet - The God of truth Psalm 31:6.

El-Emmunah - Faithful God.

El-Chaiyal - God of life.

Elohay Kedem - God of the beginning Deut. 33:27.

Elohay Mishpat - God of Justice Isaiah 30:18.

Elohay Sehchot - God of forgiveness Neh. 9:17.

Elohay Maron - God of Heights Micah 6:6.

Elohay Mikarov - God who is near Jer. 23:23.

Elohay Mauzi - God of strength Psalm 43:2.

Elohay Talilati - God of my praise Psalm109:1.

Elohay Yishi - God of my salvation Psalm 18:46.

Elohay Elohim - God of Gods Deut. 10:17.

Elohim Kedoshim - Holy God Lev. 19:2, Josh. 24:19.

Elohim Chaiyim - Living God Jer. 10:10.

El-Shaddai - All Mighty, All Sufficient Gen. 17:1.

El-Hagodol - The Great God Deut. 10:17.

Ei-Ha Kadosh - The Holy God Isaiah 5:16.

El-Yisrael - The God of Israel Psalm 68:35, Ezra 5:1.

El-De'ot - The God of knowledge 1Sam. 2:3.

El-Elyon - The Most High God Gen. 14:18.

Ehye Asher Ehye - I am that I am Exo. 3:14.

El-Emmanu - God with us Isaiah 7:14.

El-Olam - God of Eternity Gen. 21:33.

El-Echad - The One God. Mal. 2:10.

El-Sh'maya V'arah - God of Heaven and Earth Ezra 5:11.

El-Gibor (EL-Hagibor) - Mighty, Strong Valiant God.

El-Hanorah - Fearful, Dreadful, Terrible, Awful, Holy Marvelous, Wonderful God. Deut. 10:20.

Tetragramaton meaning Yahweh (YHWH) from Hebrew verb "To Be."

Melech ha Melachim - The King of Kings - His superiority to the earth rulers.

YHWH M'Kadesh - The Lord who makes Holy. Ezek. 37:28.

YHWH Yireh - The Lord who provides Gen. 22:14.

YHWH Nissi - The Lord My Banner. Exo. 17:15.

YHWH Shalom - The Lord of peace. Judges 6:24.

YHWH Tzikaynu - The Lord our righteousness Jer. 33:16.

YHWH Osaynu - The Lord our maker Psalm 95:6.

YHWH Shammah - The Lord is present.

Jesus shared the same attributes YHWH as the "I AM" when challenged by some Jewish leaders, regarding His claim of seeing Abraham. He clearly claimed to be YHWH as He presented Himself in John 8:56-59. Before Abraham was born "I AM" and those Jewish leaders understood that Jesus was claiming to be YHWH. The Holy Spirit testified this through Paul in Rom. 10:9, Rom. 10:13, also Joel 2:32, whoever will call the name of the Lord will be saved. Yeshuais YHWH (Lord) the Messiah. In the word YD;V' (Shaddai), there are three letters V,D,Y. The ancient Rabbis took those three Hebrew letters and made an acrostic. The V'(shin) stands for shaqad which means "watching." The D(dalet) Stands for delet which means "door." And the Y(yod)stands for (Israel.) So in this symbolizing name SHADDAI signifies "The One Who Watches the Doors of Israel." He is the One Who Guards Israel. We have all sinned and deserved God's judgment. God the Father, sent His Only Son to satisfy that judgment for those who believe in Him. Jesus the creator and the eternal Son of God who lived a sinless life, loved us so much that He died for our sins, taking the punishment that we deserved, was buried and rose from death the next day. If you truly believe and trust this in your heart, receiving Jesus alone as your Savior, declaring Jesus is Lord, you will be saved from judgment, and spend eternity with God in heaven.

1. God wants us to know that, He is greater than our enemy.
2. Our God is great because He is not subject to human short comings.

3. Our God is great because He defends the weak.
4. Our God is great because His works are great.

El-Shaddai (YD;V"-la) Almighty, Omnipotent, All Sufficieny, God who is enough.

tzWzm(mezuzit) - El-Shaddai - And you shall write them on the door post of your houses and on your gates. Deut. 6:9(428/4-5). El - God, Shad - who is, Dai - Enough. Isaiah 45:15 Truly, You are God who hide Yourself, O God of Israel, the Savior.

Heb. 1:3 "Who being the brightness of His glory, and upholding all things by the word of His power, when He had by Himself purged our sins, sat down on the right hand of the Majesty on high." So the brightness of the glory of God gives light to the sun and the moon, because God is Light. He is the source of the brightness of the sun and the moon, and source of all authority. And for this reason He is present everywhere; **"The Omnipresent."** Because He is present everywhere, seeing everything so He knows everything. **"The Omniscient."** And the result of the two makes Him the Most Powerful and the Most High God; **"The Omnipotent."** This is the portion of Science in God. God is the wisdom and knowledge of the universe and beyond. **"Shallom"** is a Hebrew word meaning Peace, harmony, completeness, prosperity, welfare, tranquility and wholeness, and idiomatically can mean goodbye or hello, showing the love of God. God is love. Without love there cannot be faith and without love and faith you can go nowhere with Life. Love has eyes to see what one can become in future. Love and faith is the unity in the body. It has the power to reveal the things of the spirit. Love is a spirit and sees in the spirit unto the physical dimension.

THE WORDS OF WISDOM (FACT AND TRUE).

1. As human beings, we have to understand that there is no Life without Light, and we cannot live without it. Light is the foundation of Science and without Light there is no life. Also there is no life without Science. God is light and in Him there is no darkness, meaning we cannot live without God since we cannot live without SCIENCE, because "GOD" is full of science. "SCIENCE" is the study of the proof of the wonders of GOD, which confirms the reality of the existence of "GOD." Without "GOD" there is no "SCIENCE." For this everything is proven by science.

2. Spiritual laws are more severe than physical laws. They are obeyed with all respect. Their consequences are more severe and has no mercy because spiritual laws do not guarantee celestial beings their will but terrestrial beings are given their will because the Lord knows we are flesh. For the greatest mistake a Christian will make is to quit your problem.

3. The reason why Jesus healed the sick and took out problems, was that, He saw sicknesses and problems as unclean spirits or demons and not condition. Do not see your situation as a condition. If you see your situation as a condition, you will die in that condition but if you see your situation as a spirit then you will speak against it and it shall flee from you. Situations are spirits and not conditions. Matt. 12:43-45 Dry places means (unbelievers) bodies without anointing or prayer and the word of God.

4. Christians believe in the Lord Jesus Christ, and we have everlasting life to keep us alive, for we have passed from death to life. Because we have passed from death to life through the resurrection of our Lord Jesus Christ, whoever believes on Him and dies is not dead but asleep, and when the Lord Jesus Christ comes, He will raise him up. He who sleeps is waken up again because he has life in him but he who is dead does not wake up again because there is no life in him. John 6:39-40, 44, 53-54, 50-51; 3:15-16.

5. There are so many doors without security in life, and when they are liberal, demons become real. All things originated from the

spirit and the world we see is of more spiritual than the physical. And if you do not enter into the spirit, you will die in your flesh and go to hell. All come from the heart and the desire of the heart is from the spirit.

6. The new testament is the update of the old testament. Therefore rejecting the new testament means rejecting the old testament, and it is complete rejection of God.

7. The principle of the world is seeing is believing, but the principle of God is believing is seeing which is a contradiction between the old world and the new world.

8. There cannot be human being if there is no "LIGHT" in existence. There must be Light to give Light to every man coming into this world, to stop the aggressions of the darkness. Light is made up of colors, if there is light there is color and color is the visible component in man which contributes to the reality of man. The earth belongs to God and the enemy has taken possession to plant his world on it, to manipulate the inhabitants in it.

9. The preservation of a body with identical memory and identical heart for a normal progression is meaningless in its own time because they will always duplicate, and the expectation for that body's presence on earth is needful in a physical form. There wouldn't be consistent need for it because the space between its reappearing will prolong. (Christ, Holy Ghost and the Father have resembling mind and love, thinking about how they came about is useless. Always only one represents the others. you cannot see them with your naked eyes that's why Christ have to show himself physically at times because His physical presence on earth was needful. We pray always and read His word to connect with Him because His second coming will be awhile).

10. About 70% to 75% of the earth population are being tormented with mental disabilities which is one of Satan's greatest weapons for destruction, and keeps expanding in psychological attacks against ignorant inhabitants. This confusion being cause by current civilization must be taken care of, not by human intelligence but by global spiritual solution that will bring it to an end.

11. Bear in mind that the ability to possess superiority over others around you, is an intention that leads to death. There is a world beyond this our physical world, and for them technological

inventions is natural and normal developments not learned, since those creatures don't have soul. The time of fateful choices and the height of civilization choices are destined to happen at the same time and will cause a change of the earth geophysical structure. Geophysics is the study of the Earth's physical properties and that of the physical processes acting upon, above, and within the Earth. It includes, seismology (earthquakes and elastic waves through the earth or planets), geomagnetism (geological dynamics of the magnetic fields of the earth), meteorology (stars and means of forecasting the weather and earth atmosphere) and oceanography (physical and biological properties of the sea).

12. Astronomy is the branch of science that deals with the celestial objects, space and physical universe as a whole or the study of the sun, moon, stars, planets, comets, gas, galaxies, dust, and other non-earthly bodies and phenomena, including supernova explosions, gamma rays, bursts, and cosmic rays, microwaves, radiation. It applies to mathematics, physics and chemistry in an effort to explain the origin of those objects. Astronomy is one of the oldest of the natural science. The early civilization in record history such as the Babylonians, Greeks, Indians, Egyptians and Nubians, Iranians, Chinese, Maya and many indigenous peoples of the Americas as diverse as astrometry celestial navigation and observational astronomy are considered to be synonymous with astrophysics. "ASTRO" in Greek means "STAR" and "NOMIA" means "LAW" meaning "the Law of Star." Astrophysics is the branch of physics and chemistry to ascertain the nature of astronomical objects rather than their positions or motions in space.

13. Without God there will be no light and there will be no energy as well, no light bulb will give light because the light we see is the reflection and refraction of the light from God.

14. Human point of view is limited. There is no short cut to spiritual maturity, unless earthly understanding gives way to spiritual enlightenment, the world will continue to be far behind the current cosmic advancement.

15. TIME OF LIFE: the orthodox Jewish bible says the time of life is et-chayyah (Gen. 18:10,14) and (2Kings 4:16-17) periods of conception. In every reproductive living thing, God has set a time of life and this is known as a period of conception. Every female has this periods. Some females have single period (time of life) and others have multiple periods (time of life). This has nothing to do with age. At the age of 12-21, 30, 40, 50, 60, 70, 80, 90, a woman can still have this time of life. Likewise animals and trees. For some women their et-chayyah is every two years or every three years, even one year or every four years. You have to understand "THE TIME OF LIFE OF A WOMAN" to set time frame to carry a baby.

16. Exo. 20:13 Thou shall not kill. Deuteronomy 5:17 says the same and according to John 8:44 Satan is a murderer, he is a killer and according to Isaiah 43:7 God has created human beings for His glory and in Gen. 12:2 God told Abraham, I will make you a nation, therefore every single human being constitute a nation. So if a person is killed, a nation is killed, consisting of doctors, engineers, pilots, presidents, kings, accountants, lawyers, politicians, professors etc. and regular citizens. The descendants of Abraham are

1. Ishmael which is the Arabs and
2. Isaac which is the Israelites.

Look at how the Arabs have spread in the Middle East : Saudi Arabia, Iran, Iraq, Libya, Syria, Yemen, kuwait, Oman, United Arab Emirates, etc. And look at how Israelites of the country of Israel has spread all over the world Germany, Russia, Britain, America, Canada etc. The word of God is true. If one man produce ten children, and the ten children also produce ten each, that will be hundred in the next generation, if the ten also produce ten each, that will be a thousand in the second generation so in the fifteen to twentieth generation that will be a country. If Abraham was killed when he went to Egypt, all these countries would have been killed with him. So do not kill, you will cause the end of a nation. If you don't know where you are going after this life you will do stupid things, killing, stealing, occult, etc. The whole world is confused, but with help of Jesus Christ, Christians know where we are going after this life. As you need passport and a visa to travel to another nation on earth, even so you need salvation as your passport and righteousness as your visa to enter into heaven. It is not a place, it is not life, it is not house, it is the power of identification of origin to enter into heaven. It is the passport and visa that tells where the person comes from and where the person will be determined the opportunity of permission for entry. So your salvation and your righteousness will tell your legibility to be given the opportunity for permission of entry, then Christ becomes your gateway. This is Christianity.

17. Problems and troubles are demons and when they show up they must be dealt with severely and systematically.

   (a) Do not under estimate problems or troubles.
   (b) When you encounter problems or troubles, know that they have the capacity or ability to destroy your life and when they do, you will never be the same again.
   (c) If you are the cause of the problem, check yourself and stop the cause.
   (d) If the devil is the cause of your problem, speak against him, meaning rebuke him.
   (e) If the problem was set up by God, your best action is to humble yourself and surrender to God.
   (f) The problems sometimes are your angel which transform and create a new page in life. Do not quit your problems because demons do not quit till they have seen total destruction.
   (g) The reason why Jesus healed the sick and took out problems, was that, He saw sicknesses and problems as unclean spirits or demons and not condition.
   (h) If you see your problem as a condition, then you shall die with it but if you see it as an unclean spirit then you shall speak against it and they will depart to somewhere else. Matt. 12 : 43-35. dry places means bodies without anointing or prayers.

18. When the soul is corrupt, wisdom departs and knowledge hide in your understanding to depart.

19. Wisdom is the treasure of the heart, which attracts knowledge to understand.

20. Knowledge could be purchased, but wisdom is the gift from the Lord, the creator.

21. The old testament covenant is the Jewish covenant which comes with Abrahamic blessing but the new testament covenant which is the Christian covenant is about everlasting life and heaven. Know that covenant is a treaty that cannot be broken. Therefore whoever breaks it, takes a curse upon himself and his descendants.

22. Whoever does not believe in God has no proper sense of life because he is disconnected from God, that is the reason why he does not believe in Jesus Christ not knowing JESUS CHRIST is the legal name of the TRUE GOD.

23. The devil uses what is around you, to destroy what is inside you. Satan cannot curse you because he has no flesh, so he needs a body, either yourself or another person who is a flesh around you to curse you, and this can affect the entire human being.

24. Physical exercise, Physical training or bodily training is good but of limited value, but godliness is valuable in every way, holding promise for the benefit of the present life and also the life near at hand and to come.

25. If you do not know the scripture, you also don't know how far Satan can take you to destroy you, and In short, how dangerous Satan is and who he is.

26. A father is the spiritual authority, and he who has not the Lord Jesus Christ, has no spiritual Father and easily to be sift by Satan.

27. Man has infected and polluted the creations on earth with his corruption and now seek to reach the heavens to corrupt the planets. Scientific exploration is good, it's for the change, development and prosperity of mankind but when our science which is in God, rejects God, that is a catastrophic mindset and leads to chaos and curse. There is God. The moon knows there is God. The sun knows there is God. The animals know there is God. The trees know there is God. The birds know there is God. The mountains know there is God. The stones know there is God. The stars know there is God. The planets know there is God. Only

human beings argue about God, and refuse and reject to believe in God, and have corrupted the animals, the trees, the birds, the mountains, the stones, the stars, the planets, the sun and the moon because they (human beings) sell their glory to them and make them gods and serve them to reject God. Human beings have become dangerous and corrupt and have corrupted every creation making God the creator to feel bitter and jealous. But it is not our believe or our honor to God that makes Him God. He was and is God in existence before we were made and born and sent to the world, even before creation.

28. God has life in Himself to give life and has granted the Jesus Christ to have life in Himself to give life, and whosoever believes in Him shall not perish but shall have everlasting life in himself also to give life.

29. Jesus is the True Light which gives light to every man coming into world, to see the past present and the future. But as many as are without the right perception of God, the wicked snatches and withholds their light till the high arm is broken (till salvation is received).

30. People don't live by the word of God because they do not understand the word. But when they come to understand the word of God, they will live by the word and they will serve God in spirit and in truth. Miracles are the results of perfection.

31. Man is pre-ordained god, and is God made god which is the likeness of God, The Only True, Everlasting and Living God. Hence it is the idol, the Man made god which has to worship the Pre-Ordained god, the God made god. But Satan has made the inverse for the God made god to worship the Man made god, which, by the World Standard of administration in human perspective is seen to be legal and acceptable in congruent to God's principle.

32. There is a battle, and we are fighting a battle in this our world because we are building the kingdom of God in the kingdom of Satan, and without God's spirit we will be defeated and crushed and ground, because we are pressed in every side but we are not crushed.

33. When everything has failed, OFFER IS THE THING OF THE LAST, for those who are merciful will obtain mercy because blessed are the merciful for they shall obtain mercy.
34. God is Spirit and Word is Spirit, therefore God is Word and if Jesus Christ is word, then He is God and is Spirit.
35. It is wise saying that one has to give up his beauty to establish his future that his established future will make up his beauty.
36. Words are Spirit, they are powerful, move very fast and they are sharp and wherever they can land, the result can be anything.
37. Because of the death and resurrection of Jesus Christ, those of us who believe in Christ see death as transit and not a destination.
38. Deliverance from captivity without Salvation is destructive and Salvation without Deliverance from captivity is Blindness.
39. If the mortal will touch the immortal, they shall enter into their rest and live forever.
40. Tap into the word of God for the revelation and there shall be performance.
41. It is impossible to give in your lack but the possibility to give in your lack will redeem you from lack.
42. If you believe in lack, you will always be in lack. You can not violate this. Meditate on the word and it will manifest.
43. Nobody can stop you from reaching your future, only you can stop it. God has designed your future to put your enemies in pain. God wants to change you from inside out. All is possible through believing and meditation. It is time to get rid of the limitations on yourself, wake up and allow God to do His work.
44. Once you take things beyond your mind by prayer, the spirit will take it up. Prayer is spiritual issue. Prayer goes to the root of the problem. We do the praying and God does the work. Prayer means entering into God's bedroom and you need God's spirit to enter into His bedroom. Those who worship God worship in spirit and in truth.
45. Faith takes you bound. If you are only dealing with the physical aspect of matters, you will achieve anything.
46. Anytime you deal with God, you have to deal with FAITH. You have to have physical to see the physical things likewise you have

to have the spirit to see spiritual things. God has to come to the world in the physical to take care of the physical burden. Those who have both see deeper and perform well.

47. People are poor not because they do not have money. They are poor because they do not have the knowledge. Prosperity is not potential by race or color. People deal with the flesh but dealing with the spirit is the most powerful. Tap into the spirit and there will be physical manifestation.

48. Expensive sacrifice will results in expensive breakthrough.

49. You have to experience poverty to manage blessing likewise you have to taste tribulation to manage freedom. Poverty is a curse and it takes a mighty power to break it. It could only be broken by the power of God, which is the hand of God, the blood and the name of Jesus Christ, and the power and anointing of the Holy Spirit.

50. Tribulations and afflictions are the fountains of one's life because everyone desires breakthrough, whereas disappointments sometimes is used to strengthen us.

51. How will you know the Most High God when you do not hear from Him. You have to hear from God to know Him.

52. Death is a temporally separation, which means sleep. So when a Christian dies, he or she is asleep.

53. When the anointing of God is upon you and God is using you even demons will admire you. And people do not see your education neither your personality but what they see is the anointing. Anointing is the physical aspect of the Holy Ghost. And that's what people see.

54. Patience is bitter but its fruits are sweet and appetizing.

55. Discernment is a remarkable opportunity whilst waiting is a remarkable discernment. (discernment is the gift for hearing and seeing through things. And could be obtained by waiting.)

56. As a child of God you must be strong in relationship with God, for the interesting thing about Christians is not the miracles we do perform but our intimate relationship we maintain with God.

57. You need an overflowing anointing that can break the mountains, that is the level of anointing you need as a man of God and this anointing is in different categories.

58. When you are desperate for solution, you will always be tempted and will become distracted which turns to affliction and becomes oppression and finally a demonic covenant.

59. As a Christ follower you always need to cover yourself with the blood of Jesus.

60. Prophesy is what God wants to perform in one's life. Do not ignore prophesy. Prophesy is God's taught about you. If you will live according to His will then it shall come to pass.

61. Prophesy dies when you refuse to accept it by faith. It is like accepting a pregnancy by faith, you will deliver a child unto your bosom, but if the pregnancy is aborted you may have no child. Likewise prophecy will not tarry but shall come to pass if it is accepted by faith.

62. Christians depend upon God's Spirit to serve Him, but religious worshippers serve God by traditional laws, which is a religious form of worship. If you depend upon the religious act of worship, you will never see the glory of God.

63. Lets love one another because all men have one agenda, which is the ultimate reality of mankind (shelter, food, clothing and work).

64. All life (Every Living thing) begins with birth and all life (Every Living thing) ends with death but between birth and death is life, the space of accomplishments which makes a person who he is, when completed carefully with success. Hence no one can escape these three phenomenon, birth, life and death.

65. Who is a Christian? A Christian is a committed follower of Jesus Christ, someone saved and delivered. You must be saved to need deliverance to be a true Christian. The unbeliever cannot be delivered till he or she is saved. Until the saved is delivered he cannot be faithful to God. You vow always and not fulfill it, you cannot live up to the word of God.

66. Living under the shadow of stereotype is the worst scenario in life, in otherwise listening to the negative things around you is the worst thing in life. It is the tool of action limitation.

67. If there is a man to pray, there is a God to answer. And where there is demand there is supply. And again where there is faith there is the impossibly made possible. Faith is the key.

68. If you avail yourself, God can do more with you. Distance is not a barrier with God's move.

69. Parable is the unveiling truth of God's way of doing things and His intentions in the life of man.

70. Covenant is a deal initiated by God, built on well divine time and sealed by an oath. God cannot get out of His covenant unless we fail to do our part. Once we play our part God is committed to honor His prosperity contract. Covenant is a spiritual contract and not a promise. It is an oath sworn to abide by the two parties, a binding agreement.

71. As a Christian if you refuse and reject to sow seed in your life is equivalent to praying for poverty. Spiritual men who do not do charity become poor. You need to engage in quality covenant with God. Only covenant people with God can live under the open windows of heaven. Sowing your substance will bring about reaping of your blessing. The farmer sows and reaps. So sow and reap according to your faith.

72. If you think having enough to eat and drink is prosperity, you may be deceiving yourself, that's survival. Prosperity is sharing your blessing or prosperity with other people in the form of providing education and jobs to others not only your house. That's others can see you and smile, come to you and become blessed. That's what we call prosperity, that's allowing your blessing to fall into the ground for multiplication. John 12:24. "Most assuredly, I say to you, unless a grain of wheat falls into the ground and dies, it remains alone; but if it dies, it produces much grain." This approach is the smartest way of liberating millions of people from the grip of poverty forever.

73. You need to be empowered to prosper because someone that has a greater power is holding your prosperity whom you do not see, and you will need the greatest power to overcome him. It is impossible to have financial blessing and prosper without empowerment (God's favor). Satan deceives people of the word of God. If you need to be free from lack, then you need to be empowered. Anytime you borrow, it belittles the power of God in your lives. Habitual Lack and borrowing is a sign of poverty. It needs to be broken.

Accepting to be poor means accepting to be dead. It is the dead which is poor. We are made rich but someone is sitting on it. 2Cor. 8:9. It can be done by the blood and the name of Jesus Christ, the hand of God that is word of God and the power and anointing of the Holy Spirit. PROSPERITY EMPOWERMENT:- 2Cor. 8:9; 3John 2; Deut. 26:12-15, 7:12-15; 2Cor. 9:8,10.

74. God knows beforehand that we need financial resource for everything and God grants that we must have money. Money is answer to many things but not everything. Our social life can only be catered for by financial empowerment. Money is good but the love of it is evil and sin. 1Tim. 6:7,10,17-18.

75. God created us with the dignity (respect) to transcend (to go beyond our limits). Borrowing is not sin, it is a short term relief but when it becomes a habit, it can lead to slavery and become a curse.

76. Each and everyone has an unction with God to be great, that is for you to be heard worldwide, but if you allow dream killers, if you give them the opportunity, they will kill that dream. That's the work of dream killers. They will put fear in you, they will fill you with confusion, they will put you under desperation, they will frustrate you, they will destroy your image and they will lie about you.

77. Where there is faith, there is impossibility made possible. Faith has no imitation. You can't fake the Holy Ghost. Faith arises from the heart according to the word of God. Consistency must be based on something more stronger and more solid. Faith based on consistency is a terror and nightmare to the Satanic kingdom but in these era emotions and feelings has become the spiritual experience of many believers, (people want to proof spiritual things with science, if it cannot be proved, it cannot be accepted; but life is a spiritual experience). Live a life of consistency with God and having consistent fellowship with God, and taking a relationship seriously with God, brings the anointing.

78. When you do not have God's Spirit to serve Him, is like, you are serving an idol. Depending on God's spirit to serve Him will reveal God's taught in your environment.

79. Satan is the author of complains and keep people complaining to be under his captivity, unless they are destined to be delivered, they will remain captive.

80. Your achievements in terms of wealth and possession, takes Satan no time to destroy it. Hence you need God and faith in God to protect your achievements. Faith comes by the spirit and not of the flesh. Have faith in God, for you need not to be sick to die, it's God's decision. Without God, Satan can knock you down at anytime he wants.

81. We work by time and not by faith but we walk by faith and not by sight. A disconnection in faith is a break in God. My smile represents my achievements but my heart represents my future.

82. Embracing the word of God is the most effective instrument for change and prosperity.

83. For a Christian every day is a good morning, because God's mercies and compassion fail not, they are new every morning. Never say good night for good night is for the dead. Night means darkness and refers to the grave. Good night means you've entered into Satan's arena.

84. If you speak about Jesus without righteousness which is God's Spirit, it will be an abomination.

85. Without God's Spirit, God's opinion and God's plan about your faithfulness (praise, worship, fasting, prayer, and charity) will be useless, vague and destructive.

86. Devotion is the tool for reading the bible, a God's satisfying desire which your life depends on.

87. All religions claim to be the same because they all teach and explain life and death, and life after death, but the claim of superiority makes their difference which cause division in humanity.

88. You cannot serve someone you do not know. Therefore you have to know God to serve Him. If you know that God is your creator and your life is in His hands and without him you cannot exist then you can serve Him with all perseverance.

89. If you serve God without His spirit, you will be serving a God you do not know, lifeless god, an object. If Jesus does not accept your prayer, Satan will accept your prayer. There are two powers,

Christ and Satan. We are made spiritual by living in the word and the word living in us. Philosophies and theories of the word do not cause spirituality. The holy bible becomes history without depending on God's Spirit to teach it. As well the Holy Bible is a history book in the hands of an unbeliever and the ungodly.

90. Knowing the reason why you are a Christian and being determine to achieve Salvation, but some powerful force stands your way to oppose you. The Spirit of God is the power and without Him nothing works in the universe.

91. The word of God becomes a living weapon in the lips of the believer when he depends on God's Spirit. Words are like seed, when they surround a person for far too long, they will germinate, gain root and take him captive. Satan loves to demonize and put negative trade marks on people to hold them captive. Satan knows God has put wonderful and gracious talent in people, so he visits them with discouragement, fear and inferiority to overcome God's purpose to achieve his own plan. Satan does not fight against your current situation, he fights against your future. He always plans ahead.

92. You are saved by the blood of Jesus Christ, but your prosperity depend upon your deliverance from the blood covenant (murder), the Demonic covenant (witchcraft) and the Satanic covenant (shrines) of your ancestors and generations. That scar is in there, you need to work on it to erase it, to pave the way for your prosperity.

93. Anything that has no change does not grow and anything that does not grow cannot develop. Development is change which is valuable component that brings quantity from quality. Therefore prosperity becomes an outcast where there is no change.

94. Bitterness escalates heart troubles and results in hatred. There are doors without protection in life and when they are opened Satan becomes real.

95. The more you call the name of the enemy and criticize him, and the more you advertise his name, hence the more popular he becomes and the more proud he will be. Better, do not even mention his name and let his name die.

96. COURAGE TO WITHSTAND CRITICISM:-

a.   If you fear criticism you cannot be a leader.

b.   If you fear criticism you cannot even marry, because at your wedding, you will be criticized.

c.   If you fear criticism you cannot qualify as a human being. We are the image of God, and if God is criticized, left alone image.

d.   Criticism shows your importance and your value but do not let the criticism prove that judgment to be your character.

97. SEVEN KEYS TO CHRISTIAN FAITH:

a.   a. Pray for vigorous body for evangelism. Do not let your selfish and prejudice turn you away from the work of God. It is the only means to break down your negative tendencies.

b.   If you want to free yourself from death and attain the supreme Eternal Life then you must awaken the Christ-In-You. John 14:17-21.

c.   Do not allow anyone to hinder your dedication to the great mission of spreading Christianity which will bring peace in this world and after. Remember, only by witnessing for the LORD JESUS CHRIST will your entire life be CROWNED with glory. Matt. 19:27-29.

d.   Never become a mere observer. If you do, you will never know even a fraction of the profound joy in Christ. Matt. 9 :13

e.   If your faith is weak, you will be overcome by your negative tendencies and will not see the joy in Christ. Matt. 21:21-22.

f.   If you have weak faith in Christ you will be influenced by your negative tendencies, and hold grudges against others, keeping yourself away from the world of faith in Christ. Because of the negative tendencies, you will be unable to perceive that which is valid or correct, and will feel resentment and make justifications to suit your own purpose. This is the tendency, a tragic one of people whose faith is weak and eventually they backslide in their faith in Christ and extinguish the light which Christ has lit in them. Matt. 12:1-12; 2 Cor.12: 1-6-7.

g. The benefit of the HOLY SPIRIT is mostly inconspicuous and as common mortals we tend to be always making short sighted judgment. So as a result even if one's prayer is not answered immediately, one will eventually find himself moving a positive direction towards benefits. There is profound meaning behind the fact that sometimes one's prayer seems to go unanswered. <u>Hebr. 3:7-8</u>

98. EVOLUTION: Even though people think of evolution as an independent operating faculty being the source of creation and its development, evolution itself must have source. And the source is God, who is the creator of this universe that we live in. For the bible says in Rom. 1:20 "For since the creation of the world, His invisible attributes are clearly seen being understood by the things that are made, even His eternal power and Godhead so that they are without excuse." So there is no excuse whatsoever on earth for a human being to say there is no God or I do not believe in God. Job 9:24 says, "The earth is given into the hand of the wicked. He covers the faces of its judges. If it is not He, who else could it be." Job 38:4 "Where were you when I laid the foundation of the earth? Tell Me if you have understanding." Now we see how evolution believers are deceived by the devil. They have allowed themselves to be blinded by the demon of evolution, making them to understand that there is no God who created the universe. These are some supporting quotations. Psalm 14:1; 2Cor. 4:4; John 12:40; Matt. 13:14-15; Hosea4:1-3,6.

99. ACCEPTING CHRIST: One accept out of the power of miracle unto the power of faith, then out of the power of faith repentance is made unto forgiveness to salvation. It is easy to accept, but difficult to continue but continuing faith in Christ leads to ETERNAL LIFE.

100. Science is needful, it is good to apply in daily life, it's just a contributor of worldly activities but do not put your faith in science. It could become a precarious predicament in your life. For you to be special, you must be prepared to face uncomfortable situations. If everybody is special, then no one will be special. Special is for those who can take a risk.

101. The world is of more spiritual than physical, for this reason, there is more in the spirit than the physical. There is no instance on earth which is not in the Holy Bible that exist. Anything that is not already in existence cannot be revealed or invented. It is invented because it is already in existence and one must attain a particular standard to reveal or invent such hidden ideas. All that is revealed and yet to be revealed are already in the bible.

102. Living in this world without the power of God behind you or supporting you, you become like a bait in the waters, no matter how large the bait, the smallest fish fumbles with that bait.

103. God does not judge one with who he is, but He judges with what that individual has been capable to do.

104. Where there is LIGHT, there is LIFE. And if Jesus is LIGHT then He is LIFE, who alone can give life.

105. Physical exercise, physical training, or bodily training, is of limited value, but Godliness is valuable in every way, holding the promises for the benefit of the present LIFE or LIFE near at hand and yet to come.

106. SIN is a spirit and it is Satan's most strongest and powerful agent which controls the Kingdom of Satan against our physical world.

107. Once you accept and believe in Jesus Christ, your "SOUL" becomes the likeness of God. You become "LIGHT" unto the world. God is Light and there is no darkness in HIM. So is the power and the Wisdom of God which is in Our Lord Jesus Christ.

108. The earth is full of Spiritual and Physical Entities and God has to put someone who is both Spiritual and Physical entity to control them and continue with the creation. ********

109. We were all once angels and our performance when we were angels determined the families we are born to and what mission to accomplish. Because the Deity of Jesus Christ determined which family to be born to and what mission to accomplish. The Devil is the ruler of the world and whoever comes into the world, the Devil will strip him naked of the gift of God which is for the glory of God. Unless the family into which that individual was

born is righteous and know why that person is born and resists the devil.

The Devil has blinded us from righteousness, so we do not even know why we are born into the world. This comes to fornication and consulting of occults. About 90% of the marriages were once in fornication or consulted occult before the real marriage. They had sex before the marriage or entered into occultism before the marriage. These acts gave Satan the opportunity to take advantage and take control of the marriage. The fornication acts had brought curse to couples as well as the children that are born in those marriages. This is the reason why most children are living in poverty and struggling in life. The man and the woman both are cursed for the sexual act before marriage and the children born under such sexual act had also come under curse. If the man abandons the children and the woman, his curse is multiplied, even so the woman. Your success depends upon what went on in your life, even before that person was born and for this majority of the world population need deliverance from captivity.

110. Money is needful and useful in life, in this technological era, but putting your trust in it attracts all kinds of demonic spirits.
111. Prosperity is God's plan for mankind, for honesty and complements are the beauty of wealth.
112. Keep God's word and search His word and make Him the Living bread of life, Then He shall come and abide with you and that glory will affect your community.
113. Because of the death and the resurrection of Our Lord Jesus Christ those who believe in Jesus see death not as destination but as a transit.
114. To understand life, you need the bible as your GPS (global positioning system) and as your road map, because everything that has ever happened and will happen is in the bible.
115. The bible is a "book (of) - instruction - before - life - ends" (BIBLE), the media through which God speaks to us (mankind).
116. Birthright comes with blessing (an inheritance), and goes to the one who has the birthright. Because the Jews rejected Jesus

Christ, the birthright is given to the Christian who is now the first born.

117. If God could find only two righteous persons in your family, He will do crazy miracles in your home.

118. If you need to solve mathematical problem, you need a formula and that formula must come from a mathematical book, which will give you the right answer. Even so to have the solution to the right God, you need the right religious book which is the bible that talks about the TRUE LIGHT which is the TRUE GOD.

119. Love is spirit and sees in the spirit, and has the power to reveal the things of the spirit. Without love there cannot be faith and without love and faith you shall go nowhere with God. Love and faith is the unity in the body.

120. When you dedicate your heart for God, you have that ability from God to stop looking or thinking about where you are coming from and start looking to where you are going. That is the ability from God.

121. The word of God in the New Testament is to put Satan in pain. For he is revealed and troubled by the new testament.***

122. You have to be perfect to be righteous, and you have to be righteous to be holy and holiness is God. Matt. 5:48.

123. Christians believe in Jesus Christ, and we have everlasting life to keep us alive for we have passed from death to life, and because we have passed from death to life, through the resurrection of our Lord Jesus Christ, whoever believes on Him and dies is not dead but asleep and when the Lord Jesus Christ comes, He will raise him up. He who sleeps wakes up again because he has life in him, but he who is dead does not wake up again because he has no life in him.

124. The tremendous power of your faith is the conclusive words of Jesus Christ on the subject of divine healing. Medical science is good but the science of the miracles of Jesus Christ is the greatest. Faith is the master key to everything. It is the master key that unlocks the doors of prison, the master key that breaks the chains of the captive, the master key that brings the axe to the surface of the water, the master key that raises the dead. It

is the foundation of all things. It is not something acquire but something you already have because faith is older than the person with the faith for out of faith came creations.

125. If you want to see miracles then fast and pray but if you want to hear the voice of God then read the scripture with devotion.

126. The new testament is to put Satan out of business because it is the rejection of Satan's offer.

127. Medical (earthly) science is great but Christ science is the greatest because Christ science embodies both physical and spiritual science.

128. As a Christian, treat every minute and every day as holy unto God.

129. God is invisible and work through visible things to display the invisible God.

130. Worrying is atheism and it means you have no God.

131. Blessing is always into the future, likewise curse is also always into the future.

132. Christianity is not religion but love relationship with God, while religion is established in Christianity.

133. A heart that has no assignment becomes the workshop of Satan. Give your heart assignment. If you do not give your heart assignment, your heart will give you assignment.

134. There is a real battle going on in your heart, you nourish only the flesh because that is the part of God visible to you. If you can see the part of God in you which is invisible to be visible, you will not stop nourishing it.

135. Have control over your heart, do not let your heart have control over you. If you allow your heart to have control over you, you will seize to be the image of the invisible God. Your heart is roaming about receiving all kinds of assignments because it has no purposed assignments, and this situation distances you from God.

136. If you practice religion, you will carry your problem. Only Christianity which is a love relationship with God brings deliverance.

THE BIBLE COMPANION.

This material helps and makes it easier to study the bible on these selected topics and could also be used for sermons.

ANOINTING:- Mark 5:22-23, 6:5-6, 13; 1Sam. 16:12-13, 9:16, 10:1; Exodus 30:22-30; Lev. 8:10-12; 1Kings 19:16, 1:39; 2Kings 9:1-7; James 5:13-15; Luke 9:1, 10:1; Mark 6:7; Hebr. 6:2-3; Acts 8 2-3, 17, 13:3; 2Tim. 1:6; Deut. 34:9; 1Tim. 4:14.

ABORTION:- Isa. 66:7-9, 59:7; Job 15:35; Rom. 3:15; Prov. 1:16, 6:17. Gen. 38:7-11.

ALIENS : TAKING POSSESSION OF YOUR NATION :- Isaiah 1:7; Prov. 5:10-11; Deut. 28:43-68, 32:15-21, 35; Lam. 5:1-9.

ANOINTING CLOTHES:- Acts 19:11-12, 6; Matt. 14:36; Mark 5:27-27; 2Kings 2:13-1-15.

ANOINTING OIL - PREPARATION :- Exo. 30:22-32, 37:29, 40:9-11.

ANGELS:- Rev. 10:1-2; 1Chron. 21:16,20; 1Kings 8:27-28 (angels who they are and how they look); Gen. 15:1, 18:12-16, 16:9-11, 18:2-3, 19:1-2, 28:12; John 1:51; Luke 2:9-101, 1:11-13, 1:18-19,26,30; Matt. 2:13,18:10; Hebr. 1:14; Ex. 3:2, 23:21; Gen. 31:24; Gen. 32:24,30;17:1 Matt. 1:20; 3:16; John 5:4; Luke 1:19; Hebr. 1:6,7,13; Joshua 5:13-15; Acts 5:19, 12:7-8, 16:26.

ANGELS OF THE SEVEN CHURCHES:- Rev. 2:1, 8,12,18; 3:1, 7, 14.

APPOINTMENT OF APOSTLES, PASTORS AND ELDER:- Luke 10:1, 9:1, 11:49, 3:13-19; Matt. 10:1-2. 1Tim. 2:7; 2Tim. 1:11; 1Cor. 12:28; Mark 3:13-19.

ANGER:- Eph. 4:26; James 1:19-20; Prov. 10:19, 14:17,29, 16:32; Psalm 4:4, 37:8.

ALMIGHTY GOD:- Deut. 32:39; Isaiah 43:10-11; 44:6; 45:5,18; Rev. 1:8, 11, 18; 22:13; 19:16; 4:8,11; 11:17; Zech. 14:9b; Deut. 6:4; 4:35,39; Ex. 33:20, 23; 1Timothy 6:16; Daniel 2:22; John 6:46; matt. 11:27. 1Cor. 8:6; Jer. 10:12-13; Jer. 32:17.

ADULTERY:- Deut. 22:22-27; Gal. 5:19.

APOSTLE PAUL'S SUFFERINGS:- 2Cor. 11:24-25; Acts 16:22-24, 21:30-33, 14:19-20, 23:12-13.

APOSTLE PAUL'S MIRACLES:- Acts 14:3, 14:8-12, 16:25-26, 19:11-16, 2-7, 20:19-20, 28:3-6.

ATONEMENT:- Lev. 17:11, 10:17, 23:27, 8:21,34, 16:6,30, 15:28, 10:17,4:20,9:8,14:53,4:1, 12:6-10, 5:6-10; Rom. 3:25, 5:10; Num. 15:28, 31:50, 6:11, 29:11; Exo. 30:10, 15-16; 1Cor.15:3; Hebr. 2:17, 9:14, 26; John 1:29.

ANTICHRIST :- 1John 2:22, 18, 4:3; 2John 1:7; 2Thess. 2:3-4, 9-10; Rev. 13:4-8, 13-17, 16:13-14, 19:19-20.

BUILD AND LIVE IN:- Rom. 5:12-14; Acts 5:1-15; Isaiah 65:17-25.

BUSINESS :- Luke 19:23-26; Gen. 47:13-26; 2Kings 7:1,18.

BLESSING:- Deut. 28:1-14; Rom. 4:7-8; Psalm 1:1-3; 3Jn. 2.

BOASTING:- Rom. 11:18, 12:3; Prov. 25:14, 27:1; Gal. 6:3.

BLOOD SHED:- Gen. 9:6; Rev. 13:10; Num. 35:33; Matt. 26:52; 2Sam. 16:7-8; 2Sam. 3:30.

BLOOD - EATING OF:- Gen. 9:4-5; 1Sam. 14:32-34; Lev. 17:14; Deut. 12:16, 23-25.

BATTLE BETWEEN CHRIST AND SATAN:- Luke 4:6; Matt. 28:18; John 14:30, 12:31. John 1:5, 12:31,14:30. 8:44; Gen. 1:2-3.

BIRTHRIGHT:- Rom. 9:10-13;Gen. 25:21-34, 27:21-38; Prov. 16:25, 24:4; 1Chro. 17:15.

BRIBERY:- Deut. 27:25; Ez. 22:12; Prov. 17:23, 15:27, 21:13; 1Sam. 8:2-5, 12:3; Ex. 23:8; Acts 24:24-27; Isa. 5:23, 1:23; Luke 3:12-14; Num. 35:31.

CHILD TRAINING:- Prov. 28:13, 29:17, 6:20-24, 13:24, 3:11-12, 19:18, 22:6, 5:20-26, 22:6; Eph. 6:1-3; Gen. 18:19; Deut 6:7.

CITIZENSHIP IN HEAVEN:- Hebr. 9:28, 12:28, 11:16; Matt. 26:28; Eph. 2:12,19; Hebr. 11:16; Phil. 3:20-21; 2Cor. 5:1-3.

CURSE:- Jer. 11:3; Gal. 3:10; Deut. 27:15-26, 28:15-68, 21:22-23. Prov. 20:20; Prov. 3:33, 26:2; Eccl. 10:20, 5:4-9; Lam. 5:7; Deut. 27:15-26.

CURSE-REJECTION OF THE SCRIPTURE:- Jer. 11:3; Deut. 21:22-23; 27:26; Gala. 3:10,13.

COMFORTER:- John 14:15-16, 26, 15:26, 16:7,

COMMUNION:- Exodus 12:5-14; John 6:33-35,47-58; Luke 22:15-20; Matt. 26:26-30; 1Cor. 11:23-30, 5:7-11, 10:16-17; Acts 20:7; Mark 14:22-25.

CHARITY:- 1Cor. 13:2-4, 141; Colo. 3:14; 2Tim. 2:22; 1Peter 4:8; 2Peter 1:7; 3John 6; Acts 16:25-35; Prov. 21:13,29:13, 22:2,9, 28:27.

CHRIST MADE SURETY FOR MAN:- Hebrews 7:22; Genesis 1:26; Luke 19:10.

COVENANT - NEW covenant :- Hebr. 8:8-13; Jer. 31:31 -34; John 13:34-35; Ezek. 36:26-27.

COVENANT with God :- Gen. 9:9-17; 17:1-7, 10-14, 19-21.

CURSE - JOSHUA CURSED JERICHO :- Josh. 6:26; 1Kings 16:34; Luke 19:1.

DAY OF THE LORD:- Matt. 24:36; Acts 1:7; 1Thess. 5:1; Deut. 29:29.

DEMONS :- 1Tim. 4:1; James 2:19; 1Cor. 10:20-21; 2Cor. 6:15-17; Lev. 17:7; Deut. 32:17; Rev. 9:20, 16: 13-14.

DEPRESSION :- Numb. 11:11-25; 1Kings 19:4.

DEATH is transit and not a destination :- John 6:39-40; John 11:11-15; Luke 7:11-15.

DISPUTE -SETTLE CHRISTIAN DISPUTE :- 1Cor. 6:2-6; Matt. 5:23-26, 18:15-17; 2Chron. 19:6; Deut. 1:17.

DIVORCE:- Deut. 24:1, Matt. 5:29-32,19:3-9; 1Cor. 7:10-16, 27-28,39; Mala. 2:10-12, 14-16; Mark 10:3-12; Rom. 7:2-3; Jer. 3:1. Hebr. 2:16; Ezra 9:1-3.

DIVORCE QUALIFICATION:- (bases for divorce);-1Cor. 7:15; Prov. 30:20; Matt. 19:9; Jer. 3:1; Deut. 24:1-4.

DESCRIMINATION:- Acts 10:34; Jam. 2:2-9; Rom. 2:11; Gal. 2:6; 1Tim. 5:21;Deut. 1:17, 10:17.

DIVISION:- Ex. 8:22-23; 1Cor. 1:10; John 10:18-21, 7:43; 1Cor. 11:18, 3:3; Rom. 16:17-18; Acts 15:1.

DRUNKENNESS:- Gen. 9:20-24, 19:30-38; Isaiah 5:11-12,22; Prov. 31:2-6, 23:20-21, 29-32, 20:1, 21:17; Joel 1:5; Jer. 25:27,35:5-6; Gal. 5:21; Hab. 2:15-16; Eph. 5:18; Num. 6:13; 1Tim. 5:23; Lev. 10:9-10; Eze. 44:21.

DUKES :- Gen. 36:40-43; Exo. 15:15; 1Chron. 1:51-54.

DESTRUCTION OF BABYLON :- (Joshua 9:11); Deut. 32:21-23, 16-17; Jer. 32:30,50:8, 51:6-9; Job 12:9-10, 13,16; Rev. 14:8; Isaiah 21:9; Rom. 10:19.

DOGS :- Prov. 26:11; Matt. 15:26, 7:6; Phil. 3:2; 1Sam. 17:43; Rev. 22:15.

EARTH - NEW HEAVEN:- 2Pet. 3:13; Isaiah 66:22; Isaiah 65:17; Rev. 21:1; Rev. 21:2-3.

EXPENSIVE SACRIFICE:- 2Kings 3:26-27; John 3:16-18; Rom. 5:8; 2Chro. 7:5; Judges 11:39-40.

ENVY :- Mark 15:10; Matt. 27:18, 20:6-11; Prov. 23:17, 3:31; Psalm 73:3, 106:16; 1Sam. 18:9,29; Num. 12:1-3; Jam. 3:14; Esther 5:13; Rom. 13:13; Acts 17:5; Gal. 5:26. Num. 12:1-3; James 3:14; Esther 5:13; Roman 13:13; Acts 17:5; Gal. 5:26; 1Tim. 6:4.

END:- Rev. 7:2-3, 9:1-12, 20:11-15; 1Peter 4:17-18; 2Peter 2:4-11; Matt. 24:3-7, 23-26,29-31,36-51.

EXERCISE:- 1Tim. 4:8, 6:6; 1Cor. 8:8; Psalm 37:4-7

EYE - OPENING OF THE EYE :- Gen. 21:19, 2King 6:17; Numb. 22:31; Luke 24:31.

FAMILIAR SPIRITS:- Exodus 22:18, 21:18; 2Kings23:10, 21:6, 23:24, 17:17; Lev. 19:31, 20:6, 27, 19:26, 20:27;Deut.18:10; Isaiah 8:19; 2Chron. 33:6; 1Sam. 28:7, 9, (1-7).

FORGIVENESS:- Matt. 18:21-22, 6:14-15, 18:23-35, 5:, 23-25,39-48, ; Eph. 6:12; Gal. 6:7-10, 5:25-26; Lev. 19:17-18; Deut. 32:32-35; Hebr. 10:30-31; Luke 15:20; Rom. 5:10-12, 16:20; 2Cor. 2:10-11.

FORNICATION:- Deut. 22:28-29; Gal. 5:19.

FORTY DAYS:- Acts 1:3; Luke 4:2; Exo. 34:28; 1Kings 19:8.

FACE OF GOD:- Exo. 33:20; John 6:46, 5:37,1:18.

FASTING AND PRAYER:- Acts 14:23, 9:9, 10:30, 13:23; Gal. 5:22; Matt. 4:2-4,6:16-18; Gen. 126; Exodus 34:28-30; Daniel 101:1-3; Luke 2:37; Joel 2:12; Mark 9:29; Esther 4:3; Rom. 14:17; 1Cor. 7:5,8:8; Isa.58:3-16.

FAITH:-James 1:5-8; Matt. 7:7,17:20; Mark 11:22-24, 6:2; Hebr. 11:1, 3-6, 16-17; John 3:11-12; 3:18; Gal. 3:7-11; Gen. 1:1-4, 6,9,11,14,20; Rom. 10:14-17; Eph. 2:8-10; John 3:11-12, 18; Luke 8:25, 9:41, 17:5-6.

FINANCIAL BLESSING:- 3John 2; 2Cor. 8:9, 9:6-8; Luke 6:36, Prov. 13:20, 19:17, 21:3,5,13, 22:4,7,9,20; Matt. 19:21,26,29.

FOOT - ONE FOOTED JOSHUA :- Acts 12:8, 13:25; Luke 15:22; Exo. 3:5; Josh. 5:15; 2Sam. 14:25.

FORGIVENESS:- Matt. 18:21-22, 6:14-15, 18:23-35, 5:, 23-25,39-48, ; Eph. 6:12; Gal. 6:7-10, 5:25-26; Lev. 19:17-18; Deut. 32:32-35; Hebr. 10:30-31; Luke 15:20; Rom. 5:10-12, 16:20; 2Cor. 2:10-11.

GIVING:- Prov. 11:24; 2Cor. 9:6-10; Prov. 28:8,27, 3:9-10; Eccl. 11:1; Luke 6:38; Matt. 7:2; 1Kings 17:15-16; Gen. 22:16-17; Acts 20:35, 9:6-40; Phil. 4:14-15; Dan. 4:27; Psalm 30:9; 6:5; Prov, 19:17.

GIANTS:- Deut. 2:10-12, 20; Gen. 14:5, 6:4.

GOD - UNSEEN :- John 5:35, 6:46,1:18; Exo. 33:20; 1Tim. 6:16; Eze. 39:29. Jer. 10:10; Acts 14:15; Heb. 10:31.

GODS - FOREIGN GODS :- Gen. 35:4; Hosea 2:13; Deut. 5:8; Exo. 32:1-6.

GODS - YE ARE :- Psalm 82:6; John 10:34

GOD - CHRISTIAN GOD :- John 8:12,24,27,29; 6:46, 1:1,17,18; matt. 11:27; EXo. 33:20; 1John 5:7; Gen. 1:2.

GRIEVE - THE HOLY GHOST :- Isaiah 63:10-11; Psalm 78:40; Eph. 4:30.

HOLY GHOST:- Joel 2:28; Rom. 8:11-16, 26-27, 9:1; Acts 10:38, 44-48; John 14:16-17, 25-26, 15:26, 16:7-13; 1Cor. 2:13; Exo. 31:3; Acts 1:5, 8,

4:8, 2:1-4, 19:2-6, 13:9, 7:51. Luke 11:13, 3:22, 4:1, 12:12; 1John 5:6-7; Eph. 1:13, 4:30; 1Sam. 10:10; Matt. 1:20, 3:11, 12:31; Gen. 2:18.

HOLY GHOST BAPTISM:- Acts 2:1-4; 10:44-47; 9:17-18; 19:2-7; Matt. 3:11, Rev. 2:10.

HATRED:- Gal. 5:20; Rom. 9:13; Mala. 2:16.

HEAVENLY AND EARTHLY DAYS:- 2Peter 3:8; Psalm 90:4.

HOMOSEXUALITY - Lesbian Gay Bisexual Transgender :- Lev. 18:22, 20:13; Rom. 1:24,26-27; Gen. 19:5-6; Deut. 22:5, 23:17; Judges 19:22-24; Mark 10:6-9.

I AM HE :- Isaiah 43:10,13, 25; 46:4, 9; 45:3,6; 47:10; Exo. 3:14; John 8:24,28;13:19; 18:5-6, 7, 8.

IDLE WORDS:- Matt. 5:22, 12:35-37, 15:11,17-20; 1Peter 2:12, Psalms 34:13-14, 52:2; 2Tim. 2:16; Phil. 2:14-15. Luke 6:45; James 3:5-9; Eph. 4:29-31, 5:4; Romans 6:16; Colo. 3:8-9; 4:6; Lev. 24:14; Prov. 4:23.

IDOLS:- Jer. 10:3-5,8-9,11; 50:38; Psalm 78:58, 115:4-10, 135:15-18; Ex. 32:2-14; 1John 5:21; Acts 15:20; Rev. 2:14; 1Cor. 8:4; Lev. 19:4.

IDOL WORSHIP:- 1Corinthians 8:4-5; Psalm 16:4;Psalm 14:1; Ez. 8:7-18; 23:35-39; Jer. 2:27; 50:38; Acts 14:11-16; 15:20; 17:23; Ex. 23:13,24; 20:5, 32:2-4; Deut. 4:15-20,23-24; 6:14-16, 27:15; Lev. 19:4; Rev. 2:14; 1John 5:21; Roman 1:23.

JESUS PRAYED:- Luke 18:1, 11:1, 5:16, 9:18,29, 6:12; Mark 6:46, 14:32,35, 14:36; Matt. 14:23, 26:36,41, John 17; Acts 13:3.

JESUS VANISHED:- Luke 24:31, 4:29-30; John 7:30, 10:39, 12:36,8:59.

JOSHUA - JERICHO CURSED :- Josh. 6:26; 1Kings 16:34; Luke 19:1.

JESUS AT THE RIGHT HAND OF THE FATHER:- Hebr. 1:3, 10:12, 12:2; Colo. 3:1; Eph. 1:20; Acts 2:33-34, 7:55-56; Rom. 8:34, Rev. 3:21; 1Pet. 3:22.

JUBILEE:- Lev. 25:8-9, 10-13, 14-18, 33-44.

JUDGMENT OF THE UNGODLY :- 1Peter 4:17-19; Jude 6; 2Peter 2:4; 1Thess. 4:13-18; Zeph. 1:13-18; Mala. 4:1-3; Matt. :- 24:1:32; Isaiah 13:9-16.

LAMB - LAMB OF GOD :- John 1:29,36; Rev. 5:6,8,12,13; 6:1, 7:10, 14,17, 14:4, 10; 15:2.

LAYING ON OF THE HANDS:- 1Tim. 4:14; Acts 8:17, 13:3; James 5:13-15; Hebr. 6:2; Mark 6:5-7; Rom. 10:17; 1Tim. 2:22.

LAZINESS :- Prov. 28:20, 24:33-34,6:9-11, 10:4, 19:15; Hab. 2:6; Luke 12:19-20; Dan. 4:27; Eccl. 10:18.

LOVE OF MOMEY:- Hebr. 13:5; James 5:18; 1Tim. 6:7-10; Luke 18:18-25.

LIES:- Gen. 12:11-20, 20:2, 26:7, 27:5-34, 18:12-16; Joshua 2:1-15; 1Kings 13:1-31; Prov. 12:20,22, 13:3. Prov. 26:28, 6:17; Rev. 22:15.

LIBATION:- Jer. 7:17-20, 19:13; Colo. 2:8.

LIGHT - TRUE LIGHT:- John 1:9, 5:26, 8:12, 12:46, 12:35-36, 1:4-5; 1 Tim. 6:16; Gen. 1:3-4. John 3:19.

LIGHT - GREAT LIGHT:- Isaiah 9:2; Matt. 4:16; Eph. 5:8.

LEVIATHAN:- Isaiah 27:1, 51:9; Psalm 74:13-14, 104:26; Job 41:1. Ezek. 29:3.

LOVE:- Matt. 5:43-38; 1Cor. 13:1-13, 4:1; Prov. 10:12, 11:7; Acts 2:44-45; 1Sam. 18:1-4; Rom. 13:8-10; Gal. 5:13-14; Eph. 5:2; COlo. 3:14; Lev.

19:18; Mark 12:31; 1Jn. 3:10-17, 5:1-3; 1Jn. 4:7-12,16-21, Deut. 6:5; Psalm 31:23; Jn. 13:34-35, 15:13; Zech. 8:17. Rom. 12:9,5:8-10.

MARRIAGE:- Colo. 3:18-19; Prov. 18:22, 9:13, 3:5, 19:14, 31:10, 27:2-3, 30:23, 5:18-23; Eph. 5:21-32; Gen. 2:24, 24:51-53; 1Peter. 3:2-7; Mark 12:20-25; Psalm 127:2-3; 1Cor. 7:34-39,1-16; Titus 2:2-5; 1Peter 3:1; Rev. 21:1-4; 1Tim. 3:11; Rom. 8:8-9, 26-28, 7:2-4; Matt. 5:31-32, 19:3-9, 22:23-32; Hebr. 13:4, 7:4-9;Exodus 22:16; Eccl. 4:8-12, 9:1; Jer. 29:6.

MARY - CHILDREN :- Mark 6:3.

MUSIC - power of :- 2Kings 3:15-20, 18:6-8; 1Sam. 16:14-23; 2Chron. 20:2126; Exo. 15:20-21;

NAMING:- Gen. 17:19; Luke 1:13,31; Luke 2:21-24; Lev. 12:2-4;1Chron. 4:9-10.

MORNING STARS :- Rev. 22:16; Luke 1:78; 2Pet. 1:19; Job 38:7; Psalm 19:4-5.

NINE ELEVEN - BABYLON :- Deut. 32:16-23, 35; Rev. 14:8; Isaiah 21:9, 13:14; Jer. 32:30, 51:6-9; Job 12:13, 16; Rom. 10:19

ORDINATION OF PASTORS:- Exodus 29:7-9, 28:40; Num. 11:25; Mark 3:13-14; John 13:3-4; Acts 15:23.

OVERCOMER :- Rev. 2:7, 17, 26; 3:3, 5, 11-12, 21; 16:15; 21:7; 22:12-13; John 6:46; 1:18; 1John 4:12; 14:13.

OCCUPY - TILL I COME :- Luke 19:11-27; John 12:31, 14:30;1Cor. 15:24-26.

PARADISE OF GOD :- Rev. 2:7, 22:14. Luke 23:43. (Sheol: Rev. 1:18, Luke !6:24-25).

PLANNING:- Luke 14:28-33; Prov. 24:27.

POWER OF PROPHECY:- Matt. 21:21; Ezek. 37:1-19; John 11:24-26; 2Kings 4:2-3; 1Kings 17:14-16.

POWER - All power given to Christ :- Matt. 28:18, 11:27; Dan. 7:13-14; John 3:35; 1Cor. 15:27; Phil. 2:9-11; Heb. 1:8.

PRAYER:- Acts 12:5; 16:25, 16, 14:23, 1:14,46,42; 10:2 Luke 24:53; Matt. 18:18-20; 17:21; 1Thess, 5:17-19; Eph. 6:18;Math. 26:41; Luke18:1, 17:1-4; Phil. 1:4, 4:6; Acts 12:5; Colo. 4:2, 12.

PRAYER - Jesus prayed :- Mark 1:35, 14:32, 35-38, 6:46; Matt. 14:23, 26:36; Luke 5:16, 9:18, 29, 11:1, 18:1, 22:41.

PRIESTHOOD :- Hebr. 7:1-28, 1Pet. 2:5, 9-10; Hebr. 5:1-10; Psalm 110:4.

POTENTIALS:- John 10:34-35; Eccl.10:6-7; Jer. 18:1-4; Rom. 9:20-22; 1John 4:4,13; Psalm 68:1.

POLYGAMY:- Gen. 16:3, 29:30, 28:9, 30:3-4,9; 1Sam. 30:5; 1Kings 11:1-3.

POVERTY {cause}:- Prov. 10:4; 12:24; 13:4,18; 15:27; 19:15,24,27, 20:4,13,22; 21:25; 22:7,8,13; 23:6-8; 26:13-16; 28:8,22; 1Tim. 6:17.

PREACHING:- Mark 1:14-15, 3:13-14; Luke 9:1-2; Matt. 11:1

PRIDE:- Prov. 13:10, 15:25, 16:5,18, 28:25, 8:13, 6:17, 100:5

PROMISE;- Deut. 6:10-19, 7:12-16; Eccl. 10:7; Rom. 5:1; Psalm 116:14, 76:11; Jonah 2:9,1:16; Judges 11:30.

PROPERTY ANCESTRAL (security):- Prov. 5:7-11; Gen. 20:12-14, 24:2-8, 28:1-4.

PROPHETESS:- Ex. 15:20-21; Judges 4:4; Luke 2:36-38; Neh, 6:14; Acts 21:8-9; 2Kings 22:14. Isaiah 8:3.

PROPHETS - FALSE:- Jer. 23:21, 25-26, 2:8, 23:16, 30-34, 14:14, 27: 9-10, 29:8-9; Deut. 18:20-22; Lev. 19:31,11; Mark 12:30-31. 1Kings 13:18. Rev. 2:20

PROPHETIC DIRECTION:- Heb. 12:16-17; Gen. 25:22-23, 30-34;Prov. 23:4.

PROPHETIC DIRECTION:- Heb. 12:16-17; Gen. 25:22-23, 30-34;Prov. 23:4.

REJECTION - No excuse to reject God :- Rom. 1:20; Psalm 14:1, 10:4; Deut. 32:16-18.

REJECTION - OF THE SCRIPTURE :- Jer. 11:3; Deut. 21:22-23, 27:26; Gala. 3:10,13.

REFUGEE camps:- Num. 35:6,11-15; Joshua 20:6, 20:2,7-9, 21:13,21, 27,32,38.

RETIREMENT OF THE PRIESTS:- Numbers 8:24-26, 4:3, 23, 30, 35, 43, 47.

REINCARNATION:- Matt. 17:10-13, 11:14; Mark 9:11-13. Luke 1:17. Mala. 4:5; John 1:21.

REBELLION:-

Deut.32:16,30,35;Psalm.78:56;Rom.10:19;Jer.50:31-38,51:6-7,24,26,5.

RICHES AND BLESSINGS:- Prov. 10:6,22; 11:11,24; 19:4; 24:35; 20:21; 22:2,7,9; 28:13,25,27; Gen. 24:35, 26:12-14; Deut. 15:7,11; 1Tim. 6:18-19; Rom. 12:9-11.

RAINBOW:- Gen. 9:13-17. Rev. 4:3 10:1, Ezek. 1:28.

RAPTURE:- 1Thess. 4:13-17; 2Kings 2:11; Matt. 27:60-64; Acts 1:9-11; 1Cor. 15:5-8,15:12-22,15:35-44, 15:52-54; Rev. 11:8-18, 4:7-11. 19:13-20, 16:15; 2Peter 3 -13.

RESURRECTION:- John 11:25-35, 8:56-58, 12:24, 5:28-35; Matt. 22:23-33, 27:52-53; 1Cor. 15:12-26, 35-44, 51-54; 1Thess.13:18; Matt. 27:52-53; Mark 16:6; Luke. 24:6, 24-50; 1Peter 1:3; Phil. 3:10; Acts 24:15.

SUNDAY WORSHIP:- John 20:19, 26; Acts 20:7, 1Cor. 16:2-3; Ex. 12:16.

SMOKING:- Isaiah 55:2; Job 41:19-20; Hab. 2:13; Prov. 16:25; Acts 17:16-17; 1Cor. 3:16-17.

STEALING:- Lev. 19:11; Ex. 20:15; Deut. 5:19; Romans 13:9; Josh.7:20-21; Lev. 19:11.

STUDY:- 2Tim. 2:15, 3:7, 16; Rom. 15:4.1Tim. 4:6,13; Prov. 4:13; Acts 17:11; Psalm 119:105.

SABBATH:- Mark 2:27-28, 3:4; Lev. 26:2, 19:30, 20:8-11; 25:2-7, 23:3, 8, 12, 15-16, 35-36, 28:2; Ex. 12:16, 20:8-11,9-11.23:12, 31:12-18, 35:2-3,12; Gen. 2:2-3; Isaiah 58:13-14,56:2; Deut. 5:12-15, 16:8; Luke 4:31, 13:14-16; Heb. 4:2-6; Jer. 17:21-27.

SPIRITUAL EYES:- Gen. 3:7; Num. 22:31; Gen. 21:19; 2Kings 6:17; Luke 24:30-31.

SALVATION:- Luke 19:10; Gen. 1:26; Gen. 3:1-4; Colo. 2:8-15; 2Cor. 5:21; Hebr. 7:22; Gal. 4:4-5; Ezek. 22:30; Isaiah 53:1-12, 1:18-20; Jer. 33:14-16; John 3:14-19,20-36,; Matt. 26:56, Eph. 3:9-12, 2:7-8,12-14; Isaiah 14:12-14; Rev. 12:7-11; Job 9:24; Luke 4:6; Matt. 28:18; Mark 16:16. Rom. 10:9-13, 12:1-2; 1Jn. 1:8-9; Jn. 20:31; Prov. 28:13.

SALVATION - SALVATION OF THE JEWS:- Isaiah 14:1, 45:17,25; Rom. 11:26-32, 5-7, 9:6-13, 25-28, 10:1-2; John 4:22, 12:32; Psalm 106:1-48, 105:7-45, 102:13; Ezek. 39:27-28; Gen. 26:24; Zech. 12:8-10.

SOLOMON - WISDOM :- 1Kings 3:4-28, 4:29-31.

SOLOMON - WEALTH :- 1Kings 9:26-28, 10:22,23,4-10,14-21.

SOLOMON - SACRIFICES :- 1King 3:3-4, 8:63-66, 9:25.

SYNAGOGUE - SATAN :- Rev. 3:9, 2:9, 2:13, 24, 2:15.

SIN:- Gen. 31:19; Josh. 7:20-21; Gen. 38:13-16; Gen. 39:12-18; Rom. 1:22-32, 2:11-12; Isaiah 3:16-26; Mark 12:38-40; John 3:17-18, 27; 1Sam. 2:25; Hebr. 10:26, 31,23; James 2:10-11; 1Peter 3:12-16; Acts 5:1-11; Hosea 8:2-7; Matt. 11:12.

SON OF GOD:- Isa. 9:6; Dan. 3:25; Matt. 3:17; Jn. 1:18,5:19, 9:35, 11:4, 27; Acts 8:37; Gal. 4:4; 2Peter 1:17; Heb. 5:8; Rom. 1:4,8:3,32; 1John. 5:5,10-13, 20, 2:8, 23-24, 4:15. Luke 1:32.

SON'S POWER:- Matt. 28:18, Matt. 11:27.

SONS OF GOD :- 1John 3:1-2; Job 1:6, 2:1; Gen. 6:2. Matt. 4:3,6.

SPIRITUAL WARFARE :- 2Cor. 10:3-6; Eph. 6:12-16; Josh. 5:13-15, 6:20, 7:24-26; Exo. 18:22; Josh. 6:20; Matt. 17:21, 12:43-45;Rev. 12:11; Matt. 12:43-45; Mark 3:14-15, 5:1-13, Rev. 12:7-11; Matt. 17:21; Job 38:31-32.

SPIRITUAL MARRIAGE :- Matt. 22:23-34; John 4:15-19; John 8:1-11; Joshua 2:3-5.

TATTOO :- Lev. 19:28; Rev. 14:9-11, 13:15-18.

TAXES :- Paying of Taxes :- Matt. 17:24-27; Rom. 13:5-8.

TRANSFER OF POWER:- 2Kings 2:9-15, (2Kings 5:19-27, 13:20-21); Matt. 16:19; John 20:22-23; Luke 9:1,10,10:1,17; Acts 13:3; Mark 6:7.

TELL - no one :- Matt. 8:4, 12:16, 17:9, 9:30; Mark 5:43, 7:36.

TEACHING:- Matt. 11:1, 5:2, 22:33, 7:28,29; John 7:46.

TRUE LIGHT :- Gen. 1:3-4; John 1:1-9, 3:19, 8:12, 12:35-36, 46, 5:26, 9:5; 1John 1:5, 2:8-11.

TEMA - IN THE BIBLE :- Isaiah 21:14.

TEMPTATION:- Psalm 11:4-5, 95:8; Jam. 1:2-15; 1Cor. 10:13; 1Thess. 3:5; Matt. 26:4, 6:13; Job 1:8; Heb. 4:15; 2Peter. 2:9.

TONGUES:- Joel 2:28; Acts 2:1-2, 10:44-48; Cor. 14:1-39; Eccl. 8:8.

TALENT:- Luke 19:11-27; Deut. 8:17-18, 9:3; Matt. 25:14-30.

TONGUES:- Joel 2:28; Acts 2:1-26, 19:4-6; 1Cor. 13:1, 14:1-33; Eccl. 8:8. Mark 16:17; Daniel 10:13, 11:32.

TIME - IN HEAVEN AND EARTH :- Psalm 90:4; 2Pet. 3:8.

TIME OF LIFE :- 2Kings 4:16-17; Gen. 18:10,21:2, 17:21.

TITHE:- Hebr. 7:8-9: Ex. 16:36; Num. 18:21-28; Gen. 14:20, 28:20-22; Neh. 10:35; Deut. 14:22-28, 8:18, 26:12-13; 1Cor. 16:1-2, 9:13-14; Matt. 22:21, Matt. 21:33-40, 23:23; Mala. 1:7-8, 3:8-10; Levit. 27:13, 30-34; Prov. 3:9-10. 1Cor. 16:1-2, Job 38:4; 1Sam. 25:21; Matt. 23:17.

TITHE - PASTORS:- Num. 18:26; Neh. 10:38; 1Chron. 9:26.

TREE OF LIFE :- Gen. 2:9, 3:22, 24; Rev. 2:7,17, 3:2,14, 22:2,14

TRADITION:- Mark 7:5; Matt. 15:3

VIOLENCE TO WIVES:- 1Peter 3:7; Col. 3:19; Eph. 6:8-10; Mala. 2:16; Prov. 20:29; Gen. 2:18, 21-24.

VISION:- Acts 16:9-10, 10:10-11, 19-20, 18:9-10, 23:11; Daniel 10:2-8; Hab. 2:3; Prov. 29:18; 1Kings 3:5, 15; 2Cor. 12:14.

VOW:- Eccl. 5:4-7; Job. 22:27-28; Psalm 56:12; 66:13-14; Numb, 30:2; Judges 11:30-40; Gen. 28:20.

WAIVER:- Deut. 15:1-3, 9-11, 12-118; Exo. 21:2-3; Matt. 5:42.

WOMAN TO MARRY:- Prov. 12:4, 14:1, 31:10-31, 1cor. 11:5-7,12-15.

WOMEN TO KEEP SILENT IN CHURCH:- 1Cor. 14:34-37,33,40; 1Tim 2:11-15; James 2:10-11; 1Tim. 5:20-21; 2Thess. 3:14-15; 1Tim. 5:2.

WOMEN PASTOR:- Roman 16:1.

WISDOM:- Prov. 4:5-7, 5:1-2, 14:33, 21:22,24:3-7; Isaiah 5:13; Hosea 4:6; Eze. 22:26; Matt. 13:44; Eccl. 9:13-18, 10:10.

WATER BAPTISM:- John 3:5-27, 3:22-27, 6:44; Matt. 3:6, 11, 13-17,13-16, 28:19; Mark 1:8-10, 15, 16-18; Rom. 6:3-5, 10:9-10, 8:15-16; Acts 8:13, 38-39, 2:38, 41, 16:33,10:47-48, 18:8; 1Cor. 10:2; Colo.2:12; 1Peter 3:21; Luke 3:21; Eph. 2:4-9, 4:5; 1Cor.12;13; Hebr. 6:1-2.

WASHING OF THE FEET:- Gen. 18:4, Gen. 19:2, Gen. 43:17; John 13:5.

WHO ARE CHRISTIANS:- Gal. 3:26-29; Eph. 2:4-10; Acts 11:25; Luke 15:7-10; Mark 9:39; Matt. 7:21-25; Matt. 24:5, 23-26; Hebr. 11:6; Psalm 82:6; John 10:34-35.

WORKS, I know thy:- Rev. 2:2, 9, 13, 19, 3:8-9.

0FFERING:-

Sin Offering:- Lev. 4:1-35.
Peace Offering:- Lev. 3:1-17, 7:15
Burnt Offering:- Lev. 6:9-14, 9:23-24, 7:8.
Wave Offering:- Lev. 10:14-15, 22:14, 7:30,34; Num. 18:11.

THE TWELVE PLAGUES:-

Exo. 7:10-12, 20,8:6, 8:16, 8:24, 9:6, 9:9, 9:26, 10:5, 10:21, 11:4, 14:21-30.

THE EIGHT TENENTS OF JESUS CHRIST

1. The prophecies about Jesus : a. Isaiah 9:6 b. Isaiah 53:2-12 c. Isaiah 7:14 d. Luke 1:30-35, e. Deut. 18:18-19; f. John 5:46.
2. The birth of Jesus Christ : a. Luke 2:6-7 b. Luke 2:9-14
3. The Ministry of Jesus Christ: a. Mark 1:9-11 b. Mark 1:14-20 c. Matt. 3:21-23
4. The Crucifixion of Jesus Christ: a. Mark 15:21-23 b. Mark 15:33-39 c. Exo. 26:31-33 d. Luke 23:33-38,46,53 e. John 19:30.
5. The burial of Jesus Christ : John 20:38-42; Isaiah 53:9; Luke 23:5; Matt. 27:59-60; Mark 15:45-46.
6. The resurrection of Jesus Christ: a. John 20:11-20 b. Luke 24: 6-9, 18-35 c. John 20:24-31.
7. Ascension of Jesus Christ:- Mark 16:19; Luke 24:51; Acts 1:2, 9-.11.
8. Deity of Jesus Christ:- Acts 2:33; Heb. 1:13, 10:12; Matt. 12:32; Psalm 110:1(Mark 12:36); John 17:5, 16:28.

   Jesus Christ was made an accurse of God : Deut. 21:23; Galatians 3:13.

THE SEVEN DEADLY SINS:-

LUST:- 1John 2:16; Gen. 3:6; Eccl. 5:10.

GLUTTONY:- Matt. 11:19; Luke 7:33-35; Deut. 21:20-21; Rom. 12:2; Isaiah 5:11; James 2:14-24; Prov. 23:21; Gal. 5:16-26.

GREED:- Luke 16:4, 12:15; Prov. 15:27; Matt. 5:39-40.

SLOTH :- Prov. 26:13-16, 19:24, 15:19, 13:4;Phil. 4:13; Colo. 4:1-7, 3:23; 2Thess. 3:10; Prov. 12:24.

WRATH:- Rev. 14:8; James 1:20; 1Tim. 2:8, Heb. 10:30.

ENVY:- Prov. 28:22; Mark 15:10; Matt. 27:18; Job 5:2.

PRIDE:- Prov. 8:13, 3:7, 16:5, 15:25; 16:18; 1John 2:16.

GIFT FOR PRAYER.

Prophetic prayer Isaiah 54:17.
Angelic prayer Luke 1:26-38.
Praises and Worship Psalm 99:1-3; 150:1-6.
Prayer as a custom Luke 4:16.

SPEAKING IN TONGUES

Foreign Tongues 1Cor. 14:11; Acts 2:6-8.
Worship Tongues 1Cor. 14:2, 2Chron. 20:21-23.
Angelic Tongues 1Cor. 13:1, 14:2.
Prophetic Tongues 1Cor. 14:6, 3-4.
Gift of Tongues 1Cor. 14:2; Mark 16:17.

WIVES OF DAVID :-

1Samuel 27:3; 1Chronicles 3:1-3; 2Samuel 3:2-4

The mother of David was NITZEVET (Talmud) His father was JESSE

wife sequence son <u>Quotation</u>

1. Ahinoam 1 - Amnon - 1Sam. 27:3.
2. Abigail 2 - Chileab (Daniel) - 1Chron. 3:1; 1Sam. 27:3; 2Sam. 3:3
3. Maacab 3 - Absalom - 1Sam. 19:9-11; 2Sam. 6:20-23; 1Sam. 18:25-28.
4. Haggith 4 - Adonijah - 1Sam. 27:3
5. Beshsheba 7 - Solomon(Jedidiah) - 2Sam.12:24 (Shimea, Shobab, Nathan)
6. Eglah 6 - Ithream - 1Chron. 3:3
7. Abital 5 - Shephatiah - 1Chron. 3:3
8. Michal 8 - Nil - 2Sam. 6:20-23

WIVES OF JACOB (ISRAEL) AND CHILDREN:-

Father of Jacob was ISAAC and the Mother was REBEKA (Gen. 24:67) (Gen. 30, 29:32-35).

1. LEAH - 1. Reuben, 2. Simeon, 3. Levi, 4. Judah, 5.Issachar, 6. Zebulun : 7. Dinah
2. RACHEL - 1. Joseph, 2. Benjamin (ben-oni). (Gen 35:18)
3. BILHAH (Rachel) - 1. Dan, 2. Nephtali.
4. ZILPAH (Leah) - 1. Gad, 2. Asher.

WHERE I GO YE CANNOT COME :-

John 8:21,22; John 7:34; John 13:33

GOD IS NOT RESPECTER OF PERSONS:-

Deut. 10:17; Rom. 2:11; Acts 10:34.

PARENTS OF MOSES:-

Father of Moses was AMRAM and the Mother was JOCHEBED (Num. 26:59).

Exo. 2:1-2, 6:20; Numb. 26:59; 1Chron. 23:12-17

JESUS IS GOD:- The incarnation of God, image of the Invisible God. (Col. 1:15).

Exo. 33:20; Ezek. 39:29; Luke 1:26-35, 2:1-7; Matt. 5:8; Heb. 1:6,8-9.

JESUS AND THE HOLY GHOST:-

Acts 1:5, 8; John 14:26, 1:33; Matt. 3:11, 2 8:19; mark 1:8.

PARAPHRASING THE SCRIPTURE

Paraphrasing of the scripture is the deeper interpretation and explanation of the scripture delivered by the Holy Spirit and it's important for every preacher or bible teacher to seek the help of the Holy Spirit to paraphrase. It is the gift of the Holy Spirit.

Job 1:6-7 "Now there was a day when the sons of God came to present themselves before the Lord, and Satan came also among them. And the Lord said unto Satan, hence cometh thou? Then Satan answered the Lord and said, from going to and fro in the earth, and from walking up and down in it." : *Satan was there to take the glory of God. When Satan came among the sons of God, the sons of God did not see him, because he was in the form of pillar of clouds. This means the sons of God saw him as God and he was difficult to be identified. Satan stole God's identity and came among the angels, which they did not see him. Only God saw him because He was not that pillar of cloud which is God's symbol. Satan did that for the angel to worship him to take the glory of God that God will be angry with the angels, which are the sons of God, for God to loose those angels. Even so Satan visits people with imitation forms of God and destroy their relationship with God.*

Genesis 1:1-2 "In the beginning God created the heaven and the earth. And the earth was without form, and void; and darkness was upon the face of the deep. And the spirit of God moved upon the face of the waters." *Because the earth was so precious to God and also precious in His sight, and very dear to His heart when it was created, so God did not just created it, but created it with an angel to protect it, an angel who is so mighty and ordained with all power, beauty and anointed, and that angel was Lucifer, very handsome angel. Lucifer as head of the angels took advantage of the angels and tried to take advantage to control the earth by preventing farther creation in the form of darkness, but God knew all his intention which showed his desire to take over the earth from the beginning, so when he made the war in heaven, the angels made him faced the war and was casted out of heaven and chose to land on earth. So in this way Satan landed on earth and now harasses and threatens the whole population of the earth. The earth is at war with him.*

Rom. 6:15-16 What then? Shall we sin because we are not under the law, but under grace? God forbid? *He who is obedient is on the path* *to righteousness, he who sins is on the path of death. Those who live under the law, live under the old testament, and those who live under the grace, live under the new testament. In the old testament, when you are sick is because of sin, when you are disable it's because of sin, when you lose your job it's because of sin, even death is because of sin, but under the new testament which is grace, those things come to glorify God. Because in the old testament, there is no way to deal or take out those evil situations but in the new testament deliverance is made possible. If you are sick, it's for you to rise and speak to the situation with the Christian tools eg. hope, love, faith, patience. perseverance, and endurance, and by seeing your situation not as a condition but as a spirit and you will overcome. These tools make God draw near to take the fight, go before you and destroy those enemies, Deut. 9:3. Those tools are already in the hands of the Christian. Know that the new testament is the update of the old testament and to put Satan in pain because it prevents the Christian from sinning. Anyone under the new testament can attract God but not anyone under the old testament can attract God that is the reason why God elected Noah, Abraham, Moses Elijah, Elisha and David etc. In the new testament there is no consideration for specific people but all are considered to attract God, all that you need is in the name Christian.*

Jude 6. "The angels which kept not their first estate, but left their own habitation, He hath reserved in everlasting chains under darkness unto judgment of the great day. *Spiritual laws are more severe than physical law. Those who violate those spiritual laws, their consequences are more severe and has no mercy. Spiritual laws do not guarantee celestial beings their will but terrestrial beings are given their will because God knew they are flesh.*

John 8:23-24. "And He said unto them, ye are from beneath, I am from above: ye are of this world; I am not of this world. I said therefore unto you that ye shall die in your sins; for if ye believe not that I am He, ye shall die in your sins." *You believe in your situation and you have taken your situation to be condition. Do not see your situation as a condition. If you see your situation as a condition, you will die in your condition. But if you see your situation as a spirit, you will speak against it and it shall flee. Situations are spirit and not condition.*

John 6:39. "This is the will of Him that sent Me, that everyone which sees the Son and believes on Him may have everlasting life, and

will raise him up at the last day." *As a Christian, I believe in the Lord Jesus Christ and for this I have everlasting life to keep me alive, for I have passed from death to life through the resurrection of Jesus Christ. Whoever believes on Him and dies is not dead but asleep and when Jesus comes He will wake (raise) him up. He who sleeps wakes up again because he has life in him, but he who is dead, does not wake up again because he has no life in him.*

2Cor. 4:18. While we look not at the things which are seen, but at the thing which are not seen: for the things which are seen are temporal; but the things which are seen are eternal. *Physical things are visible and the things which are seen are physical and they do die but the things which are not seen are invisible and invisible things are spiritual which do not die. Everything that dies is temporal but the things that do not die are eternal.*

Gen. 3:14." And the Lord God said unto the serpent, because thou has done this, thou art cursed above all cattle, and every beast of the field; upon thy belly shall thou go and dust shall thou eat all the days of thy life." *The snake was created by God and was normal beast but ignorantly allowed itself to be possessed by the serpent which was devil. A satanic snake is serpent. So the snake became serpent. When God curse the serpent, that curse came upon all animals also, but that of the serpent was more severe than all the species of animals. God knew what will happen to animals so He said that, we should use the herb for meat and not animals. So the present problems of mankind is from the animals. Cancer, diabetes, high blood pressure, tumor, kidney disease, heart disease, lungs etc. all are from the curse of animal which we use for food. Hence animal flesh is dangerous to our health.*

Gen. 1:28. "And God blessed them and God said unto them, be fruitful and multiply and replenish the earth, and subdue it and have dominion over the fish of the sea, and over the fowl of the air, and over every living thing that moves upon the earth." *God is a creator and an inventor, so when He created man, He blessed him and said to him, to continue with the physical creation and invention to fill the earth with his creation, and rule over them all and exercise power over all the Living Creatures. It was not about sex and creating children but being glorified to glorify God.*

WHO WERE THE PHARISEES AND THE SEDDUCEES?

The Pharisees were the expect and accurate expositors of Jewish laws. **The SANHEDRIN** *was the seventy elders Moses was directed to associate with him in the government of the Israelites* (**Numb. 11:16-17**) *and also the seventy member supreme council of the Jewish people in the time of Jesus Christ* (**Mark 14:55-56**). *The Sadducees had majority and held powerful positions eg. High Priests and chief priests and were rich and influential, the Jews highly regarded the Pharisees. The Sadducees believed the word of God but did not keep it. The Pharisees adjusted the word of God to suit them, but the Sadducees were not. They believed not the existence of angels, neither the devil nor the resurrection, not even life after death. There are still Sadducees: whoever believes the word of God or Christ and does not live by the word is a Sadducee. The Pharisees force people to keep the law and make salvation part work of righteousness, but add to the law as they like. The Pharisees believe in the law and that it was liable for amendment and keep them but the Sadducees believe and refused to live by it. That's what happen when people reject Christ and refuse to repent - they become the rebellion children of God.*

Hebr. 11:1. Now faith is the substance of things hoped for, the evidence of things not seen. FAITH :- *Faith is the divine formula that exterminates every problem which is delivered into the hands of human beings. Anything that has a name exists and faith has a name, but faith is a spirit. Spirit work miracle that's why faith works miracles. So faith is the evidence of things not seen but hope to receive and received, no matter what the situation: that's faith. When situation become spirit and not condition, miracles happen and that's by faith. It is that which recognizes the power and authority over diseases, sicknesses (demons) and witches, and capable to edify broken lives which is in Jesus Christ, the Son of the Living God. With the divine formula, there is no negativity in actions. The tremendous power of faith is the conclusive word of Jesus Christ on the subject of divine healing. It is the foundation of all things leading as far as unto salvation. Medical science is good and purposed to glorify God but the science of the miracles of Jesus Christ is the greatest. Nothing is made or created without faith, therefore faith is older than the person having the faith because through faith he was created. Faith is not something one can acquire but something one has from creation. There is no power like the power of faith. It is the master key to everything, the master key to unlock the prison* *doors, the master key that breaks the chains of the captive, the master key that brings the axe from the bottom to the surface of the water, the master key to break evry yoke, and the master key that raises the dead.*

Mark 10:27 "And Jesus looking upon them saith, With men it is impossible, but not with God: For with God all things are possible."

This means, whosoever has faith can find favor with God because that person is connected to God. And whosoever is connected to God, angels will always do him service.

THE CHARATERISTICS OF GOD:-

1. **God is not a man.**
2. **God is Light.**
3. **God is consuming fire.**

Num. 23:19 (Hosea). "God is not a man that He should lie, neither the son of a man, that He should repent; Hath He said and shall He not do it? or hath spoken and shall He not make it good."

So God is someone who even that which is corrupt, He makes it perfect. That is the reason He made man in His image, that we as human beings will be like Him and behave like Him, not lying to one another, not repenting every time making so many mistakes. That whatever we say, we will fulfill it. In this way, we shall be like Him, that is the reason why He created us for His glory. That whatever we do on earth we will give the glory to Him that He will in turn glorify us as Jesus Christ said in.

John 17:4-5. "I have glorified thee on the earth: I have finished the work which thou gave me to do. And now, O Father, glorify thou Me with thine own self with the glory which I had with thee before the world was."

So God is not a man but He had sent us on earth to declare His existence in the universe and on earth, and to show His characteristics which is in us on earth as Jesus, the only begotten Son of the Father displayed from the time He was born till the time He was take up. Jesus did not take Himself as born by a man but by God the Father, even so God does not want us to take ourselves as being born by a man. By so doing He will have direct contact with us as His children; meaning we will consider not of man's decision but of God's decision for our existence on earth. Our claim that we are born by man is the cunning operation of Satan not to accept that we are born by God. So the verse is saying that God is full of scientific proves and all scientific experimental results emanates from Him. That is the reason why we are created for His glory. So all human beings must serve the purpose of being little gods(John 10:34) to be able to serve our purpose in this our world. We do scientific research, we do great things, some which it is difficult to believe that it was created or manufactured by human beings. All these are part of God which is the energy in us and surrounding us. The mistake is, we do not give the glory to God as Christ glorified Father.

Hebr. 7:9-10. "And as I may so say, Levi also who received tithes, paid tithe in Abraham, For he yet in the loins of his father, when Melchisedec met him." *There is a proverb which says, the evil that men do lives after them, likewise the good that men do lives after them. So in the above bible verse, if one sins the children not yet born, inside him have also sinned with him and they are already under the curse of that sin or blessing according to the activities of the parents, whether of good or evil or bad. So as we pay tithe we pay tithe with the children in our loins. So before the children will come forth, they are already into the parental activities of curse or blessing. So Levi paid tithe when Abraham paid tithe and was affected with the blessing of Abraham.*

Hebr.7:28. "For the law makes men high priest which have infirmity; but the word of the oath which was since the law, makes the Son, who is consecrated for evermore. *The Jews are waiting for the Messiah to come from above, if Christ descents from above, things that will happen to purify the earth before the appearance of the Messiah will be too hectic for the inhabitants of the earth to handle, significantly majority of the inhabitants on earth (not only the Israelites will perish but the inhabitants of the whole earth) beginning with storms, earthquakes, volcanoes, hurricanes, tornados, thunderstorms, and lightning etc, to clean up the earth of every sin for six days and the seventh day, the appearance of Jesus Christ; the bible says in the above verse, the high priest have infirmity(chronic sins) in them which cannot sustain the presence of the Messiah. For this our Gracious, Merciful and Compassionate Messiah, decided to use another form that will enable us to sustain His presence by being born like one of us, but with heavenly anointing upon Him who cannot sin and never sinned till He was taken up. So Christ is* *the Messiah and the Jews who refused Him have miss the mark and the target by not accepting and believing in Him.*

Colo. 3:17. "And whatever you do in words or deed, do all in the name of the Lord Jesus Christ, giving thank to God the Father by Him." *It is normal routine and culture of the Moslems to do all things in the name of Allah; so if a Moslem is going to sit down he says, "Bismilahi rahmani rahim" meaning In the name of Allah, most gracious, most merciful. Whatever a Moslem does he has to invoke the name of Allah. But we Christians just do things without the name of Jesus Christ. We pray in Jesus name and call Jesus name when we are in trouble, especially accident. The bible says whatever we do in word or deed, we have to do all in the name of Jesus Christ the Son of the Living God, Most Gracious, Most Merciful and Most Compassionate. How many times Christians do call the name of Jesus a day and why we do not do all things in Jesus name. In Jesus name is the driven power of our prayers so without the name of Jesus, the prayer of a Christian carries no power and that prayer is in your name and not Christ and we make the name of Our Lord Jesus Christ ineffective because we blame Christ for our ignorance because that prayer was not answered. The anointing behind the name of Jesus Christ is always the same, the problem is the Christian. It is time to make the name of Jesus Christ a Christian tradition in all things. The Moslem prays five times a day, how many times a Christians prays a day? The Christian must go extra mile, if a Moslem prays five time a day the Christian must do seven times as King David said in Psalm 119:164. King David had laid the foundation to praise the Lord seven times daily. He made it his culture. King David did everything either in words or deeds in the name of the Lord and for this he was able to overcome Goliath in the name of the Lord and killed Goliath. So Christians go extra mile.*

Luke 11:1. 'And it came to pass that as He was praying in a certain place, when He ceased, one of His disciples said unto Him, Lord teach us to pray, as John also taught his disciples." *Lord teach us to pray! The apostle wanted to rely on God's strength to pray. If you rely on God's strength, you will pray as Jesus is praying. Lord teach me to depend on your strength that my prayer will be thy will and not the will of man. Without the spirit of God, that is His anointing, my prayer, my praise, my worship, my fasting and my charity will be destructive.*

Mark 5:25-26. "Now a certain woman had a flow of blood for

twelve years. And had suffered many things from many physicians, she had spent all she had and was no better but rather grew worse." *Physicians are good and good to visit but not all sicknesses they are good at. Some sicknesses can only be dealt with by God only. Only Jesus Christ and His name deal with spiritual sicknesses.*

      FATHERHOOD TO GOD :- *Because only Jesus Christ was able to live unto the will of the Father, among the inhabitants on the earth to date, so Jesus is ordained by God, His Father, to be God of the universe.* Acts 17:31 "Because He had appointed a day, in the which He will judge the world in righteousness by that MAN whom He had ORDAINED; whereof He had given assurance unto all men, in that He had raise Him from dead." Again in Acts 10:42 "And He commanded us to preach to the people, and to testify that it is He which was ORDAINED of God to be the judge of the quick and the dead." *The claim of Jesus of God as his Father is based on the creation,* Let there be Light, and there was Light, Gen. 1:3. *He was the Light that was called forth into existence in the spirit by God the Father. So Jesus was born by God at the creation, that was the meaning of His claim as THE SON OF GOD, which is not metaphor but a reality. The believe of the confirmation of His claim is found in:* John 16:27-28. "The father Himself loves you, because ye have believed that I came out from God. I came forth from the Father, and I am come into the world: again, I leave the world, and go to the Father." *And the Father sending Him physically to dwell among us on this our earth without human father. This is the reason Jesus never called Joseph, the husband of His mother, father and said human being is not our father but brought to existence through them and they do not own us.* Matt 23:9 "And call no man your father upon the earth, for one is your Father, which is in heaven. He continue to explained: John 16:27-28 "For the Father Himself loves you, because you have loved Me, and have believed that I came out from God." "I came forth from the Father and Am come into the world; again, I leave the world and go to the Father." *Meaning the Father love the disciples, because they had believed that He came out from inside the Father to join Him, and He sits with the Father. He continued to say He came from the Father who sent Him and He is come into the world for a purpose and the purpose is almost accomplished, so He was going to leave the world once again to join the Father. This gives the exact picture of His claim. Because we do not accept the claim of God our Father to* *be His sons, only Christ who was obedient to the Father has been ordained the Son and only Him Christ has whole heartedly accepted the offer of the Father as His Son,* stated in, Heb. 1:5 "For unto which of the angels said He at anytime, thou art My Son, this day have I begotten thee? And again I will be to Him a Father, and He shall be to me a Son?" and in Heb. 1:8 But unto the Son He said, Thy Throne, O God, is forever and ever: a sceptre of righteousness is the sceptre of thy kingdom." *Christ is ordained our God and the God of the universe and all power is given unto Him in heaven and the earth. Heaven and earth means the whole universe. In our time, in every family, the father or the husband who is called the father by the children and even some wives call their husbands Father, that's OK because he represents God in the family and that is great for God to reveal Himself in every family, so God is in every family as father. If we can give this Fatherhood to God by every husband or family, God will reign in Families and families will be at peace. But because husbands claim the glory of Fatherhood so we have so many troubles in families.*

THE SOURCE OF SICKNESS:

Gen. 1:29 And God said, behold I have given you every herb bearing seed, which is upon the face of all the earth, and every tree, in the which is the fruit of a tree yielding seed: to you it shall be for meat. *From Genesis chapter 4 to 5 the people live very long, ranging from 969 years to 705 years, because those people were not eating meat of animals. But in the time of Noah the people lived wickedly and ate everything and all kinds of animal meat, that which the Lord did not give them to eat, so they rebelled against the Lord.* So now the Lord said in Gen. 9:3 Every moving thing that liveth shall be meat for you; even as the green herb have I given you all things. *When the people chose to eat animal meat, then the Lord gave them their mandate to continue to eat animal meat and the curse on the animals became sickness and man attracted sickness.* Gen. 3:14 And the Lord said unto the serpent, because thou hast done this, thou art cursed above all cattle and above every beast of the field; upon thy belly shall thou go and dust shall thou eat all the days of thy life. *So when man began to eat meat of the cattle and the beast which is rebellion and wickedness that comes with curse, then man began to get all kinds of deadly sicknesses, like blood pressure,* diabetes, tumor, cancer, blindness, osteoporosis, elephantiasis, Ebola etc. etc. sickness is curse because in Gen. 3:14 the animals were cursed due to what the serpent did.

2Cor. 4:18 (Rom. 8:24) "While we look not at the things which are seen, but at the things which are not seen: for the things which are seen are temporal; but the things which are not seen are eternal. *The things which are seen are physical things which die, but the things which are not seen are spiritual things which do not die. Everything that dies is temporal but things that do not die are eternal. And in the eternal world, technological inventions are natural and normal developments, not learned.*

MOTIVATIONAL AND INSPIRATIONAL PREACHING. Matt. 23:17 "Ye fools and blind: For whether is greater, the gold or the temple that sanctifies the gold." *The salvation or the prosperity, which of the two is greater. The salvation which brings prosperity which is contained in the salvation. Most preachers are pleasing the congregation by preaching prosperity. Prosperity has become God to the churches, instead of salvation which is the heart of God. Salvation was hid in God, until He found a suitable instrument in Himself to deliver unto. Prosperity includes the package of Salvation. Eph. 3:9. There are two type of preaching; Motivational Preaching and Inspirational Preaching. The motivational preaching is about prosperity which motivate and enhance the congregation and that make Christianity a religion in motivational mindset which makes the congregation dependent on the church. But the Inspirational Preaching is all about salvation which correct the mindset of the congregation to know that Jesus Christ came to restore the missing relationship and fellowship between God and man, so that through the word of God, the people can contact God and God can also contact the people which is a progression to heaven. There is great difference between Christianity and religion, and religion is dependence on the Church. Christianity is not a religion but a love relationship with God, which depend solely on the heart. A pure heart is the conclusion. Blessed are the pure in heart for they shall see God.*

Colo. 3:17 And whatsoever you do in words or deed, do all in the name of the Lord Jesus, giving thanks to the God the Father by Him. *Do not let accident happen before you call on the name of Jesus, the accident had already happened, but if you call the name of Jesus every moment in your life, you will be protected before the accident. You need Jesus every day, every moment and He also needs you to glorify Him. Christians wait for trouble to* *hit them before they remember the name of Jesus. There is a wonderful name, which is Jesus. There is no other name like Him. In His name the blind sees, the lame walks and the dead arise. Live your life in Christ Jesus.*

James 5:13 Is any among you afflicted? let him pray. Is any merry? let him sing psalms. *The bible is saying, because of rebellion of man, God granted that we be afflicted before we pray. "Whilst Luke 18:1 says, Man ought to pray and not cease." So prayer must be a custom of a Christian. You do not have to wait for Satan to slap you with troubles: sicknesses, hardship, and all kinds of dilemma, before you pray. But attack Satan before he attacks you. Do not allow the devil to bring the battle to your gate but you as a Christian, must take the fight to Satan's gate and maintain it there until you overcome. And after the victory, rejoice with psalms and hymns, praising God.*

COMMITTING SUICIDE-:

People commit suicide because they do not have salvation and have no knowledge of the power of salvation. **Mark 14:21 "The Son of Man indeed goes just as it is written of Him, but woe to that man by whom the Son of man is betrayed! It would have been good for that man if he had never been born." Matt. 27:5 And he cast down the pieces of silver in the temple and departed, and went and hang himself.** *When one commits suicide his message is, he is not fit to continue to live in the world. He has given up on himself. If one commits suicide he had already passed judgment upon himself and condemned himself. Even in the world where there is grace, he could not spare himself, how can hell spare him after this life, meaning if you commit suicide there is no heaven for you. Judas committed suicide because he felt the punishment of what he did was condemnation by himself. Even hell does not want people who had committed suicide, meaning hell has rejected such a person. So do not commit suicide. There is no problem that has no solution. That which is impossible with man is possible with God. Christ is the solution to every problem. You think your problem is too great to handle but there is a second chance to live. You need to be born again to start a new life.* Salvation is free, seek for salvation. Matt. 11:28 "Come to me, all you that labor and are heavy laden, and I will give you rest."

Acts 3:15 And killed the Prince of Life, whom God hath raised from the dead: wherefore we are witness. *You were eager for salvation and* requested for the Son of God, for it was human who sinned and not animal and ordinary human who is contaminated and could not be used for that ransom atonement, but a righteous and holy blood and flesh was required and Jesus was the only person on earth for such sacrifice, for such He was sent.

Matt. 16:4 "A wicked and adulterous generation seeketh after a sign; and there shall no sign be given unto it, but the sign of the prophet Jonas." What is the sign of the prophet Jonah? *Jesus is just saying, a generation which is wicked and idol worshipers, request for sign before you worship and serve God. If that is what you want before you serve and worship God, then no sign will be performed unto you and take to your own way as Jonah rebelled, till he end up in the belly of the whale. Likewise all of you had also rebelled and will end up in hell, where you will regret and it will be too late for you to correct this mistake. Because you do not know and refuse to accept that, you were created for the glory of the Father. Therefore we are obliged to worship Him continuously, for such we were created. Seeking for a sign is idolatry, meaning putting one's faith and trust in signs, miracles, and wonders, and not having the love relationship with God. This act or behavior is spiritual adultery. That is the reason why Jesus said, wicked and adulterous generation.*

Printed in the United States
By Bookmasters